Elementary Level SSAT®
1000+ Practice Questions

Elementary SSAT®: 1000+ Practice Questions
January 2021

Published in the United States of America by:

The Tutorverse, LLC

222 Broadway, 19th Floor

New York, NY 10038

Web: www.thetutorverse.com

Email: hello@thetutorverse.com

For information about buying this title in bulk or to place a special order, please contact us at hello@thetutorverse.com.

ISBN-13: 978-1-7321677-3-5
ISBN-10: 1-7321677-3-7

Table of Contents

Welcome — ***7***

How to Use This Book — ***8***

3rd Grade Diagnostic Practice Test (Form A) — ***11***

4th Grade Diagnostic Practice Test (Form B) — ***36***

Quantitative — ***61***

- **Number Concepts & Operations** — **62**
  - Place Value — 62
  - Basic Concepts — 63
  - Ordering Numbers and Fractions — 65
  - Fractions — 66
  - Arithmetic Word Problems — 69
- **Algebraic Principles** — **73**
  - Solving Equations and Inequalities — 73
  - Ratios and Proportions — 74
- **Geometry** — **75**
  - Shapes and Attributes — 75
  - Area and Perimeter — 77
- **Measurement** — **79**
  - Time and Money — 79
  - Unit Analysis — 81
- **Statistics & Probability** — **83**
  - Probability — 83
  - Mean — 85
  - Interpreting Tables and Graphs — 87

Verbal — ***90***

- **Synonyms** — **92**
  - 3rd Grade — 93
  - 4th Grade — 96
- **Analogies** — **99**
  - Guided Practice — 100
  - Mixed Practice — 110

Reading — ***112***

- **Fiction** — **114**
  - 3rd Grade — 114
  - 4th Grade — 119
- **Non-Fiction** — **125**
  - 3rd Grade — 125
  - 4th Grade — 129

The Writing Sample ____ *132*

3rd Grade Final Practice Test (Form C) ____ *134*

4th Grade Final Practice Test (Form D) ____ *159*

Answer Keys ____ *184*

3rd Grade Diagnostic Practice Test (Form A) Answer Key ____ 184

4th Grade Diagnostic Practice Test (Form B) Answer Key ____ 184

Quantitative ____ 185

Number Concepts & Operations ____ 185
Algebraic Principles ____ 186
Geometry ____ 186
Measurement ____ 186
Statistics & Probability ____ 186

Verbal - Synonyms ____ 187

Verbal - Analogies ____ 187

Reading Comprehension ____ 188

3rd Grade Final Practice Test (Form C) Answer Key ____ 189

4th Grade Final Practice Test (Form D) Answer Key ____ 190

Elementary SSAT®
1000+ Practice Questions

Welcome

Dear Students, Parents, and Educators,

Welcome to The Tutorverse!

You've just taken a positive first step toward acing the Elementary SSAT - congratulations! This workbook contains the key to scoring well on the test: high-quality, test-appropriate practice materials. High-performance on this test is built on the bedrock of core learning and subject-matter proficiency. Deep content knowledge and plenty of practice are the keys to unlocking top scores.

This workbook contains over 6 exams' worth of questions – over 1,000 questions in total! We've taken a detailed look at the core content areas assessed on the Elementary SSAT. We've created questions that will introduce students to these areas and improve their proficiency with practice. Our goal is to help students master these skills, increase their knowledge, and build up their confidence. To help with this, detailed answer explanations for every question are available online at **www.thetutorverse.com**.

Let's get started! You can use this workbook for independent study or with a professional teacher or tutor. Either way, we believe these learnings will benefit you on the Elementary SSAT and beyond!

Good luck!

The Team at The Tutorverse

How to Use This Book

Overview

The purpose of this workbook is to provide students, parents, and educators with practice materials relevant to the Elementary SSAT. This workbook assumes its users have a working knowledge of the exam, including its structure and content. Though it contains tips, strategies, and suggestions, the primary goal of this workbook is to provide students with extensive practice by introducing new words, skills, and concepts. A brief overview of the exam is shown below.

This book is divided into 3rd and 4th grade content. While similar, students should begin working with their respective grade levels. If 3rd grade content is not challenging enough, move up to 4th grade. Likewise, if 4th grade content is too challenging, consider starting with 3rd grade content.

Scoring	Section	Number of Questions	Time Limit
Scored Section	Section 1: Quantitative	30	30 minutes
	Section 2: Verbal	30	20 minutes
	15-Minute Break		
	Section 3: Reading	28	30 minutes
	Total Scored Exam (Sections 1-3)	88	**1 hour, 20 minutes**
Unscored Section (sent to schools)	Section 4: Writing Sample	1	15 minutes
Unscored Section	Section 5: Experimental	15-17	15 minutes

Organization

This workbook is organized into six main sections. Each section is designed to accomplish different objectives. These sections and objectives are as follows:

- Diagnostic Practice Tests (Form A and Form B)
  The first full-length practice tests (one each for 3rd and 4th grade) are designed to help students identify the topics that require the most practice. They mirror the length and content of the actual Elementary SSAT in order to ensure that students become accustomed to the duration of the real test. These diagnostic practice tests should be used to gauge the amount of additional practice needed on each topic, **not** as an estimate of how a student will score on the actual Elementary SSAT. **NOTE:** the diagnostic practice tests include 15 questions in a mock-experimental section and, while they are useful practice, they are included only to emulate the full duration of the actual test.

- Quantitative
  The main concepts covered in this section are Number Concepts and Operations, Algebraic Principles, Geometry, Measurement, and Statistics & Probability. All of these concepts are further divided into sub-categories, which can be found in the table of contents.

- Verbal
  The material in this section covers word similarities and relationships through synonym and analogy questions. Students will encounter many new words in this section.

- Reading
  This section tests a student's ability to read passages and answer questions about them. Passages include non-fiction persuasive and informative pieces, as well as excerpts from fictional works, including poems, novels, and short stories. Questions center around understanding main idea and themes, making inferences, and understanding how details contribute to the meaning of the passage.

- Writing Sample
  This section provides information about the writing prompts and includes several practice prompts.

- Final Practice Tests (Form C and Form D)
  This workbook ends with two additional full-length practice tests (one each for 3rd and 4th grade). These tests are similar to the diagnostic practice tests in length and content and should be taken once students have completed the diagnostic practice tests and have spent sufficient time answering the appropriate questions in the practice sections. **NOTE:** the practice tests include 15 questions in a mock-experimental section and, while they are useful practice, they are included only to emulate the full duration of the actual test.

Note: The Experimental section is designed by the SSAT Test Development Team to test new questions, in order to make sure they are appropriate for use on future SSAT exams. Since this section is **not** scored, this workbook will not include content related to the Experimental section (except in the Practice Test sections). Students need **not** worry about attempting these questions on the actual exam.

At the beginning of each of the above-listed sections are detailed instructions. Students should carefully review these instructions, as they contain important information about the actual exam and how best to practice.

Strategy

Every student has different strengths and abilities. We don't think there is any one strategy that will help every student ace the exam. Instead, we believe there are core principles to keep in mind when preparing for the Elementary SSAT. These principles are interrelated and cyclical in nature.

- Evaluate
  A critical step in developing a solid study plan is to have a clear idea of how to spend your time. What subjects are more difficult for you? Which types of questions do you frequently answer incorrectly? Why? These and many other questions should be answered before developing any study plan. The diagnostic practice test is just one way to help you evaluate your abilities.

- Plan
  Once you've taken stock of your strengths and abilities, focus on actions.
    - How much time do you have before the test?
    - How many areas do you need to work on during that time?

- Which areas do you need to work on?
- How many questions (and of which type) do you need to do each day, or each week?

The answers to these and other questions will help you determine your study and practice plan.

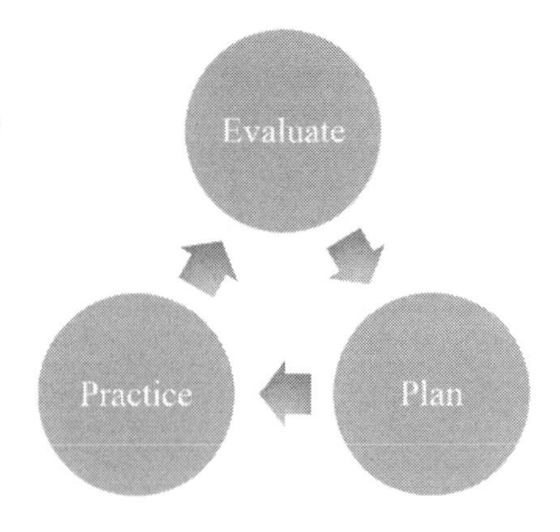

Practice

Once you settle on a plan, try to stick with it as much as you can. To study successfully requires discipline, commitment, and focus. Try turning off your phone, TV, tablet, or other distractions. Not only will you learn more effectively when you're focused, but you may find that you finish your work more quickly, as well.

Reevaluate

Because learning and studying is an ongoing process, it is important to take stock of your improvements along the way. This will help you see how you are progressing and allow you to make adjustments to your plan. The practice test at the end of this workbook is designed to help you gauge your progress.

Need Help?

Feeling overwhelmed? You're not alone! Preparing for a standardized test is often a daunting task. While students should strive to meet the challenge of the test, it's also important for students to recognize when they need extra help.

Know that since the Elementary SSAT is given to students in various grades, **students may find some material in this workbook difficult or entirely new**. It's OK! That is to be expected, as certain material may not have been taught to all students yet. Students will only be scored against other students in their grade (4th graders vs. other 4th graders, for example). Even so, mastering advanced materials often provides a competitive advantage in achieving higher scores. Give it a try!

Students are not alone. We provide detailed answer explanations online at **www.thetutorverse.com** (students should ask a parent or guardian's permission before going online). We also encourage students to reach out to trusted educators to help them prepare for the Elementary SSAT. Experienced tutors, teachers, mentors, and consultants can help students with many aspects of their preparation – from evaluating and reevaluating their needs, to creating an effective plan to help them make the most of their practice.

3rd Grade Diagnostic Practice Test (Form A)

Overview

The first step to an effective study plan is to determine a student's strengths and areas for improvement. This first practice test assesses a student's existing knowledge and grasp of concepts that may be seen on the actual exam.

Keep in mind that this practice test will be scored differently from the actual exam. On the actual Elementary SSAT, **certain questions will not count towards a student's actual score (i.e. the experimental section).** Also, the student's score will be determined by comparing his or her performance with those of other students in the same grade. On this practice test, however, every question is scored in order to accurately gauge the student's current ability level. Therefore, **this practice test should NOT be used as a gauge of how a student will score on the actual test**. This test should only be used to help students develop a study plan, and may be treated as a diagnostic test.

Format

The format of this diagnostic practice test is similar to that of the actual exam and includes 15 questions in a mock-experimental section. **For practice purposes only, students should treat the mock experimental section of the diagnostic practice test as any other.**

The format of the diagnostic practice test is below.

<table>
<tr><th>Scoring</th><th>Section</th><th>Number of Questions</th><th>Time Limit</th></tr>
<tr><td rowspan="5">Scored Section</td><td>Section 1: Quantitative</td><td>30</td><td>30 minutes</td></tr>
<tr><td>Section 2: Verbal</td><td>30</td><td>20 minutes</td></tr>
<tr><td colspan="3">15-Minute Break</td></tr>
<tr><td>Section 3: Reading</td><td>28</td><td>30 minutes</td></tr>
<tr><td>Total Scored Exam (Sections 1-3)</td><td>88</td><td>1 hour, 20 minutes</td></tr>
<tr><td>Unscored Section (sent to schools)</td><td>Section 4: Writing Sample</td><td>1</td><td>15 minutes</td></tr>
<tr><td>Unscored Section</td><td>Section 5: Experimental</td><td>15</td><td>15 minutes</td></tr>
</table>

Answering

Use the answer sheet provided on the next page to record answers. Students may wish to tear it out of the workbook.

Section 1: Quantitative

1 ⒶⒷⒸⒹⒺ	7 ⒶⒷⒸⒹⒺ	13 ⒶⒷⒸⒹⒺ	19 ⒶⒷⒸⒹⒺ	25 ⒶⒷⒸⒹⒺ
2 ⒶⒷⒸⒹⒺ	8 ⒶⒷⒸⒹⒺ	14 ⒶⒷⒸⒹⒺ	20 ⒶⒷⒸⒹⒺ	26 ⒶⒷⒸⒹⒺ
3 ⒶⒷⒸⒹⒺ	9 ⒶⒷⒸⒹⒺ	15 ⒶⒷⒸⒹⒺ	21 ⒶⒷⒸⒹⒺ	27 ⒶⒷⒸⒹⒺ
4 ⒶⒷⒸⒹⒺ	10 ⒶⒷⒸⒹⒺ	16 ⒶⒷⒸⒹⒺ	22 ⒶⒷⒸⒹⒺ	28 ⒶⒷⒸⒹⒺ
5 ⒶⒷⒸⒹⒺ	11 ⒶⒷⒸⒹⒺ	17 ⒶⒷⒸⒹⒺ	23 ⒶⒷⒸⒹⒺ	29 ⒶⒷⒸⒹⒺ
6 ⒶⒷⒸⒹⒺ	12 ⒶⒷⒸⒹⒺ	18 ⒶⒷⒸⒹⒺ	24 ⒶⒷⒸⒹⒺ	30 ⒶⒷⒸⒹⒺ

Section 2: Verbal

1 ⒶⒷⒸⒹⒺ	7 ⒶⒷⒸⒹⒺ	13 ⒶⒷⒸⒹⒺ	19 ⒶⒷⒸⒹⒺ	25 ⒶⒷⒸⒹⒺ
2 ⒶⒷⒸⒹⒺ	8 ⒶⒷⒸⒹⒺ	14 ⒶⒷⒸⒹⒺ	20 ⒶⒷⒸⒹⒺ	26 ⒶⒷⒸⒹⒺ
3 ⒶⒷⒸⒹⒺ	9 ⒶⒷⒸⒹⒺ	15 ⒶⒷⒸⒹⒺ	21 ⒶⒷⒸⒹⒺ	27 ⒶⒷⒸⒹⒺ
4 ⒶⒷⒸⒹⒺ	10 ⒶⒷⒸⒹⒺ	16 ⒶⒷⒸⒹⒺ	22 ⒶⒷⒸⒹⒺ	28 ⒶⒷⒸⒹⒺ
5 ⒶⒷⒸⒹⒺ	11 ⒶⒷⒸⒹⒺ	17 ⒶⒷⒸⒹⒺ	23 ⒶⒷⒸⒹⒺ	29 ⒶⒷⒸⒹⒺ
6 ⒶⒷⒸⒹⒺ	12 ⒶⒷⒸⒹⒺ	18 ⒶⒷⒸⒹⒺ	24 ⒶⒷⒸⒹⒺ	30 ⒶⒷⒸⒹⒺ

Section 3: Reading

1 ⒶⒷⒸⒹⒺ	7 ⒶⒷⒸⒹⒺ	13 ⒶⒷⒸⒹⒺ	19 ⒶⒷⒸⒹⒺ	25 ⒶⒷⒸⒹⒺ
2 ⒶⒷⒸⒹⒺ	8 ⒶⒷⒸⒹⒺ	14 ⒶⒷⒸⒹⒺ	20 ⒶⒷⒸⒹⒺ	26 ⒶⒷⒸⒹⒺ
3 ⒶⒷⒸⒹⒺ	9 ⒶⒷⒸⒹⒺ	15 ⒶⒷⒸⒹⒺ	21 ⒶⒷⒸⒹⒺ	27 ⒶⒷⒸⒹⒺ
4 ⒶⒷⒸⒹⒺ	10 ⒶⒷⒸⒹⒺ	16 ⒶⒷⒸⒹⒺ	22 ⒶⒷⒸⒹⒺ	28 ⒶⒷⒸⒹⒺ
5 ⒶⒷⒸⒹⒺ	11 ⒶⒷⒸⒹⒺ	17 ⒶⒷⒸⒹⒺ	23 ⒶⒷⒸⒹⒺ	
6 ⒶⒷⒸⒹⒺ	12 ⒶⒷⒸⒹⒺ	18 ⒶⒷⒸⒹⒺ	24 ⒶⒷⒸⒹⒺ	

Section 4: Writing Sample

[Use space provided in the test. Do not write your sample here]

Section 5: Experimental

1 ⒶⒷⒸⒹⒺ	5 ⒶⒷⒸⒹⒺ	9 ⒶⒷⒸⒹⒺ	13 ⒶⒷⒸⒹⒺ
2 ⒶⒷⒸⒹⒺ	6 ⒶⒷⒸⒹⒺ	10 ⒶⒷⒸⒹⒺ	14 ⒶⒷⒸⒹⒺ
3 ⒶⒷⒸⒹⒺ	7 ⒶⒷⒸⒹⒺ	11 ⒶⒷⒸⒹⒺ	15 ⒶⒷⒸⒹⒺ
4 ⒶⒷⒸⒹⒺ	8 ⒶⒷⒸⒹⒺ	12 ⒶⒷⒸⒹⒺ	

SECTION 1
30 Questions

There are five suggested answers after each problem in this section. Solve each problem in your head or in the space provided to the right of the problem. Then, look at the suggested answers and pick the best one.

Note: Any figures or shapes that accompany problems in Section 1 are drawn as accurately as possible EXCEPT when it is stated that the figure is NOT drawn to scale.

Sample Question:

11 × 12 =	●ⒷⒸⒹⒺ
(A) 132	
(B) 144	
(C) 1,112	
(D) 1,332	
(E) 1,444	

DO WORK IN THIS SPACE

1. Which of the following fractions is the largest?
   (A) $\frac{2}{9}$
   (B) $\frac{6}{9}$
   (C) $\frac{4}{9}$
   (D) $\frac{5}{9}$
   (E) $\frac{1}{9}$

2. A dart is randomly thrown at the dartboard at right. Which letter would the dart MOST likely land on?
   (A) A
   (B) B
   (C) C
   (D) D
   (E) E

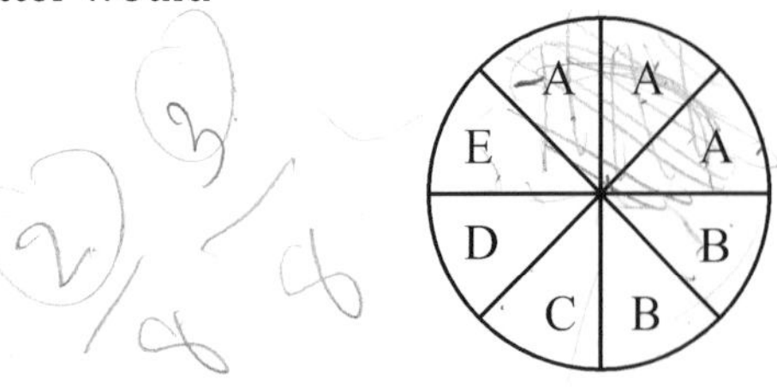

3. Tracy auditioned for the school play on October 3rd and got the part. The first day of rehearsal is 1 week and 4 days after the audition. When is the first day of rehearsal?
   (A) October 7
   (B) October 10
   (C) October 14
   (D) October 17
   (E) October 20

GO ON TO THE NEXT PAGE.

DO WORK IN THIS SPACE

4. 18 ÷ 5 =
   (A) 2
   (B) 2 R 3
   (C) 3
   (D) 3 R 3
   (E) 4 R 2

---

5. One cup of coffee costs $3. Jorge buys a coffee every weekday morning. How much does Jorge spend on coffee in one week?
   (A) $8
   (B) $9
   (C) $12
   (D) $15
   (E) $21

Questions 6 and 7 are based on the graph shown on the right:

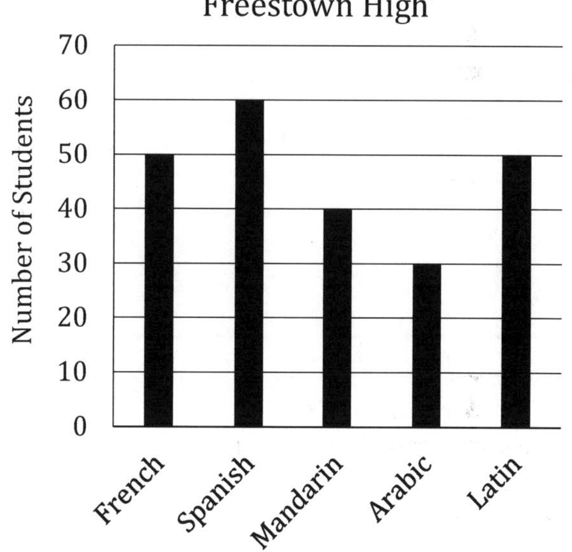

6. How many students at Freestown High School study Mandarin?
   (A) 35
   (B) 40
   (C) 45
   (D) 50
   (E) 60

7. How many students study Spanish or French?
   (A) 10
   (B) 50
   (C) 60
   (D) 110
   (E) 120

---

8. 132 + 69 =
   (A) 191
   (B) 201
   (C) 202
   (D) 211
   (E) 212

---

9. Cheryl started with 376 cents in her piggy bank. Her grandma gave her $5.55 as a gift. How much money does Cheryl now have?
   (A) $1.79
   (B) $8.21
   (C) $9.21
   (D) $9.31
   (E) $9.46

GO ON TO THE NEXT PAGE.

DO WORK IN THIS SPACE

10. What do the shapes shown at the right have in common?
    (A) They are all rectangles.
    (B) They are all parallelograms.
    (C) They are all quadrilaterals.
    (D) They are all squares
    (E) They are all trapezoids.

11. 6 yd. = ____ ft.?
    (Note: 1 yard = 3 feet)
    (A) 0.5
    (B) 2
    (C) 9
    (D) 12
    (E) 18

12. On a scale model of a city, 1 centimeter represents 250 meters. If the length of a street is 5 centimeters on the model, how long is the street, in meters?
    (A) 50
    (B) 750
    (C) 1,000
    (D) 1,250
    (E) 1,500

13. Which word best describes the triangle shown at the right?
    (A) equilateral
    (B) isosceles
    (C) scalene
    (D) right
    (E) obtuse

14. There are 30 pieces of candy in a jar: 7 green, 3 red, 8 orange, 5 yellow, and 7 purple. If you were to close your eyes and randomly select a piece of candy from the jar, which color candy would you MOST likely select?
    (A) green
    (B) red
    (C) orange
    (D) yellow
    (E) purple

15. Marissa bought $\frac{1}{2}$ pound of cheddar cheese and $\frac{3}{5}$ pound of swiss cheese. How many pounds of cheese did Marissa buy in total?
    (A) $\frac{1}{10}$
    (B) $\frac{4}{7}$
    (C) $\frac{4}{5}$
    (D) 1
    (E) $1\frac{1}{10}$

GO ON TO THE NEXT PAGE.

DO WORK IN THIS SPACE

16. A lemonade stand charges \$4 per cup of lemonade. If they collected \$48 dollars, how many cups of lemonade were sold?
    (A) 52
    (B) 44
    (C) 16
    (D) 14
    (E) 12

17. What was the average temperature of the five cities listed on the right on January 1st?
    (A) 5°
    (B) 42°
    (C) 43°
    (D) 57°
    (E) 61°

Temperature on Jan 1st

City	Temperature
Tampa Bay	72°
Montelier	15°
New Orleans	61°
Boston	19°
Richmond	43°

18. What is $\frac{22}{5}$ expressed as a mixed number?
    (A) $3\frac{3}{5}$
    (B) $4\frac{2}{5}$
    (C) $4\frac{3}{5}$
    (D) $5\frac{2}{5}$
    (E) $5\frac{3}{5}$

19. In Swanson City, there are 4 fire hydrants on each city block. If Ursula drove past 80 fire hydrants, how many blocks did she drive?
    (A) 2
    (B) 10
    (C) 20
    (D) 84
    (E) 320

20. What is the area of the triangle shown on the right?
    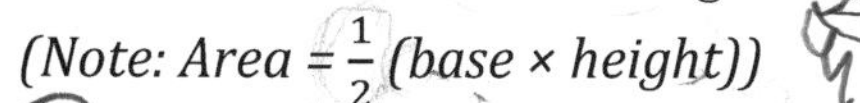
    (Note: Area = $\frac{1}{2}$(base × height))
    (A) 6 square units
    (B) 8 square units
    (C) 10 square units
    (D) 12 square units
    (E) 18 square units

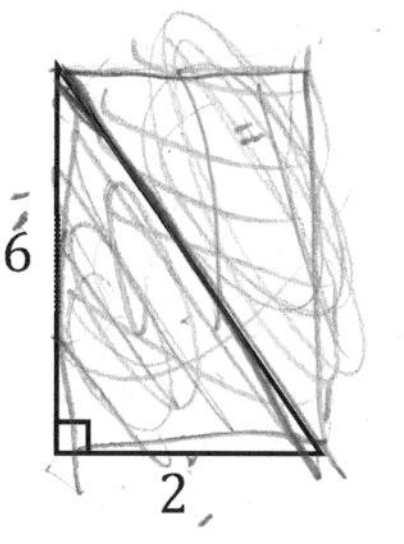

21. What is 854 minus 673?
    (A) 171
    (B) 181
    (C) 191
    (D) 221
    (E) 281

GO ON TO THE NEXT PAGE.

DO WORK IN THIS SPACE

22. A movie starts at 3:40 p.m., and is 2 hours and 5 minutes long. At what time will the movie end?
    (A) 4:05 p.m.
    (B) 5:05 p.m.
    (C) 5:35 p.m.
    (D) 5:40 p.m.
    (E) 5:45 p.m.

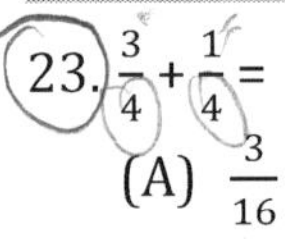

23. $\frac{3}{4} + \frac{1}{4} =$
    (A) $\frac{3}{16}$
    (B) $\frac{1}{2}$
    (C) 1
    (D) $1\frac{1}{4}$
    (E) 2

24. At a food stand, an ice cream cone costs $1.50, a burger costs $1.75, a bag of popcorn costs $0.75, a soda costs $1.00, and an apple costs $0.50. Which of the following shows the items listed from least to most expensive?
    (A) apple, soda, popcorn, burger, ice cream cone
    (B) apple, popcorn, soda, ice cream cone, burger
    (C) popcorn, apple, soda, ice cream cone, burger
    (D) popcorn, soda, apple, burger, ice cream cone
    (E) apple, popcorn, ice cream cone, burger, soda

25. What is the area of the shape shown on the right?
    (A) 32 square units
    (B) 36 square units
    (C) 40 square units
    (D) 56 square units
    (E) 60 square units

26. Karen has 123 tadpoles in her tank. Julie has 48 fewer tadpoles than Karen. Padma has 57 fewer tadpoles than Karen. How many tadpoles do they have all together?
    (A) 18
    (B) 123
    (C) 216
    (D) 264
    (E) 382

27. What is 234 rounded to the nearest ten?
    (A) 200
    (B) 230
    (C) 235
    (D) 240
    (E) 250

GO ON TO THE NEXT PAGE.

DO WORK IN THIS SPACE

28. What is twenty thousand three hundred fifty-four?
    (A) 23,544
    (B) 23,540
    (C) 23,504
    (D) 20,354
    (E) 20,345

29. Carter received money for her birthday. She put half of the money into a bank account. Then, she spent $60 on toys and books. If she has $50 left over, how much did she receive for her birthday?
    (A) 110
    (B) 120
    (C) 160
    (D) 170
    (E) 220

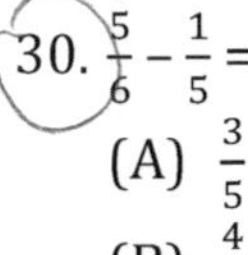

30. $\frac{5}{6} - \frac{1}{5} =$
    (A) $\frac{3}{5}$
    (B) $\frac{4}{5}$
    (C) $\frac{19}{30}$
    (D) $1\frac{1}{30}$
    (E) 4

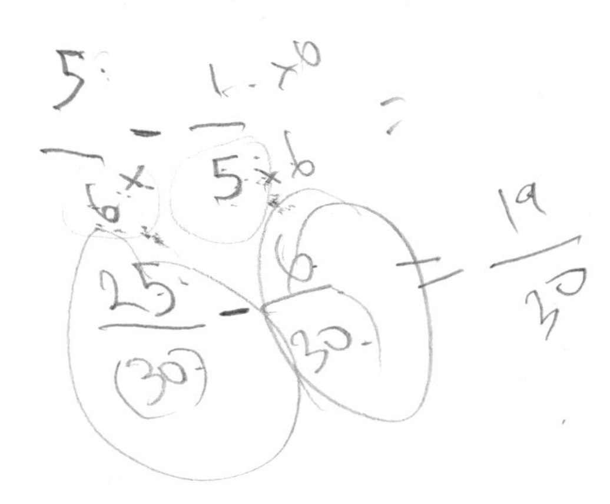

STOP

IF YOU FINISH BEFORE TIME IS UP,
CHECK YOUR WORK IN THIS SECTION ONLY.
YOU MAY NOT TURN TO ANY OTHER SECTION.

SECTION 2
30 Questions

There are two different types of questions in this section: synonyms and analogies. Read the directions and sample question for each type.

Synonyms
Each of the questions that follow consist of one capitalized word. Each word is followed by five words or phrases. Select the one word or phrase whose meaning is closest to the word in capital letters.

Sample Question:

COLD: ● Ⓑ Ⓒ Ⓓ Ⓔ

(A) chilly
(B) cloudy
(C) shady
(D) boring
(E) friendly

1. MANE:
   (A) tangle
   (B) feather
   (C) state
   (D) hair
   (E) horse

2. RECOGNIZE:
   (A) respond
   (B) classmate
   (C) know
   (D) record
   (E) familiar

3. STUMBLE:
   (A) jump
   (B) trip
   (C) stump
   (D) rock
   (E) hurt

4. BURST:
   (A) noise
   (B) born
   (C) collapse
   (D) erupt
   (E) bubble

5. DIFFERENT:
   (A) unlike
   (B) related
   (C) similar
   (D) bizarre
   (E) another

6. OCCUR:
   (A) hold
   (B) happen
   (C) think
   (D) forget
   (E) event

7. FAMOUS:
   (A) genius
   (B) unknown
   (C) greedy
   (D) star
   (E) well-known

8. RIDICULOUS:
   (A) rude
   (B) clown
   (C) disturbing
   (D) silly
   (E) noisy

GO ON TO THE NEXT PAGE.

9. COOPERATION:
   (A) interact
   (B) talk
   (C) teamwork
   (D) partners
   (E) argument

10. GIFT:
   (A) holiday
   (B) celebrate
   (C) present
   (D) family
   (E) gruff

11. TIDY:
   (A) neat
   (B) spill
   (C) mess
   (D) spray
   (E) bedroom

12. AWARE:
   (A) guarded
   (B) alive
   (C) ignorant
   (D) conscious
   (E) gaze

13. GLIDE:
   (A) shine
   (B) launch
   (C) glitter
   (D) slippery
   (E) sail

14. MARCH:
   (A) way
   (B) chase
   (C) band
   (D) month
   (E) walk

15. BOLDLY:
   (A) weakly
   (B) fearlessly
   (C) big
   (D) old
   (E) wordily

GO ON TO THE NEXT PAGE.

Analogies

The questions that follow ask you to find relationships between words. For each question, select the answer choice that best completes the meaning of the sentence.

Sample Question:

Jump is to leap as: 

(A) twirl is to spin
(B) dance is to dancer
(C) runner is to race
(D) hot is to cold
(E) happy is to sad

Choice (A) is the best answer because jump and leap are synonyms, just as twirl and spin are synonyms. This choice states a relationship that is most like the relationship between jump and leap.

---

16. Mop is to janitor as
    (A) clay is to potter
    (B) cleaner is to spray
    (C) robber is to thief
    (D) imagine is to sketch
    (E) dust is to stain

17. Banana is to fruit as pork is to
    (A) hog
    (B) beef
    (C) smoothie
    (D) meat
    (E) cooking

18. Gaze is to look as
    (A) boiling is to frozen
    (B) snooze is to doze
    (C) actual is to unreal
    (D) decay is to growth
    (E) confess is to conceal

19. Cheer is to discourage as
    (A) love is to adore
    (B) break is to repair
    (C) football is to sports
    (D) sad is to unhappy
    (E) parade is to march

20. Deer is to dear as whole is to
    (A) hole
    (B) complete
    (C) mole
    (D) whale
    (E) part

21. Square is to shape as
    (A) shoe is to sandal
    (B) triangle is to circle
    (C) pushup is to exercise
    (D) area is to perimeter
    (E) activity is to skiing

22. Goat is to herd as roof is to
    (A) top
    (B) shed
    (C) ewe
    (D) ground
    (E) open

23. Smart is to brilliant as
    (A) puddle is to lake
    (B) genius is to intelligent
    (C) dusk is to twilight
    (D) blast is to noise
    (E) beginning is to ending

GO ON TO THE NEXT PAGE.

24. Artwork is to beautiful as
    (A) sticky is to gel
    (B) bakery is to dough
    (C) overcast is to sky
    (D) awake is to sleepy
    (E) pillow is to soft

25. Shovel is to dig as
    (A) discard is to trash
    (B) ditch is to mound
    (C) lesson is to spelling
    (D) stove is to cook
    (E) mane is to tail

26. Cement is to builder as bait is to
    (A) catch
    (B) prey
    (C) construction
    (D) fisherman
    (E) accountant

27. Bulb is to lamp as
    (A) bed is to mattress
    (B) number is to equation
    (C) egg is to yolk
    (D) worker is to boss
    (E) litter is to pup

28. Banquet is to chef as
    (A) gourmet is to snack
    (B) soup is to stew
    (C) chemist is to solution
    (D) welcoming is to hostess
    (E) puppet is to toymaker

29. Hare is to hair as
    (A) bunny is to curly
    (B) rabbit is to blonde
    (C) shop is to slop
    (D) energy is to battery
    (E) grown is to groan

30. Dozen is to twelve as elegant is to
    (A) lady
    (B) beauty
    (C) lounge
    (D) stylish
    (E) private

STOP

IF YOU FINISH BEFORE TIME IS UP,
CHECK YOUR WORK IN THIS SECTION ONLY.
YOU MAY NOT TURN TO ANY OTHER SECTION.

SECTION 3
28 Questions

Carefully read each passage and then answer the questions about it. For each question, select the choice that best answers the question based on the passage.

3 astrnauts

Every American should know Neil Armstrong and Buzz Aldrin. They were the first two astronauts to walk on the moon in 1969. But who was third? The answer is Charles Conrad. He was a former U.S. Navy pilot everybody called Pete. He learned to fly airplanes while he was still in high school. He joined the Navy after college. In 1962, he was chosen for the astronaut program. (5)

conrad was tested

Conrad was an unusual character. Astronauts had to go through a lot of tests of their minds and bodies, but Conrad didn't like them. In one test, he had to look for patterns in blots of ink. He was given a card with no blots on it. Conrad looked at it for a moment and joked, "It's upside down." Some of the people choosing the astronauts didn't think he was suitable for the job. Others thought he was. In 1965, (10) he spent eight days orbiting the earth in a tiny capsule with another astronaut. He called it a "flying garbage can."

stepped on moon

In December 1969, Pete Conrad flew on America's second mission to the moon. When he stepped onto the surface, he made another joke. When Neil Armstrong first stepped onto the moon he had said, "That's a small step for a man." (15) But Pete Conrad, who was only five feet, six inches tall, said, "That may have been a small step for Neil, but it's a big one for me."

1. Which of these best describes the main idea of this passage?
   (A) Pete Conrad didn't like the astronaut tests.
   (B) The third American to walk on the moon was different from other astronauts.
   (C) Americans were the first to reach the moon.
   (D) Pete Conrad was chosen to be an astronaut for many reasons.
   (E) Astronauts must learn how to fly airplanes before they can fly in space.

2. Why did some people think Pete Conrad would not make a good astronaut?
   (A) He was too short.
   (B) He was not a good airplane pilot.
   (C) He seemed not serious about the job.
   (D) He did not like his space capsule.
   (E) He had not attended college.

3. Pete Conrad first become a pilot in
   (A) high school
   (B) college
   (C) the Navy
   (D) space
   (E) 1962

4. In line 10, what does "suitable" mean?
   (A) chosen
   (B) dressed
   (C) right
   (D) trained
   (E) tall

GO ON TO THE NEXT PAGE.

When I was five, our family moved to the other side of the country. I had only known one home, one school, one town, and one set of friends. I was worried about leaving everything. "It'll be an adventure," my mom told me. I would be taking my first trip on a huge jet. I would get to explore a brand-new place. Even my little three-
5 year-old brother Bobby was excited! But a big part of me was scared. I had no idea what my new life would be like.

The day we left, my stomach felt like caterpillars were crawling in it. The airport was crowded. We couldn't see where we were going because there were so many grown-ups in front of us. Bobby and I wheeled our own suitcases. I held my
10 mom's hand tightly. Soon, we got into our seats on the plane. They were tall and grey, and had little TVs on the back. I opened the window cover and looked out. All of a sudden, I heard the roar of the engine. And then a whooshing as we took off! I could see the world below turn slanted, and then get really small. After a while a nice lady came by and asked if we wanted headphones, pillows and snacks. Bobby and I looked
15 at each other. We started to giggle. Plane trips were fun! And my stomach ache was gone!

We got to Seattle and the exciting plane ride soon became a memory. Bobby and I got our own bedrooms. We made great new friends. We explored the outdoors with our mom and dad. I thought: what was I so scared of?

5. The narrator wrote this passage to
   (A) warn readers about airplane travel
   (B) explain why moving is scary
   (C) describe the inside of an airplane
   (D) complain about little brothers
   (E) show that trying new things can be more fun than you think

6. In line 13, "slanted" could best be replaced with
   (A) over
   (B) circles
   (C) dark
   (D) sideways
   (E) around

7. In line 14, "head phones, pillows and snacks" are examples of
   (A) what the narrator brought with her
   (B) what the plane provided
   (C) what the narrator didn't share with her brother
   (D) what the narrator's parents bought for them
   (E) what was waiting for them in Seattle

8. We can assume the narrator started to giggle in line 15 because she
   (A) thought the lady on the plane was funny
   (B) told a silly joke
   (C) was beginning to get excited about their trip
   (D) no longer had a stomach ache
   (E) saw an amusing video on the airplane's TV screen

GO ON TO THE NEXT PAGE.

Everyone loves the stories movies tell. Live plays also tell stories, but in a different way. In many ways, plays are better than movies.

One reason plays are better than movies is that plays are live. The actors are right in front of you. The performances can change every night. You never know
5 what will happen at a live play. Movies are always the same when you re-watch them. This makes plays more exciting than movies.

The sets and music are also more exciting in plays. Imagine a play set in France. The set designers must build a French street on the stage. You watch as people move one set off stage after a scene. They replace it with another set entirely.
10 In movies, these changes are done when the movie is made. You don't get to see the magic of the stage in real time. Similarly, in plays, the music is played in front of you. Musicians perform in an area right by the stage. This is called the 'pit.' In movies, the music is recorded. This is much less thrilling than live music.

Finally, you can often meet the actors after a play. This helps people feel closer
15 to the performers. You can also ask the actors questions. This helps you learn about the play and how it is made. After a movie, you just see the names of the actors on the screen. This makes plays a better learning experience.

Overall, plays are a more exciting experience than movies. You are close to the action and get to watch a world created on the stage. Next time you're by a play
20 theatre, go inside and check out the showings!

9. The author wrote this passage to
   - (A) explain how plays and movies are made
   - (B) argue that plays are better than movies
   - (C) describe actors in plays and movies
   - (D) compare music from plays and movies
   - (E) tell how plays and movies are alike

10. In line 4, "performances" could be best replaced with
    - (A) sets
    - (B) movies
    - (C) shows
    - (D) stages
    - (E) alive

11. We can assume that movies offer fewer learning opportunities than plays because the audience
    - (A) sees the sets change on screen
    - (B) cannot hear music being played
    - (C) cannot ask the actors questions
    - (D) is too close to the action on screen
    - (E) does not know the names of the actors

12. "Magic of the stage" in line 11 probably means
    - (A) spells
    - (B) stunts
    - (C) secrets
    - (D) wonder
    - (E) sorcery

GO ON TO THE NEXT PAGE.

I will be the gladdest thing
Under the sun!
I will touch a hundred flowers
And not pick one.
5 I will look at cliffs and clouds
With quiet eyes,
Watch the wind bow down the grass,
And the grass rise.
And when lights begin to show
10 Up from the town,
I will mark which must be mine,
And then start down!

13. The author wrote the poem to
(A) detail her chores
(B) show she loves nature
(C) tell about her town
(D) describe her garden
(E) explain a dream

14. The word that best describes the speaker in the poem is
(A) tired
(B) loyal
(C) bored
(D) helpful
(E) thankful

15. In line 6, "quiet eyes" could best be replaced with
(A) dislike
(B) respect
(C) fear
(D) sadness
(E) gratitude

16. According to the poem, the speaker will return to town after
(A) she finishes picking flowers
(B) the sun comes up
(C) the clouds appear
(D) the wind starts to blow
(E) the town lights come on

GO ON TO THE NEXT PAGE.

Helping others is important. Volunteering is a good way to help out. What is volunteering? It is working for free, to help others who need it.

The U.S. has a long history of volunteers. Benjamin Franklin was a volunteer. In 1736, he started a firehouse. The firefighters were not paid for their work. They did it because they wanted to keep people safe. Even today, many firefighters are volunteers.

In 1865, the Salvation Army was started. This group helps the poor. They help by collecting clothing. Volunteers sort the clothes. Then they bring them to families who need it. These clothes keep people warm in the winter. The Salvation Army also collects money for the holidays. Volunteer workers ring bells outside stores. People put money into red kettles. The money buys meals for people.

Another big volunteer group is the American Red Cross. It was started in 1881 by a nurse. Her name was Clara Barton. Today, the Red Cross raises money after disasters. It also runs blood drives. This helps injured people.

Soup kitchens are also a popular way to volunteer. People opened soup kitchens in the 1930s. At the time, many people did not have jobs. They were hungry. Soup kitchens gave them food for free. Many cities still have soup kitchens. They are run by volunteers.

Have you ever heard of the Peace Corps? John F. Kennedy founded this group in 1961. It helps poor countries. Volunteers sign up for two years. They travel to another country. There, they build hospitals. They help people farm. They also teach children. They don't do these things for money. They do it to help the countries get better.

Today, people volunteer more than ever. Everyone likes to help others. Volunteers make the world a better place.

17. The main idea of the passage is
    (A) firefighters were not paid in the past
    (B) volunteering is a good way to earn money
    (C) people should volunteer in other countries
    (D) the Salvation Army collects clothes for needy people
    (E) people have volunteered in many different ways through history

18. We can assume soup kitchens were first started because
    (A) soup is expensive to make
    (B) volunteers hoped to find work
    (C) soup is a popular type of food
    (D) many people lost their jobs
    (E) the president asked people to help

19. According to the passage, the Peace Corps is different from the Salvation Army because people in the Peace Corps
    (A) are volunteers
    (B) travel to other countries
    (C) do their work for free
    (D) try to help needy people
    (E) collect money from others

20. In line 14, "disasters" could best be replaced with
    (A) illnesses
    (B) journeys
    (C) gatherings
    (D) arguments
    (E) emergencies

GO ON TO THE NEXT PAGE.

By now the dragon realized that my father was coming to rescue him. He ran out of the bushes and jumped up and down yelling. "Here I am! I'm right here! Can you see me? Hurry, the pig is coming over on the crocodiles, too. They're all coming over!"

5 My father ran up to the dragon, and took out his very sharp knife. "Steady, old boy, steady. We'll make it. Just stand still," he told the dragon as he began to saw through the big rope.

By this time both pigs, all seven tigers, the two lions, and the monkey were all on their way across the crocodiles. There was still a lot of rope to cut through.

10 "Oh, hurry," the dragon kept saying, and my father again told him to stand still. "If I don't think I can make it," said my father, "we'll fly over to the other side of the river and I can finish cutting the rope there."

My father finished cutting the rope and the dragon raced around in circles. He was the most excited baby dragon that ever lived. My father was in a hurry to fly

15 away, and when the dragon finally calmed down a bit my father climbed up onto his back.

"All aboard!" said the dragon. "Where shall we go?"

"We'll spend the night on the beach, and tomorrow we'll start on the long journey home."

20 But my father and the dragon knew that nothing in the world would ever make them go back to Wild Island.

21. The main problem the father faces is
   - (A) trying to rescue the dragon in time
   - (B) escaping the pig chasing him
   - (C) never returning to Wild Island
   - (D) making sure the dragon knows about the rescue
   - (E) flying on the dragon's back

22. The dragon raced around in circles because
   - (A) he was trying to scare the other animals away
   - (B) he was trying to leave Wild Island
   - (C) he wanted the father to ride on his back
   - (D) he was so happy that he was free from the rope
   - (E) he was having trouble taking flight

23. The word that best describes the father is
   - (A) cowardly
   - (B) gloomy
   - (C) brave
   - (D) excitable
   - (E) loud

24. We can assume that Wild Island is not a real place because
   - (A) this is a nonfiction passage
   - (B) there are fantastical characters like dragons living there
   - (C) there are pigs, monkeys, crocodiles, tigers and lions living there
   - (D) the father and dragon do not want to go back there
   - (E) it has a strange name

GO ON TO THE NEXT PAGE.

In gardens, bees fly from flower to flower. Bees make honey, but that isn't all they do! They are very important to humans. Unfortunately, bees have been dying. Experts say some things that humans do are killing them. It is important to do what we can to help keep bees healthy.

What exactly are bees good for? Each time a bee visits a different plant, it pollinates it. This means the bee is sharing pollen between plants. Sharing the pollen helps plants make seeds. And these seeds create most of the food that people eat. So, bees are important because they help feed the world.

Scientists say there is not just one reason that bees are dying. But they do know that humans play a part. Many chemicals people use are not good for bees. If bees bring chemicals back to the hive, the queen bee might die. If the queen dies, the rest of the colony will, too. Killing plants also hurts bees. It takes away their food source. Scientists have said that building on open land is making them die off, too.

It will not be easy, but together, in small ways, we can save the bees. Start by using fewer chemicals at home. Clean using natural products like water and vinegar. To kill pesky bugs, use natural pesticides. Also, grow a garden with plants like pansies, marigold and lavender, which bees enjoy. Bees do so much for us, shouldn't we try to return the favor?

25. The author wrote this passage to
    - (A) convince people that bees are only good for making honey
    - (B) inform that pollen is healthy food for humans
    - (C) persuade people to save bees
    - (D) tell an entertaining story about bees
    - (E) show how humans need to use chemicals to survive

26. From the passage, we can assume that the queen bee
    - (A) is larger than the other bees
    - (B) has a natural defense against chemicals
    - (C) often kills other bees
    - (D) is dangerous to humans
    - (E) is important to the health of the colony

27. In line 12, what does the word "colony" most likely mean?
    - (A) chemicals
    - (B) king
    - (C) bee
    - (D) food
    - (E) group

28. In line 17, "pansies, marigold and lavender" are mentioned as examples of
    - (A) flowers that bees like
    - (B) natural pesticides
    - (C) plants that harm bees
    - (D) salad ingredients
    - (E) beautiful garden plants

STOP

IF YOU FINISH BEFORE TIME IS UP,
CHECK YOUR WORK IN THIS SECTION ONLY.
YOU MAY NOT TURN TO ANY OTHER SECTION.

SECTION 4
Writing Sample

Look at the picture and tell a story about what happened. Make sure your story includes a beginning, middle, and an end.

GO ON TO THE NEXT PAGE.

STOP

IF YOU FINISH BEFORE TIME IS UP,
CHECK YOUR WORK IN THIS SECTION ONLY.
YOU MAY NOT TURN TO ANY OTHER SECTION.

SECTION 5
15 Questions

New Orleans became a musical city in the 1800s. It sits on the edge of the Mississippi River. This made it a popular place for entertainment. But it was also a place of natural disasters. Floods and diseases happened often. Many people used music for comfort. Music became a symbol of the city's toughness. One musical form became the most popular. It was known as jazz. *5*

Jazz began in Congo Square. A musician named Buddy Bolden mixed musical styles there. He sprinkled in his own ideas. All of a sudden, the world started raving about his jazz.

Bolden's jazzy style spread throughout the nation. In the early 1900s, many jazz musicians moved to the North. They moved to places like Chicago, Kansas City, and Harlem. These cities became the new centers of jazz. Many people in the cities heard this new genre for the first time. *10*

Records began blaring jazz over the radio in the 1920s. Americans enjoyed the music together. They danced in jazz joints across the country. Jazz brought different races and cultures together. It became America's musical melting pot of sounds and cultures. *15*

1. The author wrote this passage to
   (A) inform readers about jazz history
   (B) persuade readers to listen to jazz
   (C) debate the importance of jazz
   (D) discuss the role of jazz on the radio in the 1920s
   (E) explain the history of New Orleans

2. According to the passage, "many people used music for comfort" (lines 3-4) in New Orleans because
   (A) the city sits by the Mississippi River
   (B) floods and diseases happened often
   (C) many musicians were moving North
   (D) the city was known for being tough
   (E) jazz was moving to other places like Chicago, Kansas City, and Harlem

3. What did the author mean by "He sprinkled in his own ideas" (line 7)?
   (A) He was inspired by rainfall.
   (B) He listened to many radio stations.
   (C) He thought a lot about music.
   (D) He played a very fast, light rhythm.
   (E) He played things differently than how they were played before.

4. In line 7, what does "raving" most likely mean?
   (A) spreading
   (B) praising
   (C) blending
   (D) blaring
   (E) melting

5. When did jazz musicians begin moving to northern cities?
   (A) early 1700s
   (B) early 1800s
   (C) early 1900s
   (D) early 1920s
   (E) early 1930s

6. Jazz is an important part of American history because it
   (A) comforted people
   (B) was invented in America
   (C) was invented by Buddy Bolden
   (D) spread all over the country
   (E) brought different races and cultures together

GO ON TO THE NEXT PAGE.

7. ALERT:
   (A) tired
   (B) red
   (C) attention
   (D) watchful
   (E) panic

8. IMITATE:
   (A) same
   (B) move
   (C) fake
   (D) bother
   (E) copy

9. SYMBOL:
   (A) sign
   (B) division
   (C) computer
   (D) mystery
   (E) language

10. Blur is to focus as
    (A) chair is to couch
    (B) asleep is to napping
    (C) realistic is to fantastic
    (D) wizard is to magic
    (E) drink is to thermos

11. Cliff is to steep as
    (A) playful is to dolphin
    (B) snail is to slow
    (C) tall is to skyscraper
    (D) unsurprised is to shocked
    (E) honeyed is to sugary

12. Snowflake is to blizzard as
    (A) cupcake is to icing
    (B) student is to class
    (C) balance is to dance
    (D) follower is to leader
    (E) climate is to weather

13. Julia has two weeks to finish an art project for school. If today is February 19th, and it is not a leap year, what day is her project due? *(Note: There are 28 days in the month of February.)*
    (A) February 1st
    (B) February 4th
    (C) February 5th
    (D) March 4th
    (E) March 5th

14. A square tile has a side of 14 inches long. What is the perimeter of the tile?
    (A) 14 in.
    (B) 24 in.
    (C) 46 in.
    (D) 56 in.
    (E) 196 in.

15. Luna helps her mom at the shop after school. How much money does she earn on average each day?

Luna's Earnings

Day	Amount Earned
Monday	$1.50
Tuesday	$2.00
Wednesday	$1.75
Thursday	$2.50
Friday	$2.25

    (A) $1.25
    (B) $1.50
    (C) $1.75
    (D) $2.00
    (E) $2.25

STOP
IF YOU FINISH BEFORE TIME IS UP,
CHECK YOUR WORK IN THIS SECTION ONLY.
YOU MAY NOT TURN TO ANY OTHER SECTION.

Scoring the 3rd Grade Diagnostic Practice Test (Form A)

Sections 1-3 – Scored

Score the test using the answer sheet and *referring to the answer key in the back of the book (see Table of Contents).*

For each section, record the number of questions answered correctly. This will give you the raw score for each section. Note that the actual test will convert the raw score to a scaled score by comparing the student's performance with all other students in the same grade who took the test.

Section	Questions Correct (Raw Score)
Quantitative *Section 1*	__________
Verbal *Section 2*	__________
Reading *Section 3*	__________

Carefully consider the results from the diagnostic practice test when forming a study plan. Remember, the Elementary SSAT is given to students in grades 3-4. Unless the student has finished 4th grade, chances are that there is material on this test that he or she has not yet been taught. If this is the case, and the student would like to improve beyond what is expected of his or her grade, consider working with a tutor or teacher, who can help the student learn more about new topics.

Section 4 – Writing Sample – Unscored

Have a parent or trusted educator review the essay or story written for the writing sample. Important areas to focus on include organization, clarity of ideas, originality, and technical precision (spelling, grammar, etc.).

Section 5 – Unscored

On the real test, the Experimental section will NOT be scored. Consider the student's performance on this section for practice purposes only. Did he or she do better on one section than another? Use this information along with the information from Sections 1-3 to form the study plan.

4th Grade Diagnostic Practice Test (Form B)

Section 1: Quantitative

1	A B C D E	7	A B C D E	13	A B C D E	19	A B C D E	25	A B C D E
2	A B C D E	8	A B C D E	14	A B C D E	20	A B C D E	26	A B C D E
3	A B C D E	9	A B C D E	15	A B C D E	21	A B C D E	27	A B C D E
4	A B C D E	10	A B C D E	16	A B C D E	22	A B C D E	28	A B C D E
5	A B C D E	11	A B C D E	17	A B C D E	23	A B C D E	29	A B C D E
6	A B C D E	12	A B C D E	18	A B C D E	24	A B C D E	30	A B C D E

Section 2: Verbal

1	A B C D E	7	A B C D E	13	A B C D E	19	A B C D E	25	A B C D E
2	A B C D E	8	A B C D E	14	A B C D E	20	A B C D E	26	A B C D E
3	A B C D E	9	A B C D E	15	A B C D E	21	A B C D E	27	A B C D E
4	A B C D E	10	A B C D E	16	A B C D E	22	A B C D E	28	A B C D E
5	A B C D E	11	A B C D E	17	A B C D E	23	A B C D E	29	A B C D E
6	A B C D E	12	A B C D E	18	A B C D E	24	A B C D E	30	A B C D E

Section 3: Reading

1	A B C D E	7	A B C D E	13	A B C D E	19	A B C D E	25	A B C D E
2	A B C D E	8	A B C D E	14	A B C D E	20	A B C D E	26	A B C D E
3	A B C D E	9	A B C D E	15	A B C D E	21	A B C D E	27	A B C D E
4	A B C D E	10	A B C D E	16	A B C D E	22	A B C D E	28	A B C D E
5	A B C D E	11	A B C D E	17	A B C D E	23	A B C D E		
6	A B C D E	12	A B C D E	18	A B C D E	24	A B C D E		

Section 4: Writing Sample

[Use space provided in the test. Do not write your sample here]

Section 5: Experimental

1	A B C D E	5	A B C D E	9	A B C D E	13	A B C D E
2	A B C D E	6	A B C D E	10	A B C D E	14	A B C D E
3	A B C D E	7	A B C D E	11	A B C D E	15	A B C D E
4	A B C D E	8	A B C D E	12	A B C D E		

Overview

The first step to an effective study plan is to determine a student's strengths and areas for improvement. This first practice test assesses a student's existing knowledge and grasp of concepts that may be seen on the actual exam.

Keep in mind that this practice test will be scored differently from the actual exam. On the actual Elementary SSAT, **certain questions will not count towards a student's actual score (i.e. the experimental section).** Also, the student's score will be determined by comparing his or her performance with those of other students in the same grade. On this practice test, however, every question is scored in order to accurately gauge the student's current ability level. Therefore, **this practice test should NOT be used as a gauge of how a student will score on the actual test**. This test should only be used to help students develop a study plan, and may be treated as a diagnostic test.

Format

The format of this diagnostic practice test is similar to that of the actual exam and includes 15 questions in a mock-experimental section. **For practice purposes only, students should treat the mock experimental section of the diagnostic practice test as any other.**

The format of the diagnostic practice test is below.

Scoring	**Section**	**Number of Questions**	**Time Limit**
Scored Section	Section 1: Quantitative	30	30 minutes
	Section 2: Verbal	30	20 minutes
	15-Minute Break		
	Section 3: Reading	28	30 minutes
	Total Scored Exam (Sections 1-3)	88	**1 hour, 20 minutes**
Unscored Section (sent to schools)	Section 4: Writing Sample	1	15 minutes
Unscored Section	Section 5: Experimental	15	15 minutes

Answering

Use the answer sheet provided on the previous page to record answers. Students may wish to tear it out of the workbook.

SECTION 1
25 Questions

There are five suggested answers after each problem in this section. Solve each problem in your head or in the space provided to the right of the problem. Then, look at the suggested answers and pick the best one.

Note: Any figures or shapes that accompany problems in Section 1 are drawn as accurately as possible EXCEPT when it is stated that the figure is NOT drawn to scale.

Sample Question:

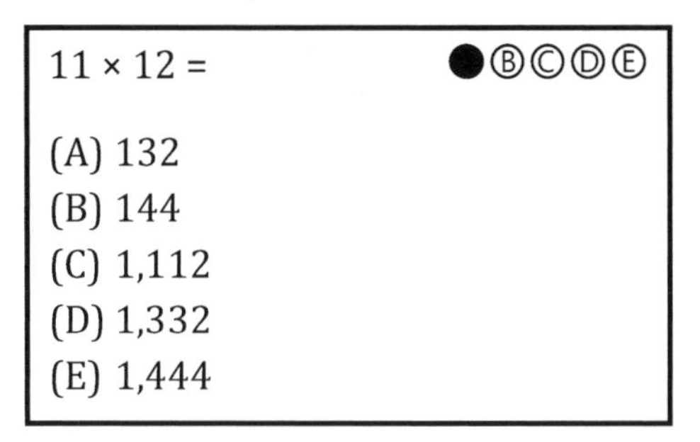

DO WORK IN THIS SPACE

1. What is 6,499 rounded to the nearest thousand?
   (A) 6,000
   (B) 6,400
   (C) 6,500
   (D) 7,000
   (E) 10,000

2. A hat contains 10 pieces of paper, each with a number 1 through 10 written on it. If one piece of paper is selected from the hat at random, which best describes the chance the number on the paper will be less than 7?
   (A) There is no chance the number will be less than 7.
   (B) The number can only be less than 7.
   (C) The number has the same chance of being less than 7 as it does greater than 7.
   (D) The number has a bigger chance of being less than 7 than it does greater than 7.
   (E) The number has a smaller chance of being less than 7 than it does greater than 7.

3. 9 is to 36 as 7 is to ___
   (A) 21
   (B) 26
   (C) 28
   (D) 30
   (E) 35

GO ON TO THE NEXT PAGE.

DO WORK IN THIS SPACE

4. Elias has 18 geodes in his collection. Sabrina has 6 less than four times as many geodes as Elias. How many geodes does Sabrina have?
   (A) 24
   (B) 48
   (C) 66
   (D) 72
   (E) 78

5. If the area of the triangle shown on the right is 18 square units, what is the triangle's vertical height? *(Note: Area =* $\frac{1}{2}$ *(base × vertical height))*
   (A) 3
   (B) 6
   (C) 7.5
   (D) 9
   (E) 12

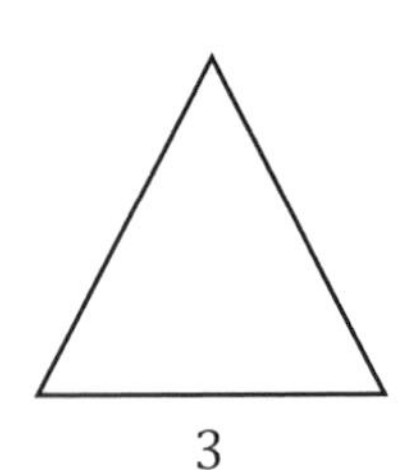

Questions 6-7 are based on the following chart

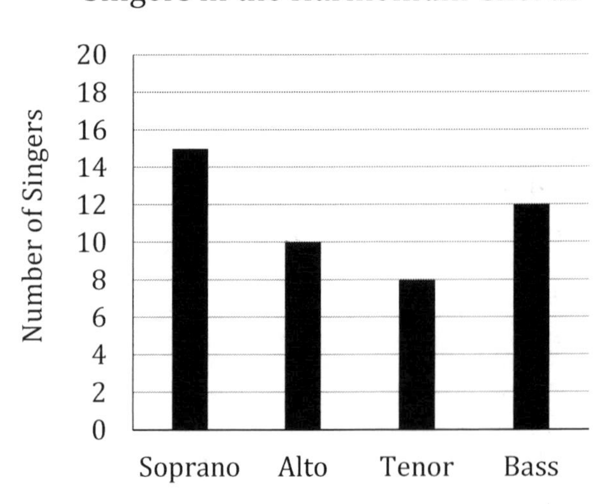

6. The number of tenors in the chorus is:
   (A) 5
   (B) 6
   (C) 8
   (D) 9
   (E) 10

7. If two altos leave the chorus, how many more sopranos will there be than altos?
   (A) 3
   (B) 4
   (C) 5
   (D) 6
   (E) 7

8. Which describes a shape that could be a rectangle but could NOT be a square?
   (A) a quadrilateral with two pairs of parallel sides and four right angles
   (B) a quadrilateral with four right angles and with two opposite sides measuring 2 inches and two opposite sides measuring 4 inches
   (C) a quadrilateral with four sides that measures 8 inches each and four right angles
   (D) a quadrilateral with two pairs of parallel sides that have the same measure and four equal angles
   (E) a quadrilateral with four equal angles and four equal sides

9. 88 + 8 = 90 + ___
   (A) 2
   (B) 6
   (C) 10
   (D) 16
   (E) 18

GO ON TO THE NEXT PAGE.

DO WORK IN THIS SPACE

10. Jenny's last day of school is 2 weeks and 5 days from today. If today is May 29th, on what day is the last day of school?
(Note: There are 31 days in the month of May.)
(A) June 3
(B) June 12
(C) June 17
(D) June 19
(E) June 23

11. Lisa measured the distance in yards from her house to her favorite restaurants. She made a table of the distances she recorded, which is shown on the right. What is the average distance from her house to the restaurants?
(A) 39 yards
(B) 48 yards
(C) 54 yards
(D) 56 yards
(E) 81 yards

Restaurant	Distance (yds.)
Joe's Pizza	42
Shanghai Garden	85
Sushi Deluxe	66
Bombay Palace	13
Venus Diner	36
Pita Prince	94

12. What is $\frac{25}{8}$ expressed as a mixed number?
(A) 3
(B) $3\frac{1}{8}$
(C) $3\frac{5}{8}$
(D) $4\frac{1}{8}$
(E) $4\frac{5}{8}$

13. A teacher randomly divides all the students in her class into four groups: The Owls, The Tigers, The Wolves, and The Sharks. A new student enters the class. In which of these four groups would they MOST likely be placed?
(A) The Owls
(B) The Tigers
(C) The Wolves
(D) The Sharks
(E) There is an equal chance of the student being placed into any of the four groups.

14. 3.4 m = _____ cm?
(A) 0.034
(B) 0.34
(C) 34
(D) 340
(E) 3,400

GO ON TO THE NEXT PAGE.

DO WORK IN THIS SPACE

15. Which set of lines is parallel?

(A)

(B)

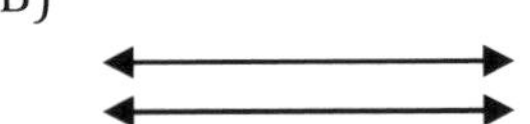

(C)

(D)

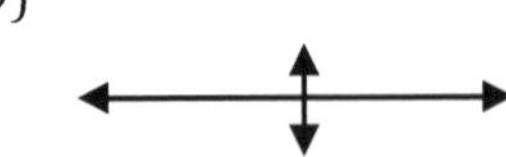

(E)

16. Ruby City has three art museums. If the Institute of Modern Art has a collection of 118 artworks, the Museum of Fine Art has a collection of 293 artworks, and the Museum of Sculpture and Design has a collection of 184 artworks, how many total works of art are there in Ruby City?
(A) 595
(B) 486
(C) 485
(D) 477
(E) 411

17. If $12 \div s = 3$, then $9 \times s = ?$
(A) 3
(B) 4
(C) 13
(D) 27
(E) 36

18. Natasha has a collection of porcelain vases, which weigh 82 ounces, 35 ounces, 64 ounces, 68 ounces, 26 ounces, and 73 ounces. What is the average weight of her vases?
(A) 54 ounces
(B) 56 ounces
(C) 58 ounces
(D) 66 ounces
(E) 348 ounces

19. Mr. Rodriguez bought a sofa that is 72 inches long. What is the length of his sofa, in feet? *(Note: 1 foot = 12 inches.)*
(A) 3
(B) 6
(C) 24
(D) 216
(E) 864

GO ON TO THE NEXT PAGE.

DO WORK IN THIS SPACE

20. Which of the following is the largest fraction?
   (A) $\frac{1}{3}$
   (B) $\frac{1}{4}$
   (C) $\frac{1}{5}$
   (D) $\frac{1}{6}$
   (E) $\frac{2}{3}$

21. A shoe store has 187 pairs of shoes. How many individual shoes does the store have?
   (A) 264
   (B) 272
   (C) 274
   (D) 374
   (E) 464

22. Gina takes 15 minutes to eat breakfast and 25 minutes to wash and dress in the morning. The school bus comes for Gina at 7:50 a.m. If Gina eats, washes, and dresses before the school bus comes for her, what is the latest time Gina must wake up in order to be ready in time for the bus?
   (A) 7:10 a.m.
   (B) 7:15 a.m.
   (C) 7:25 a.m.
   (D) 7:35 a.m.
   (E) 7:50 a.m.

23. $\frac{1}{4} + \frac{5}{6} + \frac{2}{3} =$
   (A) $\frac{8}{13}$
   (B) $\frac{11}{12}$
   (C) $1\frac{1}{12}$
   (D) $1\frac{7}{12}$
   (E) $1\frac{3}{4}$

24. Yuri and Ben buy a bag of 86 pretzels to share. They split the bag evenly and then Yuri gives 27 pretzels to his younger brother. How many pretzels does Yuri have left to eat?
   (A) 16
   (B) 26
   (C) 43
   (D) 70
   (E) 145

GO ON TO THE NEXT PAGE.

DO WORK IN THIS SPACE

25. A square is formed by putting together two equal rectangles. If the perimeter of the square is 64 centimeters, what is the perimeter of either rectangle?
    (A) 24 centimeters
    (B) 32 centimeters
    (C) 48 centimeters
    (D) 64 centimeters
    (E) 128 centimeters

26. Which fractions below are ordered from largest to smallest?
    (A) $\frac{9}{2}, \frac{7}{2}, \frac{5}{2}, \frac{3}{2}, \frac{1}{2}$
    (B) $\frac{1}{2}, \frac{5}{2}, \frac{3}{2}, \frac{9}{2}, \frac{7}{2}$
    (C) $\frac{3}{2}, \frac{1}{2}, \frac{5}{2}, \frac{7}{2}, \frac{9}{2}$
    (D) $\frac{1}{2}, \frac{3}{2}, \frac{5}{2}, \frac{7}{2}, \frac{9}{2}$
    (E) $\frac{1}{2}, \frac{5}{2}, \frac{3}{2}, \frac{9}{2}, \frac{7}{2}$

27. At the school wide meeting, there are 3 students to every 1 teacher. If there are 36 teachers, then how many students are there?
    (A) 12
    (B) 98
    (C) 108
    (D) 118
    (E) 144

28. Find the value of 152 – 139.
    (A) 7
    (B) 13
    (C) 17
    (D) 23
    (E) 27

29. Chris has a $\frac{3}{4}$ of an hour to finish a homework assignment. He spends $\frac{1}{6}$ of an hour playing video games instead. What fraction of an hour does he have left to work on the homework assignment?
    (A) $\frac{1}{6}$
    (B) $\frac{7}{12}$
    (C) $\frac{3}{4}$
    (D) $\frac{11}{12}$
    (E) 1

30. If $x > 5$ and $x < 9$, then x could equal
    (A) 4
    (B) 5
    (C) 7
    (D) 9
    (E) 10

STOP

IF YOU FINISH BEFORE TIME IS UP,
CHECK YOUR WORK IN THIS SECTION ONLY.
YOU MAY NOT TURN TO ANY OTHER SECTION.

SECTION 2
30 Questions

There are two different types of questions in this section: synonyms and analogies. Read the directions and sample question for each type.

Synonyms
Each of the questions that follow consist of one capitalized word. Each word is followed by five words or phrases. Select the one word or phrase whose meaning is closest to the word in capital letters.

Sample Question:

COLD: ●ⒷⒸⒹⒺ

(A) chilly
(B) cloudy
(C) shady
(D) boring
(E) friendly

---

1. VAST:
   (A) distance
   (B) huge
   (C) sea
   (D) compact
   (E) tall

2. LANTERN:
   (A) red
   (B) hanging
   (C) wish
   (D) light
   (E) flame

3. FRAGILE:
   (A) breakable
   (B) fancy
   (C) glass
   (D) heavy
   (E) tough

4. SOAR:
   (A) airplane
   (B) topple
   (C) clamber
   (D) hover
   (E) eagle

5. INSTANT:
   (A) noodles
   (B) made
   (C) immediate
   (D) slow
   (E) delay

6. AROMA:
   (A) coffee
   (B) smell
   (C) soup
   (D) nose
   (E) perfume

7. ORGANIZED:
   (A) closet
   (B) elegant
   (C) messy
   (D) drawer
   (E) ordered

8. WONDERFUL:
   (A) proud
   (B) curious
   (C) admire
   (D) awesome
   (E) awful

GO ON TO THE NEXT PAGE.

9. DEMONSTRATE:
   (A) presentation
   (B) teacher
   (C) direct
   (D) example
   (E) show

10. HARDSHIP:
   (A) poor
   (B) difficulty
   (C) solid
   (D) experience
   (E) simple

11. BEVERAGE:
   (A) dinner
   (B) drink
   (C) snack
   (D) food
   (E) restaurant

12. INTENSE:
   (A) forceful
   (B) concerned
   (C) passion
   (D) strict
   (E) dilute

13. MINIATURE:
   (A) large
   (B) duplicate
   (C) toy
   (D) average
   (E) tiny

14. POISONOUS:
   (A) toxic
   (B) smelly
   (C) enormous
   (D) darts
   (E) frogs

15. GRACEFULLY:
   (A) kindness
   (B) beauty
   (C) smoothly
   (D) roughly
   (E) angrily

GO ON TO THE NEXT PAGE.

Analogies

The questions that follow ask you to find relationships between words. For each question, select the answer choice that best completes the meaning of the sentence.

Sample Question:

Jump is to leap as: ●ⒷⒸⒹⒺ

(A) twirl is to spin
(B) dance is to dancer
(C) runner is to race
(D) hot is to cold
(E) happy is to sad

Choice (A) is the best answer because jump and leap are synonyms, just as twirl and spin are synonyms. This choice states a relationship that is most like the relationship between jump and leap.

---

16. Hornet is to hive as grape is to
    (A) wasp
    (B) bunch
    (C) violet
    (D) seedless
    (E) sting

17. Rays is to raise as
    (A) shall is to hall
    (B) sunshine is to elevate
    (C) sunglasses is to elevator
    (D) limp is to blimp
    (E) waste is to waist

18. Hearty is to filling as
    (A) come is to leave
    (B) new is to worn
    (C) mock is to encourage
    (D) destiny is to fate
    (E) minor is to major

19. Painting is to artist as
    (A) gadget is to inventor
    (B) canvas is to brush
    (C) butler is to bowtie
    (D) ballerina is to tutu
    (E) knight is to armor

20. Blanket is to cover as compass is to
    (A) lost
    (B) neck
    (C) navigate
    (D) East
    (E) treasure

21. Axe is to lumberjack as
    (A) sleep is to nap
    (B) conqueror is to emperor
    (C) hammer is to nail
    (D) wheelbarrow is to gardener
    (E) spy is to wig

22. Shabby is to derelict as
    (A) momentary is to temporary
    (B) resentful is to forgiving
    (C) important is to vital
    (D) dazzling is to brilliant
    (E) plenty is to few

23. Uncle is to relative as penny is to
    (A) coin
    (B) five
    (C) savings
    (D) nephew
    (E) piggybank

24. Monkey is to nimble as
    (A) criminal is to arrest
    (B) keepsake is to precious
    (C) chimp is to ape
    (D) sluggish is to sloth
    (E) loud is to thunderbolt

GO ON TO THE NEXT PAGE.

25. Eliminate is to rid as inside is to
    (A) outside
    (B) room
    (C) exterior
    (D) within
    (E) house

26. Graceful is to awkward as
    (A) fail is to decline
    (B) critical is to important
    (C) queen is to princess
    (D) suspend is to stop
    (E) total is to partial

27. Second is to minute as
    (A) hiccup is to cough
    (B) bookcase is to shelf
    (C) pen is to ink
    (D) page is to magazine
    (E) cube is to corner

28. Brain is to think as
    (A) model is to represent
    (B) evaluate is to test
    (C) dream is to fantasy
    (D) measure is to ruler
    (E) veil is to silk

29. Dress is to clothing as
    (A) fashionable is to design
    (B) texture is to fuzzy
    (C) skirt is to pants
    (D) spice is to cinnamon
    (E) fantasy is to genre

30. Happy is to overjoyed as unkind is to
    (A) nice
    (B) bully
    (C) enemy
    (D) compassion
    (E) cruel

STOP

IF YOU FINISH BEFORE TIME IS UP,
CHECK YOUR WORK IN THIS SECTION ONLY.
YOU MAY NOT TURN TO ANY OTHER SECTION.

SECTION 3
28 Questions

Carefully read each passage and then answer the questions about it. For each question, select the choice that best answers the question based on the passage.

How beautiful is the rain!
After the dust and heat,
In the broad and fiery street,
In the narrow lane,
5 How beautiful is the rain!

How it clatters along the roofs,
Like the tramp of hoofs!
How it gushes and struggles out
From the throat of the overflowing spout!

10 Across the window pane
It pours and pours;
And swift and wide
With a muddy tide,
Like a river down the gutter roars
15 The rain, the welcome rain!

In the country, on every side
Where far and wide
Like a leopard's yellow and spotted hide,
Stretches the plain,
20 To the dry grass and the drier grain
How welcome is the rain!

1. The main argument of the first stanza is
   (A) too much rain causes floods
   (B) rain is a welcome change from the heat
   (C) raindrops look like little lights setting the street on fire
   (D) rain can make the land dustier and dry
   (E) rain is beautiful, but makes lanes narrower

2. Together, lines 6-9 are known as
   (A) an epic
   (B) a haiku
   (C) a simile
   (D) a stanza
   (E) an idiom

3. In line 7, 'tramp' is best replaced with
   (A) race
   (B) roar
   (C) slide
   (D) tap
   (E) stomp

4. The author refers to a "leopard's yellow and spotted hide" (line 18) to refer to
   (A) the dirty window pane
   (B) how the ground looks with puddles of mud
   (C) the leopard living in the countryside
   (D) the color and texture of dried grass
   (E) the color of dirty raindrop

GO ON TO THE NEXT PAGE.

Jemima Puddle-duck was not much in the habit of flying. She ran downhill a few yards flapping her shawl, and then she jumped off into the air.

She flew beautifully when she had got a good start.

She skimmed along over the treetops until she saw an open place in the
5 middle of the wood, where the trees and brushwood had been cleared.

Jemima alighted rather heavily and began to waddle about in search of a convenient dry nesting place. She rather liked a tree stump amongst some tall foxgloves.

But—seated upon the stump, she was startled to find an elegantly dressed
10 gentleman reading a newspaper. He had black prick ears and sandy colored whiskers.

"Quack?" said Jemima Puddle-duck, with her head and her bonnet on the one side—"Quack?"

The gentleman raised his eyes above his newspaper and looked curiously at
15 Jemima—

"Madam, have you lost your way?" said he. He had a long bushy tail which he was sitting upon, as the stump was somewhat damp.

Jemima thought him mighty civil and kind. She explained that she had not lost her way, but that she was trying to find a dry nesting place.

20 "Ah! Is that so? Indeed!" said the gentleman with sandy whiskers, looking curiously at Jemima. He folded up the newspaper and put it in his coattail pocket.

"But as to a nest—there is no difficulty: I have a sackful of feathers in my woodshed. No, my dear madam, you will be in nobody's way. You may sit there as long as you like," said the bushy long-tailed gentleman.

5. The main problem Jemima faces is
   (A) avoiding the gentleman
   (B) remembering how to fly
   (C) identifying a place to land
   (D) finding a good place to nest
   (E) seeing someone on her stump

6. In line 4, what does "skimmed" mean?
   (A) glided
   (B) arrived
   (C) climbed
   (D) escaped
   (E) disappeared

7. We can assume the gentleman is a
   (A) fox
   (B) duck
   (C) child
   (D) snake
   (E) ranger

8. According to the passage, Jemima Puddle-duck will most likely make her nest
   (A) on top of the hill
   (B) in one of the treetops
   (C) beside the brushwood
   (D) on the gentleman's stump
   (E) in the gentleman's woodshed

GO ON TO THE NEXT PAGE.

More schools these days are getting rid of art and music classes. People believe that subjects like math and reading are more important. They are the only subjects that are tested. However, art, music and theater classes can help students in many ways. Experts say that learning the arts can even raise students' test scores.

5 Research shows that the arts can help students do better in school. For example, kids who draw or play an instrument are more likely to win math and science awards. Also, young children who draw or paint have more control in their fingers. And did you know that children who spend time doing art also do better at reading charts and graphs? This skill is important in math and reading.

10 Art and music classes help students in other important ways as well. Kids enjoy showing their feelings and ideas in art. It helps them become more creative. Practicing an instrument and rehearsals teach kids to not give up. Group efforts like band, choir and theater teach teamwork. These performances can also build confidence.

15 It is easy to see that letting kids explore subjects like art and music can help them in many ways. All schools should keep giving arts classes. Without them, students will be missing an important part of their education.

9. The author would most likely agree with which statement?
   (A) Practicing the arts is more important than studying reading and math.
   (B) Practicing sports should be required for all students.
   (C) Reading charts and graphs is the most important ability.
   (D) Practicing the arts can lead to skills in other areas.
   (E) Memorizing math facts can make students more artistic.

10. According to the passage, which of the following is a possible advantage of learning art and music?
   (A) Young children develop better control in their fingers.
   (B) Schools with arts programs have the top test scores.
   (C) Children learn that conflicts are natural.
   (D) Students become better actors.
   (E) Children become better at reading texts.

11. In line 13, "band, choir and theater" are mentioned as examples of
   (A) activities performed in front of an audience
   (B) types of musical instruments
   (C) clubs every student can join
   (D) classes that schools are getting rid of
   (E) group efforts that build confidence

12. In line 2, "subjects" could best be replaced with
   (A) citizens
   (B) classes
   (C) objects
   (D) lessons
   (E) tests

GO ON TO THE NEXT PAGE.

The lottery is a way for an ordinary person to win lots of money. Recently, people had the chance to win over 1 billion dollars in the lottery. Some people say money makes people happy. But sometimes winning the lottery doesn't make people's lives better. Winning can actually make their lives worse.

5 The first reason is that winners do not get to keep all the money. They have to pay millions of dollars to get it all at once. Otherwise, they receive the money over 29 years. Second, winners have to pay very high taxes on the money. They have to give some of the money to the government. In the end, they might end up with half of the money they had won.

10 Many lottery winners lose all of their money in less than five years. This is because they spend their money buying more lottery tickets. It is very hard to win the lottery. Each person has the same chance as anyone else in the United States of America. Winning the lottery also puts stress on relationships. Friends and family might ask for money. One lottery winner said that he wished he tore his ticket up.
15 Many others feel the same way. Winning the lottery might not be dreadful, but it also might not be good.

13. The author would most likely agree with which statement?
    - (A) Money makes people happy.
    - (B) Things that look good aren't always what they seem.
    - (C) No one needs to work after winning the lottery.
    - (D) Being rich will make you lose friends.
    - (E) Winning the lottery is always worth it.

14. What is one reason lottery winners do NOT receive their full winnings?
    - (A) They pass away before they can receive the money.
    - (B) The lottery company doesn't have enough money to pay them.
    - (C) They end up with half of the money they had won.
    - (D) They have to pay taxes to the government.
    - (E) They have to split it with other winners.

15. What do lottery winners often spend all their prize money on?
    - (A) Making their dreams come true.
    - (B) Donating to charity.
    - (C) Nothing; they tear up their tickets.
    - (D) Helping their friends and family.
    - (E) Buying new lottery tickets.

16. In line 15, what does the word "dreadful" mean?
    - (A) bad
    - (B) pleasant
    - (C) lucky
    - (D) happy
    - (E) scary

GO ON TO THE NEXT PAGE.

I've given a lot of speeches about schooling. I've talked a lot about responsibility – what each of us should make sure we do. I've talked about how your teachers should work on inspiring you. I've talked about how your community should make sure you stay on track to get your homework done. I've talked about
5 how parents have to make sure you just don't play Xbox for hours.

I've talked a lot about the government's responsibility as well. I've said that the government needs to set high standards. I said that the government needs to support teachers and principals. It needs to turn-around schools that aren't working for students.

10 But none of these things will mean anything unless all of you fulfill your own responsibilities. You need to show up to those schools. You need to pay attention to those teachers. You need to put in the hard work it takes to succeed.

And that's what I want talk about today. I want to start with the responsibility you have to yourself.

15 Every single one of you has something you're good at. Every single one of you has something to offer. And it is your job to discover what that is. That's the opportunity an education can provide.

And no matter what you want to do with your life, I promise you'll need an education to do it. You want to be a doctor, or a teacher, or a police offer? You want
20 to be a nurse or an architect? You want to be a lawyer or a soldier? You're going to need a good education for every single one of those careers. You can't drop out of school and just drop into a good job. You've got to work for it. And train for it. And learn for it. It is your responsibility to make something of your life.

17. Which phrase is the best definition for "responsibility" (lines 2)?
    (A) "what each of us should make sure we do" (line 2)
    (B) "set high standards" (line 7)
    (C) "show up to those schools" (line 11)
    (D) "You've got to work for it" (line 22)
    (E) "make something of your life" (line 23)

18. The main idea of the passage is
    (A) you can only get a job if you are educated
    (B) every student has the responsibility to turn-around schools
    (C) every student is responsible for their own education
    (D) every parent has the responsibility to educate their children
    (E) the government needs to set high standards

19. According to the passage, who is responsible for "support[ing] ...principals" (line 8)?
    (A) teachers
    (B) parents
    (C) students
    (D) the community
    (E) the government

20. When the author says that "it is your job to discover what that is" (line 16), the author is talking about how every person should find
    (A) a good school
    (B) what they are good at
    (C) what it takes to be a doctor
    (D) a responsible government
    (E) ways to get homework done

GO ON TO THE NEXT PAGE.

Why do hurricanes have names? For the same reason that people do: so that we can tell them apart.

Hurricanes are extreme storms that do a lot of damage. They hit the United States many times in a year. Once, they were called by numbers. That was confusing to people. Names are shorter and easier to remember. As a result, the government began giving names to hurricanes in 1950. Some of the first names used were Able, Baker, and Charlie. Every year they used the same names. That was also confusing. To help, the government began using different girls' names. The first major storm that year was called Alice. Every hurricane had a girl's name until 1979. Then boys' names were added to the list. The first hurricane with a boy name was called Bob.

Today, names are no longer selected by the government. A world weather group picks the names. There are six lists of names. One list is used in each year. In 2018, the first three hurricanes were named Alberto, Beryl, and Chris. Lists are repeated after six years. You won't see a Hurricane Chris again until the year 2024.

If a storm is very bad, its name is retired. In 2005, Hurricane Katrina was the worst one ever to strike the United States. For that reason, there will never be another hurricane named Katrina. In 2011, when Katrina's turn came again, the 'K' hurricane was called Katia.

You can find the list of hurricane names online. Would you like one named after you?

21. The author wrote this passage to
    (A) explain how hurricanes get their names
    (B) make jokes about hurricane names
    (C) explain how Hurricane Chris got its name
    (D) tell about an important event in world history
    (E) describe the worst hurricanes to hit the United States

22. According to the passage, the worst hurricane in the United States was named
    (A) Alice
    (B) Bob
    (C) Alberto
    (D) Chris
    (E) Katrina

23. According to the passage, who chooses hurricane names today?
    (A) the government
    (B) weather scientists
    (C) the Navy
    (D) a world weather group
    (E) people who use the Internet

24. If there is not a hurricane named Chris in 2024, we can assume that

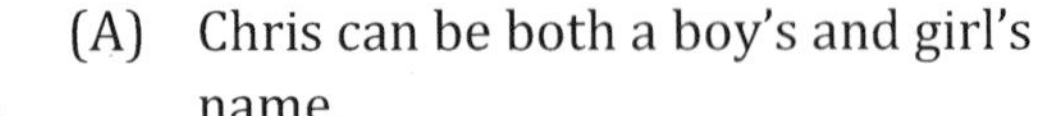

    (A) Chris can be both a boy's and girl's name.
    (B) Someone named Chris did not want a hurricane named after them
    (C) Chris was a very bad hurricane in 2018.
    (D) Chris will be on the list for 2025 instead.
    (E) Hurricanes will have numbers in 2024.

GO ON TO THE NEXT PAGE.

Home is the place where we are safe. It's where we get to relax and be ourselves. As a kid, my grandparents' house was a second home for me. When I was there, I felt loved and protected. I also had fun doing things I didn't usually do at my home.

5 Before I started school, I spent most days at my grandparents while my parents worked. I always had fun at their house. Grandma taught me how to bake cookies and sew buttons. Grandpa showed me how to work clay. I made many objects. A new mixing bowl for Grandma. A paperweight for my father. A mug for my mother.

10 My grandparents also loved nature. Grandma and I watched birds with her binoculars. Grandpa and I tended the vegetable garden. One time while watering plants, we saw a rabbit caught underneath the fence. Grandpa very gently held the rabbit's body. He let me pet it carefully so that it would not be scared. Then he lifted the fence up so the rabbit could get free. It ran away unhurt. I felt really good about
15 helping the rabbit escape and go back to his family.

I still love my memories of being at my grandparents' house. I got to do many neat things. I also learned how to do many useful things. And being there with my grandparents, I even learned some things about life.

25. The narrator made all of the following things with her grandparents EXCEPT a
    - (A) batch of cookies
    - (B) clay animal
    - (C) mixing bowl
    - (D) mug
    - (E) paperweight

26. From the passage, we can assume that the narrator's grandparents were all of the following EXCEPT
    - (A) hardworking
    - (B) creative
    - (C) wise
    - (D) loving
    - (E) impatient

27. In line 7, "work" most nearly means.
    - (A) play
    - (B) hard
    - (C) exercise
    - (D) shape
    - (E) job

28. From the passage, what is one thing we can assume the narrator "learned...about life" (line 18)?
    - (A) Home is a safe place for children.
    - (B) Girls should learn to bake and sew.
    - (C) Vegetable gardens should have fences.
    - (D) Birdwatching is fun.
    - (E) People should respect all living things

STOP

IF YOU FINISH BEFORE TIME IS UP,
CHECK YOUR WORK IN THIS SECTION ONLY.
YOU MAY NOT TURN TO ANY OTHER SECTION.

SECTION 4
Writing Sample

Look at the picture and tell a story about what happened. Make sure your story includes a beginning, a middle, and an end.

GO ON TO THE NEXT PAGE.

STOP

IF YOU FINISH BEFORE TIME IS UP,
CHECK YOUR WORK IN THIS SECTION ONLY.
YOU MAY NOT TURN TO ANY OTHER SECTION.

SECTION 5
15 Questions

The Renaissance began in Italy, more than 600 years ago. The word Renaissance means "born again." It was a time of rebirth. Italian artists traveled for inspiration. They studied the art of Ancient Greece and Rome. The ancient Romans believed that the human body was beautiful. This inspired Renaissance artists like
5 Michelangelo and da Vinci. They made many paintings and sculptures. With art, they tried to honor the human body in a realistic way. This new way of thinking was called humanism.

Humanism focused on science as well. Renaissance thinkers changed the world with this new focus. How? Well, they made new scientific discoveries.
10 Scientists like Galileo studied the stars. People began to understand that the earth spins around the sun. The scientists also made new inventions. Their greatest invention was the printing press. It was created by Johannes Gutenberg. It printed books at a faster rate. This allowed ideas to spread throughout Europe. The result was a new era in history.

1. The author would most likely agree with which statement?
   (A) The Renaissance was inspired by old ideas, but created a new era in history.
   (B) The Renaissance honored old scientific inventions.
   (C) Renaissance scientists argued that the Sun was not the center of the universe.
   (D) The Renaissance was focused on paintings and sculptures.
   (E) The Renaissance was only about science.

2. All of the following historical figures are listed in the passage as Renaissance thinkers EXCEPT
   (A) Michelangelo
   (B) Martin Luther
   (C) Leonardo da Vinci
   (D) Galileo Galilei
   (E) Johannes Gutenberg

3. According to the passage, the Renaissance in Italy began in the
   (A) 1400s
   (B) 1500s
   (C) 1600s
   (D) 1700s
   (E) 1800s

4. In the author's opinion, the Renaissance was a rebirth of
   (A) great painters
   (B) scientific study
   (C) Greek and Roman ideas
   (D) Italy
   (E) the printing press

5. In order for a sculpture to fall in the category of "humanism" (line 8), it would have to be
   (A) Greek or Roman in origin
   (B) representative of the human body
   (C) made by Michelangelo or Leonardo da Vinci
   (D) focused on science
   (E) highly unrealistic

6. In line 14, what does the word "era" most likely mean?
   (A) discovery
   (B) place
   (C) figure
   (D) idea
   (E) time

GO ON TO THE NEXT PAGE.

7. SUBTRACT:
   (A) amounts
   (B) add
   (C) math
   (D) minus
   (E) equal

8. GLIMPSE:
   (A) mysterious
   (B) reflect
   (C) glare
   (D) crack
   (E) spy

9. PITIFUL:
   (A) apologetic
   (B) selfish
   (C) thoughtful
   (D) pathetic
   (E) excellent

10. Seldom is to often as carefree is to
    (A) worried
    (B) entertained
    (C) delighted
    (D) drained
    (E) amused

11. Khadi has $5.00 in her savings, and her older sister Allie has three times as much. They pool their money to buy a present for their mother, which costs $19.52. How much will they have left over?
    (A) $0.48
    (B) $0.58
    (C) $1.58
    (D) $4.52
    (E) $5.58

12. If the perimeter of the rectangle shown below is 20 units, what is its area?

    8

    (A) 8 square units
    (B) 16 square units
    (C) 32 square units
    (D) 64 square units
    (E) 160 square units

13. After giving away 2 packs of baseball cards, Veronica has 3 packs left. If each pack contains 12 cards, how many baseball cards did Veronica have originally?
    (A) 5
    (B) 24
    (C) 36
    (D) 48
    (E) 60

14. David is reading a long chapter book. Each day, he reads 8 more pages than the day before. He reads for three days at this rate, and on Day 1 he read 36 pages. How many pages does he read on average each day?
    (A) 20 pages
    (B) 33 pages
    (C) 44 pages
    (D) 52 pages
    (E) 132 pages

15. Which inequality is NOT correct?
    (A) $5 \leq 5$
    (B) $9 > 2$
    (C) $9 > 11$
    (D) $12 < 15$
    (E) $13 < 17$

STOP

IF YOU FINISH BEFORE TIME IS UP,
CHECK YOUR WORK IN THIS SECTION ONLY.
YOU MAY NOT TURN TO ANY OTHER SECTION.

Scoring the 4th Grade Diagnostic Practice Test (Form B)

Sections 1-3 – Scored

Score the test using the answer sheet and *referring to the answer key in the back of the book (see table of contents).*

For each section, record the number of questions answered correctly. This will give you the raw score for each section. Note that the actual test will convert the raw score to a scaled score by comparing the student's performance with all other students in the same grade who took the test.

Section	Questions Correct (Raw Score)
Quantitative *Section 1*	________
Verbal *Section 2*	________
Reading *Section 3*	________

Carefully consider the results from the diagnostic practice test when forming a study plan. Remember, the Elementary SSAT is given to students in grades 3-4. Unless the student has finished 4th grade, chances are that there is material on this test that he or she has not yet been taught. If this is the case, and the student would like to improve beyond what is expected of his or her grade, consider working with a tutor or teacher, who can help the student learn more about new topics.

Section 4 – Writing Sample – Unscored

Have a parent or trusted educator review the essay or story written for the writing sample. Important areas to focus on include organization, clarity of ideas, originality, and technical precision (spelling, grammar, etc.).

Section 5 – Unscored

On the real test, the Experimental section will NOT be scored. Consider the student's performance on this section for practice purposes only. Did he or she do better on one section than another? Use this information along with the information from Sections 1-3 to form the study plan.

Quantitative

Overview

The Quantitative section assess a student's command over various mathematics topics, including number concepts, algebraic principles, geometry, measurements, probability and statistics.

There is one Quantitative section on the Elementary SSAT, which is scored.

On the Actual Test

Students have 30 minutes to complete 30 questions in this section.

Every question in the Quantitative section is multiple choice. There will be one question followed by five answer choices (A through E). Students are given blank space to the right of each question where they can do their work.

In This Practice Book

Below are the main content areas that are included in the Elementary SSAT. A list of subtopics can be found in the table of contents.

- Numbers Concepts & Operations
- Algebraic Principles
- Geometry
- Measurements
- Statistics & Probability

Considering the results of your diagnostic practice test, we recommend that students focus on the topics that are most challenging to them. Since there may be material in this workbook that they have not yet learned in school, we also encourage students to seek additional help from a trusted teacher or tutor to enhance their knowledge of those subjects.

The questions in each section are progressive, which means they start out easier, and become more and more difficult as they build on the concepts related to that topic. If students find that some questions are tricky, they should consider asking an educator for help. Don't be discouraged!

Tutorverse Tips!

You won't be able to use a calculator on the test. If, as you are answering a question, things start to get more and more complicated, take a step back and think about what the question is asking you to do. If necessary, use the answer choices themselves to help you arrive at the correct answer by plugging them into formulas or expressions.

You do **not** have to memorize customary unit conversion tables (for instance, the number of feet in a mile), as any such information will be provided. However, metric unit conversions will **not** be provided (i.e. the number of milliliters in a liter).

Remember: if you don't know the answer, skip it and come back to it. If you still don't know, and you're running out of time, just guess!

Number Concepts & Operations

Place Value

3rd Grade

1. Which of the following is farthest in value from 2.5?
   (A) 2.49
   (B) 2.45
   (C) 2.48
   (D) 2.54
   (E) 2.53

2. The digit 9 in the decimal 0.901 is equivalent to which of the following?
   (A) 900
   (B) 90
   (C) 9
   (D) $\frac{9}{10}$
   (E) $\frac{9}{100}$

3. In the decimal 0.58291, the digit 8 is equivalent to which of the following?
   (A) $\frac{8}{10}$
   (B) $\frac{8}{100}$
   (C) $\frac{8}{1,000}$
   (D) $\frac{8}{10,000}$
   (E) $\frac{8}{100,000}$

4. In the decimal 189.037, in which position is the digit 3?
   (A) hundreds
   (B) tens
   (C) ones
   (D) tenths
   (E) hundredths

5. 0.23476
   In the number above, the digit 4 is equal to which of the following?
   (A) 400
   (B) 4
   (C) $\frac{4}{10}$
   (D) $\frac{4}{100}$
   (E) $\frac{4}{1,000}$

6. In which position is the digit 9 in the decimal 193.762?
   (A) hundreds
   (B) tens
   (C) ones
   (D) tenths
   (E) hundredths

7. What is 1,385 rounded to the nearest ten?
   (A) 1,300
   (B) 1,380
   (C) 1,385
   (D) 1,390
   (E) 1,400

8. What is 960 rounded to the nearest hundred?
   (A) 800
   (B) 900
   (C) 950
   (D) 960
   (E) 1,000

4th Grade

1. Which of the following is closest in value to 26?
   (A) 25.498
   (B) 25.899
   (C) 25.909
   (D) 26.057
   (E) 26.1

2. Which of the following is farthest in value from 89?
   (A) 89.099
   (B) 88.898
   (C) 88.919
   (D) 89.09
   (E) 89.101

3. Which of the following is farthest in value from 102?
   (A) 101.09
   (B) 101.9
   (C) 101.97
   (D) 102.02
   (E) 102.11

4. 0.24982
   In the decimal above, the digit 8 is equal to which of the following?
   (A) $\frac{8}{10}$
   (B) $\frac{8}{100}$
   (C) $\frac{8}{1,000}$
   (D) $\frac{8}{10,000}$
   (E) $\frac{8}{100,000}$

5. In the decimal 0.30178, in which position is the digit 1?
   (A) tenths
   (B) hundredths
   (C) thousandths
   (D) ten-thousandths
   (E) hundred-thousandths

6. In which position is the digit 3 in the decimal 0.49283?
   (A) tenths
   (B) hundredths
   (C) thousandths
   (D) ten-thousandths
   (E) hundred-thousandths

7. What is 27,894 rounded to the nearest thousand?
   (A) 27,000
   (B) 27,800
   (C) 27,890
   (D) 27,900
   (E) 28,000

8. What is 19,961 rounded to the nearest hundred?
   (A) 19,000
   (B) 19,500
   (C) 19,800
   (D) 19,900
   (E) 20,000

Basic Concepts

3rd Grade

1. What is nine thousand three hundred two?
   (A) 932
   (B) 9,302
   (C) 90,302
   (D) 90,320
   (E) 900,302

2. What is six thousand seventy-four?
   (A) 647
   (B) 674
   (C) 6,074
   (D) 60,074
   (E) 60,740

3. What is 545 plus 317?
   (A) 228
   (B) 232
   (C) 238
   (D) 852
   (E) 862

4. 761 – 322 =
   (A) 429
   (B) 437
   (C) 439
   (D) 449
   (E) 549

5. What is 308 minus 199?
   (A) 101
   (B) 109
   (C) 110
   (D) 201
   (E) 209

6. 104 + 342 = 100 + ___
   (A) 246
   (B) 338
   (C) 346
   (D) 366
   (E) 446

7. Find the value of 37×26.
   (A) 296
   (B) 862
   (C) 956
   (D) 962
   (E) 972

8. Which of the following is NOT a prime number?
   (A) 2
   (B) 7
   (C) 11
   (D) 23
   (E) 27

9. $70 \div 7 =$
   (A) 0
   (B) 1
   (C) 7
   (D) 10
   (E) 12

10. Which of the following is a prime number?
   (A) 9
   (B) 13
   (C) 25
   (D) 49
   (E) 58

4th Grade

1. Which of the following is a prime number?
   (A) 21
   (B) 15
   (C) 10
   (D) 9
   (E) 2

2. $1{,}089 + 2{,}352 =$
   (A) 2,365
   (B) 2,731
   (C) 3,331
   (D) 3,441
   (E) 3,455

3. $1{,}842 - 752 =$
   (A) 1,190
   (B) 1,010
   (C) 1,090
   (D) 1,110
   (E) 1,190

4. $2{,}765 - 389 =$
   (A) 2,376
   (B) 2,424
   (C) 2,486
   (D) 3,154
   (E) 3,256

5. $71 + 94 =$ __ $+ 100$
   (A) 165
   (B) 115
   (C) 85
   (D) 77
   (E) 65

6. $388 + 505 =$ __ $+ 500$
   (A) 283
   (B) 383
   (C) 393
   (D) 883
   (E) 893

7. $92 \times 18 =$
   (A) 1,576
   (B) 1,646
   (C) 1,650
   (D) 1,656
   (E) 1,666

8. $168 \times 27 =$
   (A) 1,176
   (B) 3,360
   (C) 4,436
   (D) 4,516
   (E) 4,536

9. $804 \div 10 =$
   (A) 10 R 4
   (B) 10 R 8
   (C) 60 R 14
   (D) 80 R 4
   (E) 84

10. $324 \div 8 =$
   (A) 4 R 4
   (B) 40 R 3
   (C) 40 R 4
   (D) 42
   (E) 42 R 5

11. $(2 \times 5) - \_\_ = 7$
   (A) 3
   (B) 4
   (C) 5
   (D) 6
   (E) 7

12. $(10 - 4) \times \_\_ = 18$
   (A) 2
   (B) 3
   (C) 4
   (D) 5
   (E) 6

13. $(12 + 6) \div \_\_ = 2$
   (A) 3
   (B) 6
   (C) 9
   (D) 10
   (E) 12

14. $(7 + 5) \div \_\_ = 3$
   (A) 2
   (B) 3
   (C) 4
   (D) 5
   (E) 6

Ordering Numbers and Fractions

3rd Grade

1. Benito spends more than $2.25 but less than $2.75 on a hot dog. A possible price for the hot dog is:
   (A) $2.00
   (B) $2.25
   (C) $2.50
   (D) $2.75
   (E) $3.00

2. Jake earns $6.25 an hour raking leaves, $7.00 an hour delivering papers, $5.50 an hour washing cars, $8.75 an hour babysitting, and $6.75 an hour walking dogs. How many of Jake's jobs pay more than $7.25 an hour?
   (A) 0
   (B) 1
   (C) 2
   (D) 3
   (E) 4

3. Which of the following fractions is the smallest?
   (A) $\frac{1}{4}$
   (B) $\frac{3}{4}$
   (C) $\frac{6}{4}$
   (D) $\frac{2}{4}$
   (E) $\frac{8}{4}$

4. Which is the smallest fraction?
   (A) $\frac{1}{10}$
   (B) $\frac{1}{5}$
   (C) $\frac{1}{20}$
   (D) $\frac{1}{15}$
   (E) $\frac{1}{4}$

5. Jasper read more than $\frac{1}{5}$ of his book but less than $\frac{1}{3}$. Which fraction of the book could he have possibly read?
   (A) $\frac{1}{6}$
   (B) $\frac{1}{5}$
   (C) $\frac{1}{4}$
   (D) $\frac{1}{3}$
   (E) $\frac{1}{2}$

6. Of the fruits in a cart, $\frac{1}{4}$ are apples, $\frac{1}{3}$ are oranges, $\frac{1}{8}$ are pears, $\frac{1}{6}$ are bananas, and $\frac{1}{8}$ are melons. The cart contained the largest amount of which kind of fruit?
   (A) apples
   (B) oranges
   (C) bananas
   (D) melons
   (E) pears

7. Frances spent $\frac{1}{2}$ of an hour studying math, $\frac{1}{3}$ of an hour studying social studies, $\frac{1}{4}$ of an hour studying English, $\frac{1}{5}$ of an hour studying science, and $\frac{1}{6}$ of an hour studying French. On which subject did she spend the most time studying?
   (A) English
   (B) French
   (C) Math
   (D) Science
   (E) Social Studies

4th Grade

1. A beach ball costs \$5.50, a towel costs \$8.00, and an umbrella costs \$10.25. Sunscreen costs less than an umbrella but more than a towel. Which of the following is a possible price for sunscreen?
   (A) \$5.25
   (B) \$7.00
   (C) \$8.00
   (D) \$10.00
   (E) \$10.50

2. Which of the following is the smallest fraction?
   (A) $\frac{1}{7}$
   (B) $\frac{1}{9}$
   (C) $\frac{1}{6}$
   (D) $\frac{1}{8}$
   (E) $\frac{1}{5}$

3. Which of the following numbers has the least value?
   (A) $\frac{1}{500}$
   (B) $\frac{3}{300}$
   (C) $\frac{1}{100}$
   (D) $\frac{2}{500}$
   (E) $\frac{1}{1{,}000}$

4. Which fractions below are ordered from smallest to largest?
   (A) $\frac{1}{10}, \frac{1}{20}, \frac{1}{50}, \frac{1}{100}, \frac{1}{1{,}000}$
   (B) $\frac{1}{20}, \frac{1}{10}, \frac{1}{50}, \frac{1}{100}, \frac{1}{1{,}000}$
   (C) $\frac{1}{100}, \frac{1}{1{,}000}, \frac{1}{50}, \frac{1}{20}, \frac{1}{10}$
   (D) $\frac{1}{1{,}000}, \frac{1}{100}, \frac{1}{50}, \frac{1}{10}, \frac{1}{20}$
   (E) $\frac{1}{1{,}000}, \frac{1}{100}, \frac{1}{50}, \frac{1}{20}, \frac{1}{10}$

5. Which fractions below are ordered from greatest to least?
   (A) $\frac{8}{7}, 1, \frac{2}{3}, \frac{1}{3}, \frac{1}{7}$
   (B) $\frac{8}{7}, \frac{1}{7}, 1, \frac{2}{3}, \frac{1}{3}$
   (C) $1, \frac{8}{7}, \frac{1}{7}, \frac{2}{3}, \frac{1}{3}$
   (D) $\frac{8}{7}, 1, \frac{2}{3}, \frac{1}{7}, \frac{1}{3}$
   (E) $\frac{1}{7}, \frac{1}{3}, \frac{2}{3}, 1, \frac{8}{7}$

6. Five friends ordered a pizza. Lisa ate $\frac{1}{8}$ of the pizza, Bob ate $\frac{1}{5}$ of the pizza, Kim ate $\frac{1}{3}$ of the pizza, Kyra ate $\frac{1}{10}$ of the pizza, and Mateo ate $\frac{1}{6}$ of the pizza. Which friend ate the least amount of pizza?
   (A) Bob
   (B) Kim
   (C) Kyra
   (D) Lisa
   (E) Mateo

7. Roxanne has a large book collection. $\frac{1}{5}$ of her books are biographies, $\frac{2}{10}$ are science books, $\frac{3}{10}$ are poetry books, $\frac{5}{50}$ are art books, and $\frac{4}{20}$ are fiction. Roxanne has the largest amount of which type of book?
   (A) Art
   (B) Biography
   (C) Fiction
   (D) Poetry
   (E) Science

Fractions

3rd Grade

1. Written as a mixed number, $\frac{8}{5} =$
   (A) $4\frac{2}{5}$
   (B) $3\frac{3}{5}$
   (C) $2\frac{2}{5}$
   (D) $1\frac{1}{5}$
   (E) $1\frac{3}{5}$

2. What is $\frac{24}{36}$ expressed in SIMPLEST form?
   (A) $\frac{4}{6}$
   (B) $\frac{12}{18}$
   (C) $\frac{2}{3}$
   (D) $\frac{3}{4}$
   (E) $\frac{1}{6}$

3. What is $\frac{1}{3}$ plus $\frac{3}{5}$?
   (A) $\frac{4}{8}$
   (B) $\frac{3}{5}$
   (C) $\frac{4}{5}$
   (D) $\frac{14}{15}$
   (E) $1\frac{1}{15}$

4. $\frac{1}{2} + \frac{3}{8} =$
   (A) $1\frac{1}{2}$
   (B) $\frac{7}{8}$
   (C) $\frac{5}{8}$
   (D) $\frac{4}{10}$
   (E) $\frac{3}{16}$

5. $\frac{1}{5} + \frac{3}{8} =$
   (A) $\frac{5}{8}$
   (B) $\frac{4}{5}$
   (C) $\frac{7}{40}$
   (D) $\frac{4}{13}$
   (E) $\frac{23}{40}$

6. Find $\frac{3}{5} - \frac{1}{4}$.
   (A) $\frac{7}{20}$
   (B) $\frac{2}{5}$
   (C) $\frac{7}{10}$
   (D) $\frac{17}{20}$
   (E) $\frac{2}{1}$

7. What is $7\frac{1}{6}$ plus $3\frac{5}{6}$?
   (A) 15
   (B) 12
   (C) 11
   (D) $10\frac{5}{6}$
   (E) 10

8. What is $\frac{7}{10}$ minus $\frac{3}{8}$?
   (A) $\frac{13}{40}$
   (B) $\frac{1}{2}$
   (C) $\frac{37}{40}$
   (D) $1\frac{3}{40}$
   (E) $\frac{4}{2}$

9. Jake ordered a pizza for lunch. The pizza was divided into 8 slices. After lunch, Jake had 5 slices leftover. If he ate 2 slices for dinner, what fraction of the pizza is left?
   (A) $\frac{1}{8}$
   (B) $\frac{2}{8}$
   (C) $\frac{3}{8}$
   (D) $\frac{3}{4}$
   (E) $\frac{7}{8}$

10. After a party, Paul had the amount of pizza represented by the grey slices in the diagram below leftover. Which equation shows the amount of pizza Paul has left?

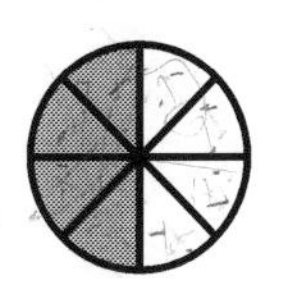

   (A) $\frac{6}{8} - \frac{4}{8} = \frac{2}{8}$
   (B) $\frac{6}{8} + \frac{4}{8} = 2\frac{2}{8}$
   (C) $\frac{6}{8} + \frac{4}{8} = 1\frac{2}{8}$
   (D) $\frac{5}{8} + \frac{3}{8} = 1$
   (E) $\frac{6}{8} - \frac{3}{8} = \frac{3}{8}$

11. Jane is making trail mix. She adds $\frac{3}{4}$ cup of peanuts and $\frac{2}{3}$ cup of cashew nuts. How many cups of nuts did Jane add to her trail mix?
   (A) $\frac{7}{12}$
   (B) $\frac{5}{7}$
   (C) $\frac{5}{12}$
   (D) $\frac{11}{12}$
   (E) $1\frac{5}{12}$

12. Craig has $\frac{3}{4}$ pounds of apples. He eats $\frac{1}{6}$ pound. How many pounds of apples are left?
    (A) $\frac{1}{2}$
    (B) $\frac{3}{8}$
    (C) $\frac{5}{24}$
    (D) $\frac{11}{12}$
    (E) $\frac{7}{12}$

13. There is $\frac{3}{4}$ of a pie available at a bakery. If someone buys $\frac{1}{8}$ of the pie, what fraction of the pie will remain?
    (A) $\frac{1}{8}$
    (B) $\frac{1}{4}$
    (C) $\frac{1}{2}$
    (D) $\frac{5}{8}$
    (E) $\frac{7}{8}$

4th Grade

1. What is $\frac{45}{8}$ written as a mixed number?
   (A) $4\frac{3}{8}$
   (B) $5\frac{3}{5}$
   (C) $5\frac{5}{8}$
   (D) $6\frac{3}{8}$
   (E) $6\frac{7}{8}$

2. Written as a mixed number, $\frac{35}{9}$ =
   (A) $3\frac{8}{9}$
   (B) $4\frac{1}{9}$
   (C) $7\frac{5}{9}$
   (D) $9\frac{1}{9}$
   (E) $10\frac{1}{63}$

3. $\frac{2}{5} + \frac{3}{8} =$
   (A) $\frac{3}{20}$
   (B) $\frac{13}{40}$
   (C) $\frac{5}{13}$
   (D) $\frac{11}{20}$
   (E) $\frac{31}{40}$

4. What is $5\frac{3}{8} + 7\frac{1}{4}$?
   (A) $8\frac{3}{8}$
   (B) $9\frac{5}{8}$
   (C) $11\frac{3}{8}$
   (D) $12\frac{1}{3}$
   (E) $12\frac{5}{8}$

5. What is $4\frac{3}{4}$ plus $6\frac{1}{8}$?
   (A) $10\frac{1}{8}$
   (B) $10\frac{3}{4}$
   (C) $10\frac{7}{8}$
   (D) $11\frac{1}{8}$
   (E) $11\frac{3}{4}$

6. $\frac{1}{8} \times \frac{1}{3} =$
   (A) $\frac{1}{8}$
   (B) $\frac{3}{8}$
   (C) $\frac{1}{24}$
   (D) $\frac{5}{24}$
   (E) $\frac{11}{24}$

7. What is $\frac{2}{3} \times \frac{3}{5}$?
   (A) $\frac{1}{5}$
   (B) $\frac{2}{5}$
   (C) $\frac{5}{8}$
   (D) $\frac{7}{15}$
   (E) $1\frac{4}{15}$

8. Evaluate: $\frac{3}{7} \times \frac{1}{2}$
   (A) $\frac{3}{14}$
   (B) $\frac{3}{7}$
   (C) $\frac{11}{14}$
   (D) $\frac{4}{9}$
   (E) $\frac{13}{14}$

9. $\frac{3}{7} \times \frac{3}{8} =$
   (A) $\frac{3}{5}$
   (B) $\frac{2}{5}$
   (C) $\frac{1}{5}$
   (D) $\frac{45}{56}$
   (E) $\frac{9}{56}$

10. Jessica is mixing paint for an art project. She adds $\frac{3}{8}$ cup of blue paint to $\frac{2}{3}$ cup of yellow paint to make green paint. How many cups of green paint does Jessica have in total?
   (A) $\frac{5}{24}$
   (B) $\frac{5}{11}$
   (C) $1\frac{1}{24}$
   (D) $1\frac{1}{8}$
   (E) 2

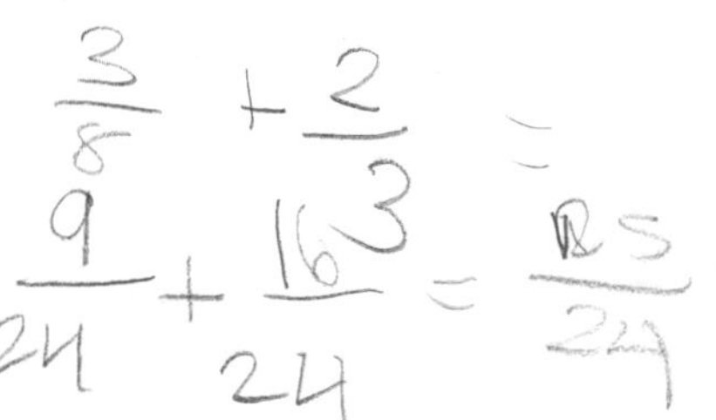

11. Manuel spent a total of $2\frac{1}{4}$ hours on homework. He spent $\frac{1}{3}$ of an hour on math homework. How much time, in hours, did he spend on the rest of his homework?
   (A) $\frac{3}{4}$
   (B) $\frac{11}{12}$
   (C) 1
   (D) $1\frac{11}{12}$
   (E) $2\frac{7}{12}$

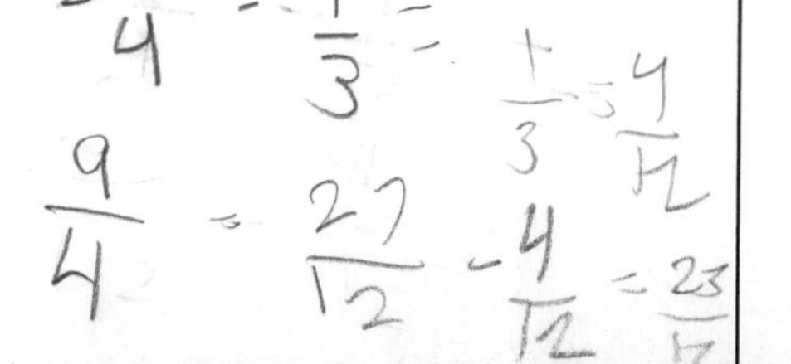

12. A baker has 2 cups of sugar. She uses $\frac{1}{2}$ cup for one recipe and $\frac{3}{4}$ cup for another recipe. How many cups of sugar does she have left?
   (A) $1\frac{1}{2}$
   (B) $1\frac{1}{4}$
   (C) 1
   (D) $\frac{3}{4}$
   (E) $\frac{1}{2}$

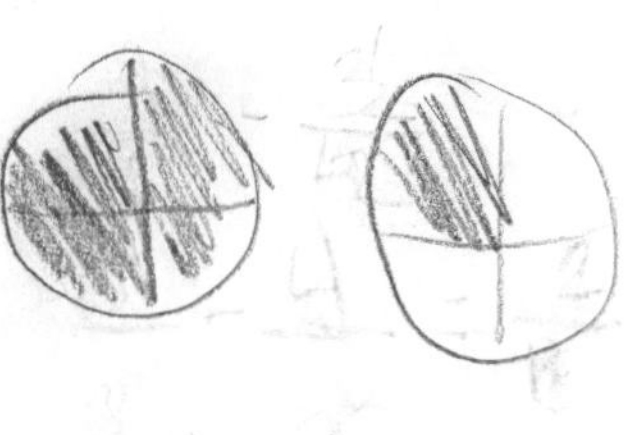

13. Juice is sold by the whole liter. Mimi estimates that each person at a party will drink $\frac{3}{5}$ liter of juice. If 8 people will be at the party, how many liters of juice should Mimi buy so that everyone has enough juice?
   (A) 2
   (B) 3
   (C) 4
   (D) 5
   (E) 6

14. There is a pizza that is cut into 8 equal slices. If Jamila eats $\frac{1}{4}$ of the pizza and Lulu eats $\frac{3}{8}$, how many slices will remain?
   (A) 1
   (B) 2
   (C) 3
   (D) 4
   (E) 5

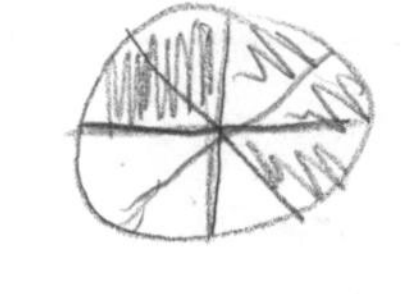

Arithmetic Word Problems

3rd Grade

1. What is the mass of 5 kiwis if one kiwi has a mass of 8 grams?
   (A) 13 grams
   (B) 35 grams
   (C) 40 grams
   (D) 45 grams
   (E) 48 grams

2. 13 students go on an ice-skating field trip. If it costs $3 to rent a pair of ice skates, how much will it cost for all the students to rent ice skates?
   (A) $52
   (B) $42
   (C) $39
   (D) $36
   (E) $16

3. If Santi eats 4 melons a day, how many melons does he eat in one week?
   (A) 11
   (B) 28
   (C) 32
   (D) 36
   (E) 48

4. Every time Cameron eats toast, he puts exactly 6 teaspoons of jam on the toast. If he has used 72 teaspoons of jam this month, how many pieces of toast has he eaten?
   (A) 6
   (B) 8
   (C) 10
   (D) 12
   (E) 14

5. A bucket holds up to 6 basketballs. How many buckets are needed to hold 76 basketballs?
   (A) 9
   (B) 10
   (C) 11
   (D) 12
   (E) 13

6. A carriage is pulled by a team of 4 horses. How many carriages can be pulled by 98 horses?
   (A) 14
   (B) 16
   (C) 19
   (D) 24
   (E) 26

7. It takes 2.5 teaspoons of baking soda to make a batch of brownies. How many teaspoons of baking soda does it take to make 7 batches of brownies?
   (A) 7.5
   (B) 9.5
   (C) 14
   (D) 14.5
   (E) 17.5

8. There are 6 students in a study group. On average, each student has 9 pencils. How many total pencils does the study group have?
   (A) 15
   (B) 36
   (C) 54
   (D) 63
   (E) 72

9. What is the fewest number of cartons needed to hold 36 eggs if one carton holds a dozen?
   (A) 2
   (B) 3
   (C) 4
   (D) 6
   (E) 24

10. Jemma has 240 gemstones. If one box holds a dozen gemstones, how many boxes does Jemma need to store all her gemstones?
   (A) 20
   (B) 24
   (C) 30
   (D) 40
   (E) 60

11. A grocery store has 262 boxes of whole grain crackers, 89 boxes of gluten-free crackers, and 127 boxes of cheesy crackers. How many total boxes of crackers does the grocery store have?
   (A) 351
   (B) 368
   (C) 378
   (D) 468
   (E) 478

12. In Belacqua Lake, there are three taxi companies. Speedy AB has a fleet of 54 taxis, Red Cab has a fleet of 162 taxis, and Wheels For Hire has a fleet of 143 taxis. How many taxis are there in Belacqua Lake?
   (A) 216
   (B) 259
   (C) 350
   (D) 359
   (E) 360

13. Pam traded away half of her baseball card collection. If she has 79 cards now, how many did she have to begin with?
    (A) 40
    (B) 140
    (C) 146
    (D) 148
    (E) 158

14. Tammy went to the arcade and traded half of the tickets she won for a basketball. If she has 62 tickets left, how many did she have to begin with?
    (A) 31
    (B) 62
    (C) 124
    (D) 142
    (E) 248

15. Carlos received 84 pieces of candy for Halloween. He gave half of his candy to his friend and then ate two pieces. How many pieces of candy does he have left?
    (A) 40
    (B) 41
    (C) 42
    (D) 43
    (E) 44

16. Seamus went to the beach and collected shells. He gave half of his shells to his mother and then half of the remaining shells to his sister. If he has 16 shells left, how many did he have to begin with?
    (A) 2
    (B) 4
    (C) 8
    (D) 32
    (E) 64

17. Glen has 50 more marbles than Adam. Adam has 30 fewer marbles than Carl. If Carl has 120 marbles, how many marbles does Glen have?
    (A) 40
    (B) 80
    (C) 100
    (D) 140
    (E) 200

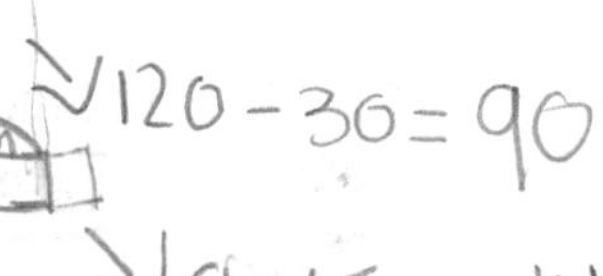

4th Grade

1. Abdul has 346 pennies in his piggy bank. If he removes 159 of them, how many are left?
    (A) 187
    (B) 197
    (C) 213
    (D) 297
    (E) 505

2. Maria makes and sells bracelets. She made 408 bracelets and sold 362. How many bracelets are left?
    (A) 36
    (B) 46
    (C) 56
    (D) 146
    (E) 166

3. Tanya is reading a book which is 617 pages long. If she has already read 248 pages, how many pages are left?
    (A) 369
    (B) 371
    (C) 431
    (D) 469
    (E) 471

4. Zach, Tina, and Elan all collect stamps. Zach has 213 stamps, Tina has 68 stamps, and Elan has 182 stamps. How many stamps do they have all together?
    (A) 281
    (B) 353
    (C) 363
    (D) 453
    (E) 463

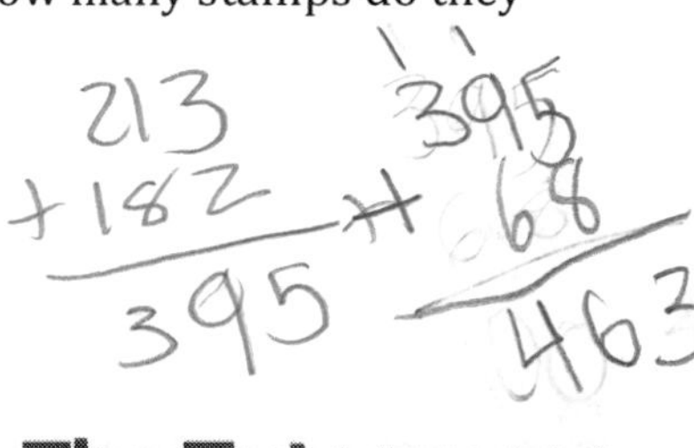

5. Dale, Alicia, and Carmen went trick-or-treating for Halloween. Dale received 88 pieces of candy, Alicia received 114 pieces of candy, and Carmen received 97 pieces of candy. How many pieces of candy did they receive altogether?
   (A) 189
   (B) 202
   (C) 211
   (D) 289
   (E) 299

6. A crate holds exactly 28 oranges. How many oranges are in three crates?
   (A) 64
   (B) 76
   (C) 84
   (D) 87
   (E) 112

7. If an album holds exactly 45 photographs, how many photographs are in 4 albums?
   (A) 49
   (B) 160
   (C) 162
   (D) 180
   (E) 200

8. If a delivery man delivers exactly 38 packages a day, how many packages can he deliver in three days?
   (A) 94
   (B) 104
   (C) 106
   (D) 114
   (E) 124

9. In a theater, a row has 7 seats. How many rows are needed to seat 140 people, if exactly one person sits in each seat?
   (A) 16
   (B) 17
   (C) 18
   (D) 19
   (E) 20

10. How many boxes are needed to hold 156 chocolates if each box holds exactly 6 chocolates?
   (A) 25
   (B) 26
   (C) 27
   (D) 28
   (E) 29

11. A delivery truck carries 127 packages. If 39 packages are delivered, how many are left in the truck?
   (A) 88
   (B) 98
   (C) 112
   (D) 166
   (E) 188

12. Samson has a collection of 146 baseball cards. He gives half his collection to his sister and then he gives 22 cards to his brother. How many cards does he have left?
   (A) 51
   (B) 62
   (C) 73
   (D) 95
   (E) 124

13. Carly has $144. She spends half of her money on a new bike and $17 on a helmet. How much money does she have left?
   (A) $55
   (B) $72
   (C) $89
   (D) $121
   (E) $127

14. Vikrant has 272 stamps in his stamp collection. If he doubles his collection and then sells 98 stamps, how many stamps does he have left?
   (A) 38
   (B) 136
   (C) 446
   (D) 544
   (E) 642

15. Trisha has 33 quarters. Aisha has 20 fewer than 3 times as many quarters as Trisha. How many quarters does Aisha have?
    (A) 13
    (B) 27
    (C) 79
    (D) 99
    (E) 119

16. If Ajax had 203 baseball cards and he sold 78 of them, how many cards does he have left?
    (A) 35
    (B) 125
    (C) 135
    (D) 225
    (E) 275

Algebraic Principles

Solving Equations and Inequalities

3rd Grade

1. James rides his bike 2 miles each day. He rides 5 days each week. Which equation tells how many miles he rides each week?
   (A) $m = 2 + 5$
   (B) $5 \div m = 2$
   (C) $m \div 2 = 5$
   (D) $2 \times 5 = m$
   (E) $5 \times m = 2$

2. If $7 \times a = 56$, then $a \div 2$ must equal
   (A) 2
   (B) 4
   (C) 7
   (D) 8
   (E) 16

3. If $33 - 15 = y$, then $y + 33 = ?$
   (A) 15
   (B) 33
   (C) 41
   (D) 51
   (E) 55

4. If $7 + 7 = 3 + m$, them m equals
   (A) 3
   (B) 10
   (C) 11
   (D) 14
   (E) 24

5. Given the equation $4 \times 10 = 2 \times k$, find k.
   (A) 4
   (B) 5
   (C) 8
   (D) 20
   (E) 40

4th Grade

1. What is the quotient of 12 and 12?
   (A) 0
   (B) 1
   (C) 12
   (D) 24
   (E) 144

2. Which inequality is NOT correct?
   (A) $8 < 10$
   (B) $10 > 9$
   (C) $0 > 4$
   (D) $7 \leq 7$
   (E) $1 < 5$

3. Five friends competed in a frog jumping competition. Mark's frog jumped 4 inches. Pete's frog jumped $\frac{1}{2}$ feet. Kylie's frog jumped 8 inches. Jane's frog jumped 6 inches. David's frog jumped $\frac{1}{2}$ feet. Which inequality is NOT correct?
   (A) Distance Mark's frog jumped < Distance Pete's frog jumped
   (B) Distance Jane's frog jumped > Distance David's frog jumped
   (C) Distance Kylie's frog jumped > Distance Jane's frog jumped
   (D) Distance Pete's frog jumped = Distance David's frog jumped
   (E) Distance Mark's frog jumped < Distance Kylie's frog jumped

4. Determine if the following is true:
   If $x < 7$, then $7 > x$.
   (A) always
   (B) cannot be determined
   (C) never
   (D) only when $x = 7$
   (E) sometimes

5. Sue has 15 crayons. She will split the crayons evenly among 3 boxes. Which equation tells how many crayons Sue will put in each box?
   (A) $c = 3 \div 15$
   (B) $3 \times c = 15$
   (C) $15 - 3 = c$
   (D) $c \div 15 = 3$
   (E) $15 \times c = 3$

Ratios and Proportions

3rd Grade

1. In a recipe, a picture of a small spoon represents 15 grams. If there are 6 spoons of sugar pictured, then how many grams of sugar will be needed for the recipe?
   (A) 30 grams
   (B) 45 grams
   (C) 60 grams
   (D) 75 grams
   (E) 90 grams

2. On a map, each inch represents 12 kilometers. If an island is 3 inches long on the map, how many kilometers is its actual length?
   (A) 12
   (B) 15
   (C) 24
   (D) 36
   (E) 48

3. In a floor pattern, there is 1 circle for every 4 squares. If there are 60 circles, then how many squares are there?
   (A) 120
   (B) 180
   (C) 200
   (D) 240
   (E) 300

4. On a pepperoni pizza, there are 8 pieces of pepperoni on each slice. If the chef uses 96 pieces of pepperoni, how many slices of pizza did he make?
   (A) 8
   (B) 12
   (C) 16
   (D) 88
   (E) 104

4th Grade

1. 12 is to 24 as 8 is to ___
   (A) 14
   (B) 16
   (C) 18
   (D) 24
   (E) 36

2. 56 is to 8 as ___ is to 7
   (A) 7
   (B) 14
   (C) 28
   (D) 49
   (E) 57

3. If I know that one handful of sand has a mass of 12 grams, how much mass do 8 handfuls have?
   (A) 80 grams
   (B) 88 grams
   (C) 96 grams
   (D) 104 grams
   (E) 108 grams

4. In a bowl, there is 1 red fruit to every 5 green fruits. If there are 30 green fruits in the bowl, then how many red fruits are there?
   (A) 5
   (B) 6
   (C) 120
   (D) 150
   (E) 180

5. A jar contains 1 clear marble for every 8 colorful marbles. If there are 72 marbles in the jar altogether, how many clear marbles are there?
   (A) 1
   (B) 7
   (C) 8
   (D) 9
   (E) 64

Geometry

Shapes and Attributes

3rd Grade

1. Which best describes the triangle shown on the right?
   (A) scalene
   (B) isosceles
   (C) equilateral
   (D) right
   (E) obtuse

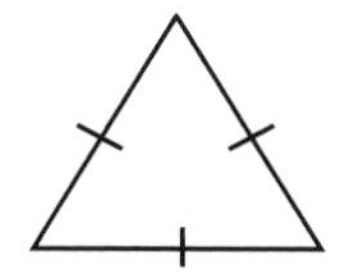

2. Which list below contains only quadrilaterals?
   (A) parallelogram, rhombus, triangle
   (B) pentagon, square, rectangle
   (C) trapezoid, parallelogram, square
   (D) hexagon, heptagon, octagon
   (E) kite, triangle, rhombus

3. A classroom window has four right angles and is 3 feet tall and 2 feet wide. Which CANNOT be used to describe the window?
   (A) square
   (B) rectangle
   (C) quadrilateral
   (D) parallelogram
   (E) polygon

4. Which shape is not a parallelogram?
   (A) (B)

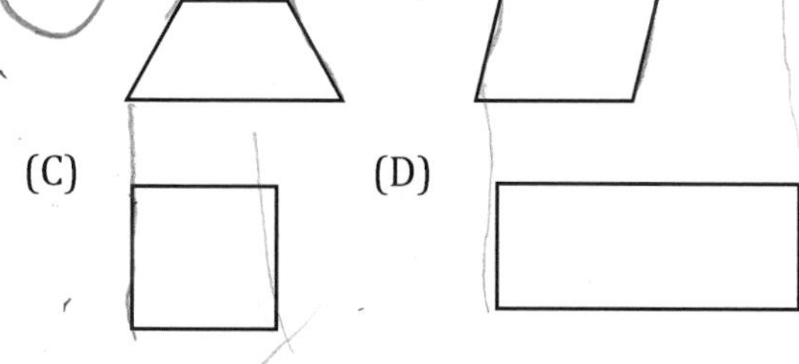

   (C) (D)

   (E)

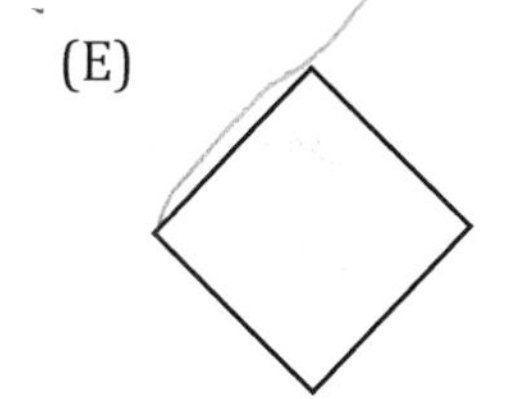

5. Which shape is NOT a rectangle?
   (A) (B)

   (C) (D)

   (E)

6. Which shape is NOT a square?
   (A) (B)

   (C) (D)

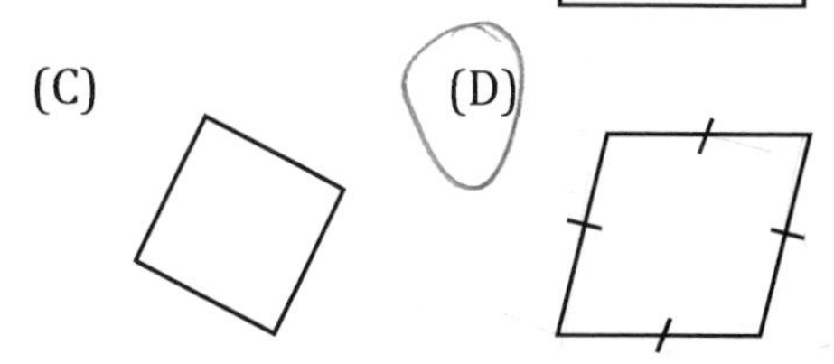

   (E)

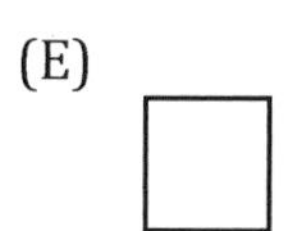

7. Which of the following shapes is a parallelogram but not a rhombus?
   (A) (B)

   (C) (D)

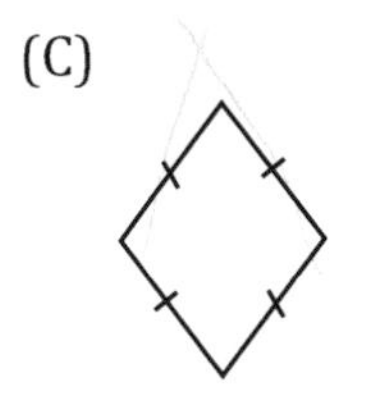

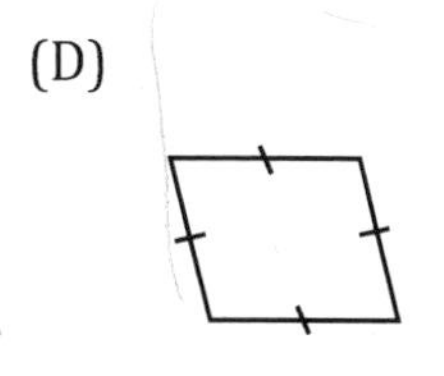

   (E)

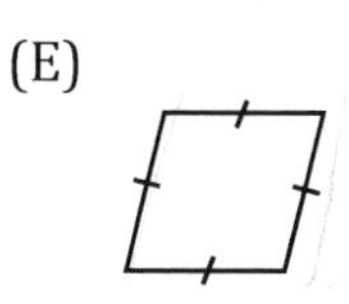

4th Grade

1. Which shape does NOT have two pairs of parallel sides?–
   (A) square
   (B) parallelogram
   (C) trapezoid
   (D) rectangle
   (E) rhombus

2. Which best describes a ray?
   (A) a line that continues forever in two directions
   (B) a line segment with two end points
   (C) a line segment with one end point that continues forever in one direction
   (D) a set of parallel lines
   (E) a set of perpendicular lines

3. Which angle has the greatest measure?
   (A) (B)

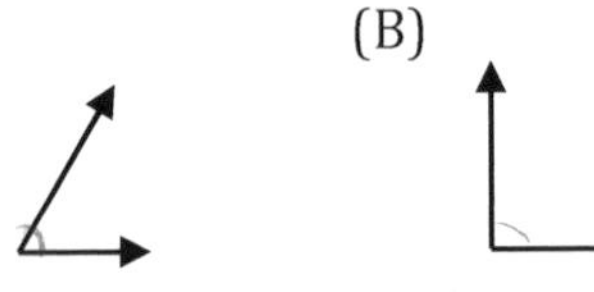

   (C) (D)

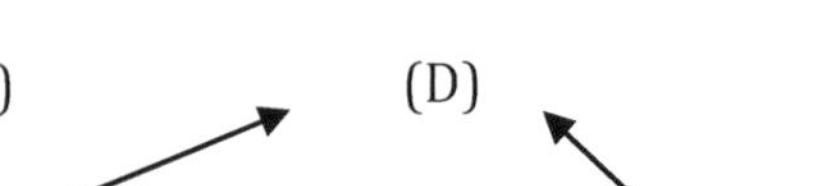

   (E)

4. Which shows a right angle?
   (A)

   (B)

   (C) (D) (E)

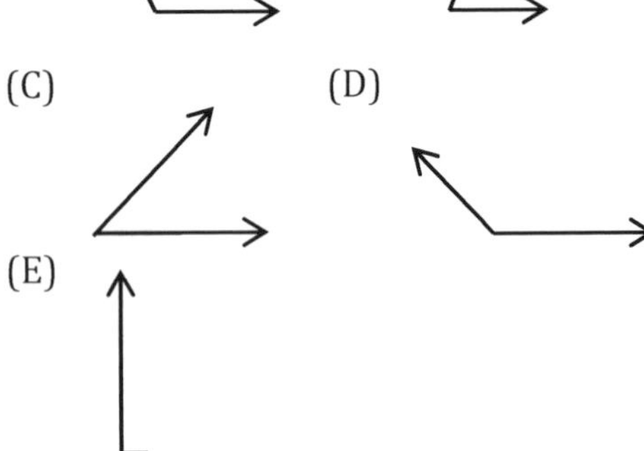

5. Which best describes the angle?

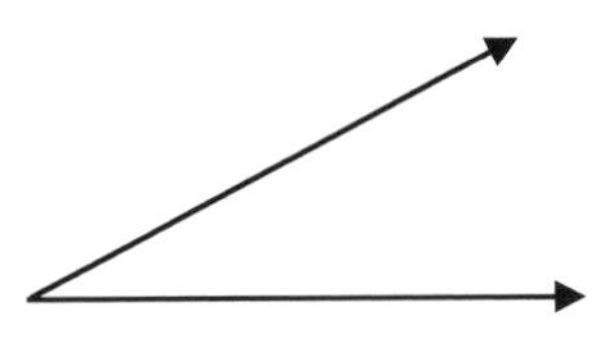

   (A) obtuse
   (B) acute
   (C) right
   (D) parallel
   (E) perpendicular

6. The image below shows the flag of Denmark. Which best describes the white lines on Denmark's flag?

   (A) perpendicular
   (B) parallel
   (C) rays
   (D) acute angles
   (E) neither parallel nor perpendicular

7. Which shape is NOT symmetrical?
   (A)

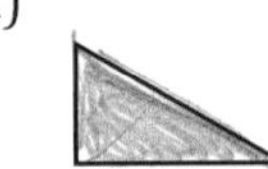

   (B)

   (C)

   (D)

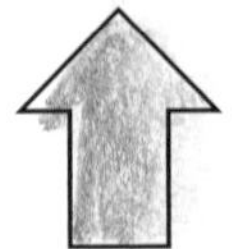

   (E)

Area and Perimeter

3rd Grade

1. What is the perimeter of this rectangle?

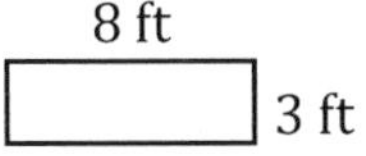

(A) 11 ft.
(B) 12 ft.
(C) 16 ft.
(D) 22 ft.
(E) 24 ft.

2. What is the perimeter of this shape shown on the right?

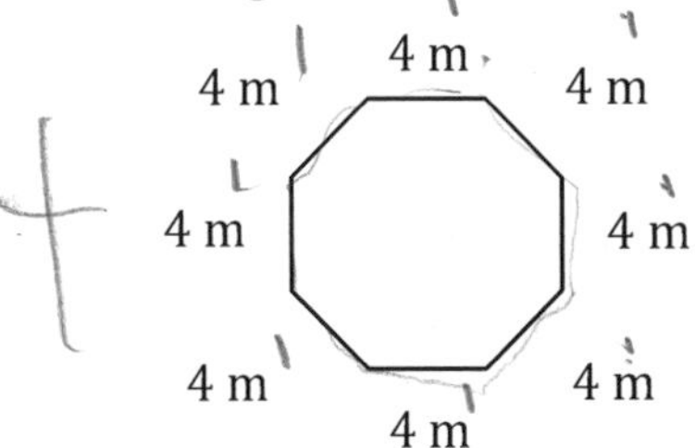

(A) 24 m
(B) 28 m
(C) 32 m
(D) 36 m
(E) 64 m

3. What is the perimeter of the shape below?

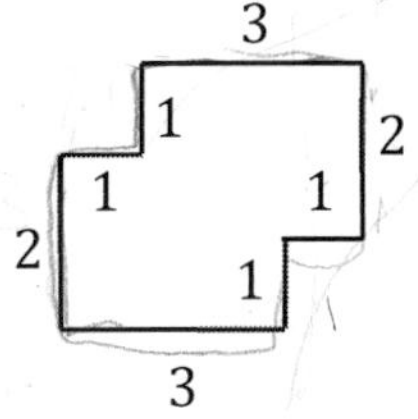

(A) 12
(B) 14
(C) 16
(D) 18
(E) 20

4. If the area of this rectangle is 30 square units, what is the length of x?

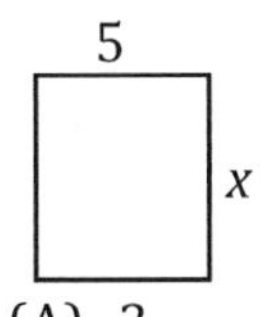

(A) 3
(B) 6
(C) 12
(D) 22
(E) 25

5. If the area of this rectangle equals 12 square units, what is its perimeter?

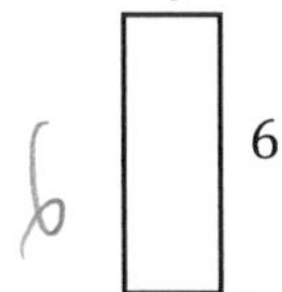

(A) 8
(B) 16
(C) 22
(D) 24
(E) 36

6. If these two rectangles have the same area, what is the length of W?

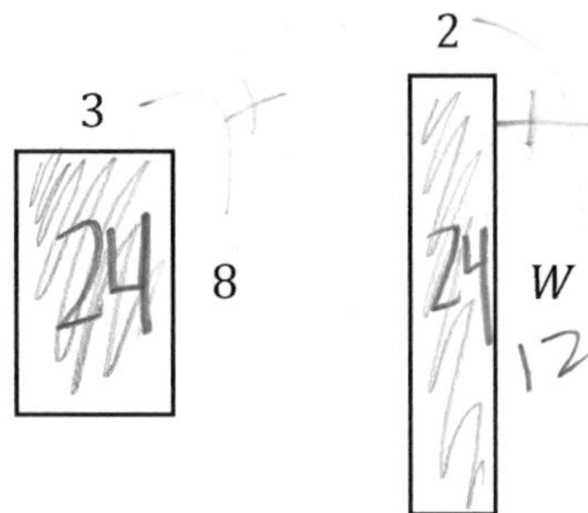

(A) 9
(B) 10
(C) 12
(D) 16
(E) 22

7. If the area of this rectangle is 42 square units, what is the length of x?

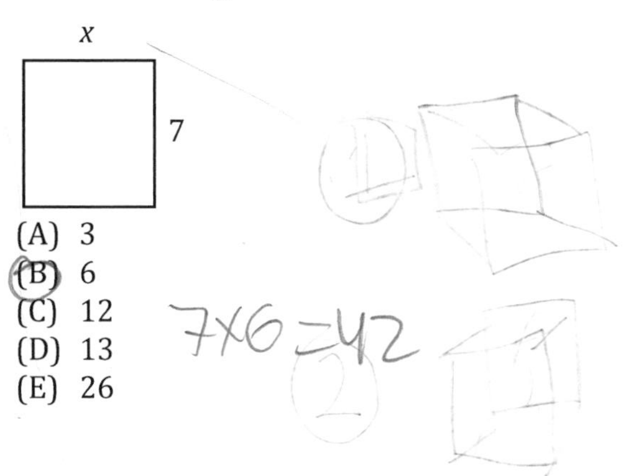

(A) 3
(B) 6
(C) 12
(D) 13
(E) 26

4th Grade

1. What is the area of this parallelogram?
(Note: Area = base × vertical height)

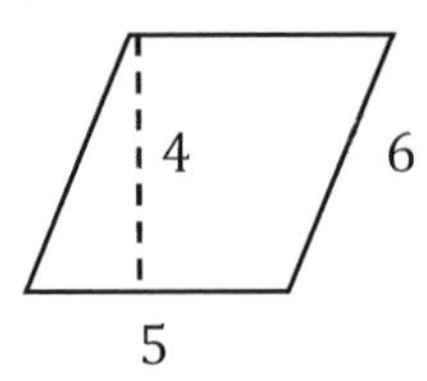

(A) 10 square units
(B) 15 square units
(C) 20 square units
(D) 24 square units
(E) 30 square units

2. If the perimeter of this rectangle is 24 units, what is its area?

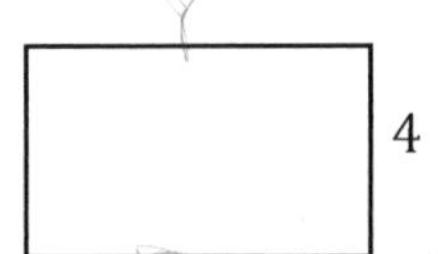

(A) 12 square units
(B) 16 square units
(C) 20 square units
(D) 32 square units
(E) 80 square units

3. If the perimeter of this rectangle is 18 inches, what is the length of x?

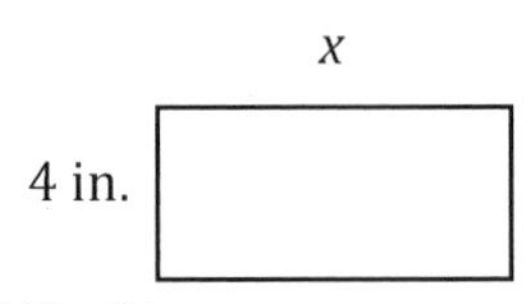

(A) 5 in.
(B) 9 in.
(C) 10 in.
(D) 14 in.
(E) 17 in.

4. If the perimeter of this rectangle is 22 feet, what is the length of x?

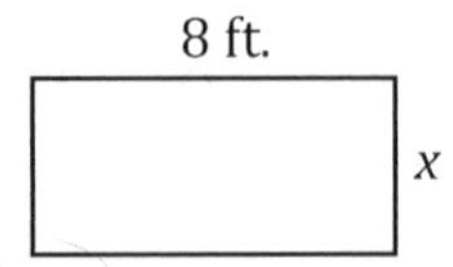

(A) 3 ft.
(B) 4 ft.
(C) 6 ft.
(D) 11 ft.
(E) 22 ft.

5. A square is formed by putting together two equal rectangles. If the perimeter of the square is 24 ft., what is the perimeter of one of the rectangles?
(A) 12 ft.
(B) 18 ft.
(C) 24 ft.
(D) 30 ft.
(E) 36 ft.

6. What is the area of this triangle?
(Note: Area of a triangle = $\frac{1}{2}$ *(base × vertical height))*

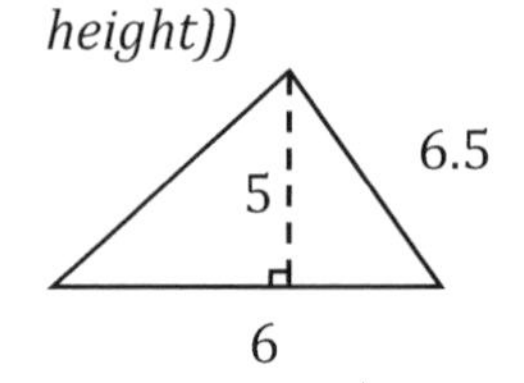

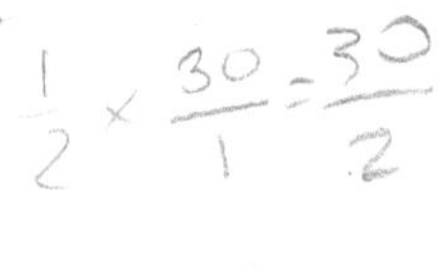

(A) 8 square units
(B) 15 square units
(C) 17.5 square units
(D) 30 square units
(E) 32.5 square units

7. If the area of this triangle is 24 square units, what is its perimeter?
(Note: Area = $\frac{1}{2}$ *(base × vertical height))*

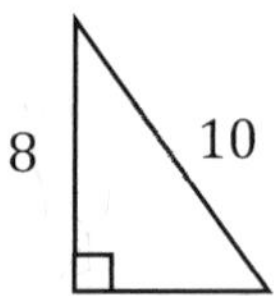

(A) 6
(B) 21
(C) 24
(D) 28
(E) 30

8. If the perimeter of the shape shown on the right is 84 meters and all side lengths are equal, what is the measure of one side length?
(A) 7 meters
(B) 10.5 meters
(C) 12 meters
(D) 14 meters
(E) 21 meters

9. Two identical triangles are put together to make a larger triangle, as shown below. If the area of the large triangle is 48 square units, what is the perimeter of either of the smaller triangles?
(Note: Area of a triangle = $\frac{1}{2}$ (base × vertical height))

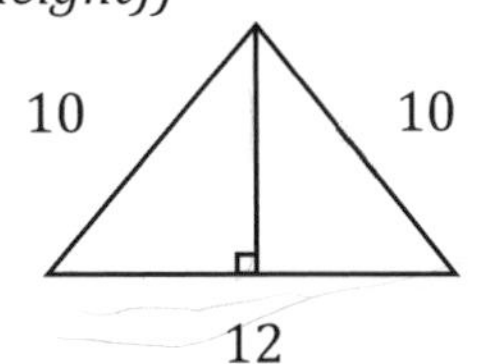

(A) 8
(B) 20
(C) 22
(D) 24
(E) 30

10. Two identical triangles are put together to make a rectangle as shown below. The area of each triangle is 21 square units. What is the perimeter of the rectangle?
(Note: Area = $\frac{1}{2}$ (base × vertical height))

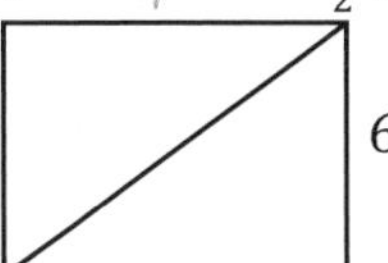

(A) 13
(B) 21
(C) 26
(D) 42
(E) 52

Measurement

Time and Money

3rd Grade

1. The first day of school is 2 weeks and 3 days from today. If today is August 10, on which day will school start?
(A) August 17
(B) August 24
(C) August 27
(D) August 30
(E) September 1

2. Celia and her family have been vacationing for 2 weeks and 5 days. If today is July 21st, on which day did their vacation start?
(A) June 30
(B) July 2
(C) July 4
(D) July 7
(E) July 14

3. Marie is having a party 3 weeks and 2 days from today. Today is May 2. On which day is Marie's party?
(A) May 23
(B) May 25
(C) May 29
(D) May 31
(E) June 5

4. Rhonda has $3.25 and Sharae has $4.67. How much money do they have together?
(A) $1.67
(B) $6.92
(C) $7.82
(D) $7.92
(E) $8.02

5. Melissa wants to buy a granola bar from a vending machine. The granola bar costs $1.15. Which coins can she use to make the EXACT cost of the granola bar?
(A) 3 quarters, 2 dimes, and 1 nickel
(B) 3 quarters and 5 dimes
(C) 4 quarters, 1 dime, and 1 nickel
(D) 5 quarters and 1 nickel
(E) 6 quarters and 1 dime

6. Briar's math test began at 10:30 a.m. and it ended 45 minutes later. At what time did her test end?
(A) 10:15 a.m.
(B) 10:45 a.m.
(C) 11:15 a.m.
(D) 11:30 a.m.
(E) 11:45 a.m.

7. Garrett buys a sandwich for $4.50 and a bottle of juice for $1. How much money did he spend in total?
   (A) $3.50
   (B) $4.49
   (C) $4.51
   (D) $4.60
   (E) $5.50

8. Nick had $4.50 and he spent 26¢ on a new pen. How much money does he have left?
   (A) $1.90
   (B) $4.24
   (C) $4.34
   (D) $4.76
   (E) $21.50

9. Dan has $6.78 to spend on lunch. He buys a wrap for $4.50. How much money does he have left?
   (A) $1.28
   (B) $1.88
   (C) $2.28
   (D) $6.33
   (E) $11.28

10. Amin buys a movie ticket for $7.65. He pays with a ten-dollar bill. How much change will he receive?
   (A) $1.35
   (B) $2.35
   (C) $2.45
   (D) $3.45
   (E) $7.55

11. Hallie wants to buy a book that costs $12.55. However, she only has $10.80. Which coins could her sister give her so Hallie has exactly $12.55?
   (A) 5 quarters
   (B) 5 quarters and 3 dimes
   (C) 6 quarters
   (D) 6 quarters and 2 dimes
   (E) 7 quarters

12. Jeff wants to buy a book that costs $6.50 but he only has $5.20. What coins could Jeff's brother give him so that Jeff would have exactly $6.50?
   (A) 2 quarters and 2 dimes
   (B) 3 quarters and 3 nickels
   (C) 3 quarters and 3 dimes
   (D) 4 quarters, 1 dime, and 1 nickel
   (E) 5 quarters and 1 nickel

13. Maria bought some snacks at the corner store for $3.55. She handed the cashier a 5-dollar bill. Which coins should the cashier give Maria as change?
   (A) 2 quarters, 1 dime, and 1 nickel
   (B) 4 quarters and 1 dime
   (C) 5 quarters and 1 dime
   (D) 5 quarters and 2 dimes
   (E) 6 quarters and 1 dime

14. Ben bought a bag of chips at a vending machine. If the chips cost $1.45 and he fed $2.00 into the machine, which coins could he have received as proper change?
   (A) 1 quarter and 3 nickels
   (B) 1 quarter and 3 dimes
   (C) 2 quarters and 1 dime
   (D) 2 quarters and 2 dimes
   (E) 3 quarters and 1 nickel

4th Grade

1. Eric's birthday party is on April 5. If his party is in 12 days, what is today? *(Note: There are 31 days in the month of March.)*
   (A) March 7
   (B) March 14
   (C) March 24
   (D) April 5
   (E) April 17

2. What day is today if Valentine's Day, February 14, is 1 week and 3 days away?
   (A) January 31
   (B) February 4
   (C) February 10
   (D) February 11
   (E) February 24

3. The last game of the soccer season was 2 weeks and 5 days ago. Today is December 21. On which day was the last game of the soccer season?
   (A) November 26
   (B) December 2
   (C) December 26
   (D) January 9
   (E) January 10

4. This year's 5-mile Turkey Trot race began at 11:43 a.m. The first runner crossed the finish line 37 minutes later. At what time did the first runner cross the finish line?
   (A) 11:06 a.m.
   (B) 11:20 a.m.
   (C) 11:50 a.m.
   (D) 12:30 p.m.
   (E) 12:20 p.m.

5. So far, Jack has saved $8.65 towards a game that costs $10.00. He decides to look around his room for loose change. Which combination of coins would help Jack reach his goal of exactly $10.00?
   (A) 3 dimes and 1 nickel
   (B) 4 quarters, 3 dimes, and 1 nickel
   (C) 4 quarters and 5 dimes
   (D) 5 quarters
   (E) 5 quarters and 1 nickel

6. Luke, Jenny, and Sam want to buy candy to share. Luke has 80¢, Jenny has $1.30, and Sam has $1.95. What is the total amount they can spend on the candy?
   (A) $2.25
   (B) $3.33
   (C) $3.96
   (D) $4.05
   (E) $4.50

7. Jay and Liam each have $10. They put their money together to buy popcorn and 2 drinks. The popcorn and drinks cost $14.58. How much money do they have left?
   (A) $4.58
   (B) $5.42
   (C) $6.42
   (D) $6.58
   (E) $14.58

8. Katie, Adam, and Lily want to put their money together to buy a gift for their mother. Katie has $4.35, Adam has $1.88, and Lily has $2.64. If the gift costs six dollars and fifty cents, how much money will they have leftover?
   (A) $1.27
   (B) $2.37
   (C) $2.73
   (D) $7.77
   (E) $8.87

9. Colin wants to buy an action figure that costs $8.90. However, he only has $7.35. Which coins could his mother give him so that he would have exactly $8.90?
   (A) 4 quarters and 2 nickels
   (B) 4 quarters and 3 dimes
   (C) 5 quarters
   (D) 5 quarters and 2 dimes
   (E) 6 quarters and 1 nickel

10. Ryan bought a few groceries that cost a total of $9.34. He paid with a ten-dollar bill. Which group of coins could be his proper change?
   (A) 1 quarter, 2 dimes, and 1 penny
   (B) 1 quarter, 3 dimes, and 4 pennies
   (C) 2 quarters, 1 nickel, and 4 pennies
   (D) 2 quarters, 3 nickels, and 1 penny
   (E) 3 quarters and 1 penny

Unit Analysis

3rd Grade

1. Miranda measures the length of her bedroom. If the room is 400 centimeters long, how long is the room in meters?
   (A) 4 meters
   (B) 40 meters
   (C) 400 meters
   (D) 4,000 meters
   (E) 40,000 meters

2. Samantha bought a 1,800-gram bag of flour. Judy bought a 1-kilogram bag of flour. How many more grams of flour did Samantha buy than Judy?
   (A) 80
   (B) 200
   (C) 800
   (D) 1,700
   (E) 1,799

3. Tracy has 16 pints of milk. How many gallons of milk does Tracy have?
(Note: 1 gallon = 8 pints)
(A) 2
(B) 4
(C) 8
(D) 32
(E) 128

4. Jaheem bought an aquarium that can hold up to 5 liters. He has a 500-milliliter jug that he uses to carry water. If he wants to make the fewest number of trips possible, how many times does he need to fill his jug in order to fill the tank?
(A) 2
(B) 5
(C) 10
(D) 100
(E) 1,000

5. Will's backpack has a mass of 1,400 grams and Toby's has a mass of 2 kilograms. How much more mass does Toby's backpack have than Will's, in grams?
(A) 0.6
(B) 600
(C) 1,200
(D) 1,380
(E) 1,398

6. A racetrack is 4 kilometers long. What is the length of the racetrack in centimeters?
(A) 40
(B) 400
(C) 4,000
(D) 40,000
(E) 400,000

4th Grade

1. $3\frac{1}{2}$ kg = ___ g?
(A) 0.0035
(B) 0.35
(C) 350
(D) 3,500
(E) 35,000

2. Tim bought 10 bottles of juice. He has 4.7 liters of juice total. How many milliliters of juice are in each bottle?
(A) 0.047
(B) 0.47
(C) 47
(D) 470
(E) 4,700

3. Donnie tossed a beanbag 80 centimeters. Hector tossed the beanbag 0.75 meters. Maya tossed the beanbag 90 centimeters. Emma tossed the beanbag 0.82 meters. Kyle tossed the beanbag 50 centimeters. Who tossed the beanbag the GREATEST distance?
(A) Donnie
(B) Hector
(C) Maya
(D) Emma
(E) Kyle

4. Kirsten's desk is 3 feet wide. Mike's desk is 40 inches wide. How much wider is Mike's desk than Kirsten's?
(Note: 1 foot = 12 inches)
(A) 2 inches
(B) 4 inches
(C) 12 inches
(D) 31 inches
(E) 37 inches

5. Chris measured the masses of his textbooks. He wrote: Math book mass of 2.1 kilograms. His science book has a mass of 3,200 grams. His English book has a mass of 3.8 kilograms. His spelling book has a mass of 1,800 grams. His music book has a mass of 2.4 kilograms. Which book has the smallest mass?
(A) Math
(B) Science
(C) English
(D) Spelling
(E) Music

6. 7 ft 6 in. = ____ in?
(Note: 1 foot = 12 inches)
(A) 78
(B) 80
(C) 84
(D) 90
(E) 92

Statistics & Probability

Probability

3rd Grade

1. Each of the six letters of the word "SCHOOL" is written on a piece of paper and placed in a bag. If one piece of paper is selected at random, which of the following would have the GREATEST chance of being selected?
   (A) the letter S
   (B) the letter C
   (C) the letter H
   (D) the letter O
   (E) the letter L

2. In a jar, there are 8 red candies, 10 yellow candies, 6 green candies, 8 blue candies, and 5 brown candies. If you remove one candy without looking, which color will it MOST likely be?
   (A) red
   (B) green
   (C) yellow
   (D) blue
   (E) brown

3. In a bag of marbles, there are 7 green, 2 red, 5 orange, 7 yellow, and 10 purple marbles. If you were to close your eyes and pick a marble from the bag at random, which color is LEAST likely to be picked?
   (A) green
   (B) red
   (C) orange
   (D) yellow
   (E) purple

4. Jane, Tim, John, Chris, Mike, Jim, Sue, and Tina are all hoping to be picked to be the teacher's weekly classroom assistant. Each of their names is placed in a paper bag and one name is randomly selected. It is MOST likely that the student chosen has a name that starts with which letter?
   (A) J
   (B) T
   (C) C
   (D) M
   (E) S

5. If one shape is selected at random, which would have the LEAST chance of being selected?

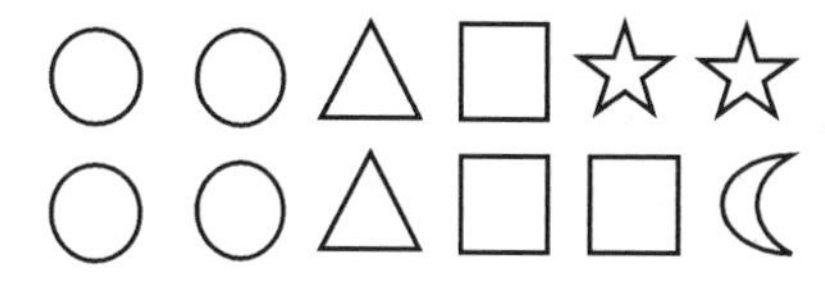

   (A) a circle
   (B) a moon
   (C) a square
   (D) a star
   (E) a triangle

4th Grade

1. One penny, three nickels, two dimes, and one quarter are placed in a piggy bank. If a coin is chosen at random, which coin would have the GREATEST chance of being selected?
   (A) penny
   (B) nickel
   (C) dime
   (D) quarter
   (E) they each have an equal chance

2. Maria has a bag full of yarn. She has 3 balls of red yarn, 2 balls of blue, and 3 balls of yellow, and 4 balls of green yarn. If she grabs a thread out without looking, what color will she MOST likely pull out?
   (A) red
   (B) blue
   (C) yellow
   (D) green
   (E) red or yellow

3. There are eight states representing the central part of the United States. Those states are Minnesota, Wisconsin, Michigan, Iowa, Illinois, Indiana, Ohio, and Missouri. The Smith family lives in Indiana. They decided to take a vacation in one of the OTHER central states. If they randomly selected a central state to visit, the letter the state begins with is MOST likely
   (A) an I
   (B) an M
   (C) an O
   (D) a W
   (E) They each of have an equal chance of going to a state beginning with I or M.

4. The checkboard below is made up of 64 squares. Tashi tossed a chip on the board and it landed within a square without overlapping. Which statement about the chip's placement is true?

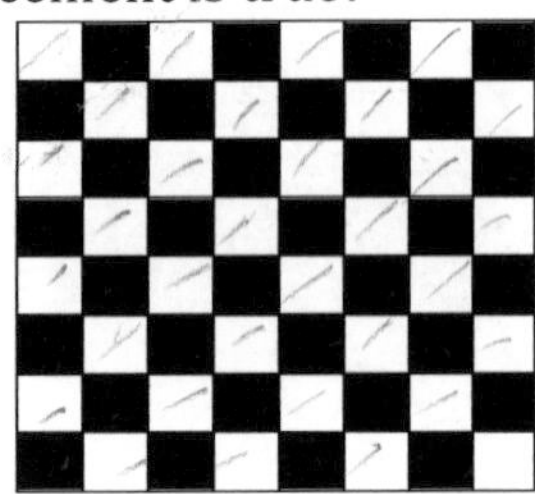

   (A) It is more likely to be on a black square than a white square.
   (B) It is more likely to be on a white square than a black square.
   (C) The chip has an equal chance of being on either a black or a white square.
   (D) It is twice as likely to be on a black square than a white square.
   (E) It is twice as likely to be on a white square than a black square.

5. John is holding a deck of flashcards labeled from 1 through 9. Which of the following is MOST likely to happen?
   (A) He will pull out an odd number.
   (B) He will pull out an even number.
   (C) He will pull out a multiple of 3.
   (D) He will pull out a number greater than 5.
   (E) He will pull out a number less than 5.

6. A box contains 5 pieces of paper each with a letter A through E written on it. One piece of paper is randomly selected from the box. Which statement about the letter written on the selected paper is true?
   (A) There is no chance the letter will be a vowel.
   (B) There is no chance the letter will be a consonant.
   (C) The letter has the same chance of being a vowel as it does a consonant.
   (D) The letter has a greater chance of being a vowel than it does a consonant.
   (E) The letter has a smaller chance of being a vowel than it does a consonant.

7. If a coin is tossed, which of the following statements is true?
   (A) It is more likely to land on a head.
   (B) It is more likely to land on a tail.
   (C) It is least likely to land on a tail.
   (D) It has an equal, or same, chance of landing on a head or tail.
   (E) It would depend if the coin is a penny, nickel, dime, or quarter.

8. The chart shows the favorite pizza toppings of 20 students in a 4th grade class at Bedford Elementary School. If a new student came to class, which pizza topping would MOST likely be his or her favorite?

Favorite Pizza Toppings

cheese	✓✓✓✓
mushroom	✓✓✓
sausage	✓✓✓✓
pepperoni	✓✓✓✓✓✓✓✓✓

   (A) cheese
   (B) mushroom
   (C) sausage
   (D) pepperoni
   (E) no topping would likely to be the student's favorite

Mean

3rd Grade

1. Sylvia counted the number of red cars she passed on the way to school during the week. What is the average number of red cars she saw per day over the course of the week?

Day	Cars
Monday	11
Tuesday	15
Wednesday	12
Thursday	10
Friday	12

(A) 10
(B) 11
(C) 12
(D) 13
(E) 14

2. What was the average temperature of the five cities listed below on January 1st?

Temperature on Jan 1st

Coin Type	Price for One
Tampa Bay	72°
Montelier	15°
New Orleans	61°
Boston	19°
Richmond	43°

(A) 22°
(B) 42°
(C) 43°
(D) 57°
(E) 61°

3. What was the average annual rainfall in Willow City over the period represented in the table?

Willow City Annual Rainfall

Year	Rainfall (in.)
2011	62
2012	43
2013	23
2014	28
2015	29

(A) 29 in.
(B) 36 in.
(C) 37 in.
(D) 39 in.
(E) 49 in.

4. Stacy has a collection of semi-precious stones. The mass of the stones are 27 grams, 19 grams, 17 grams, 21 grams, 27 grams, and 15 grams. What is the average mass of her semi-precious stones?

(A) 12 grams
(B) 18 grams
(C) 20 grams
(D) 21 grams
(E) 27 grams

4th Grade

1. Alex is a dog-walker. The dogs she walks weigh 25 lbs., 56 lbs., 18 lbs., 41 lbs., 27 lbs., 63 lbs., 33 lbs., and 25 lbs. What is the average weight of the dogs Alex walks?
(A) 25 lbs.
(B) 30 lbs.
(C) 32 lbs.
(D) 35 lbs.
(E) 36 lbs.

2. Ellen is weighing rocks for her science project. The rocks weigh 22 kg, 13 kg, 28 kg, 10 kg, and 12 kg. What is the average weight of the rocks?
(A) 13 kg
(B) 17 kg
(C) 18 kg
(D) 19 kg
(E) 21 kg

3. Abe lives in a very rainy city. Over a 9-month period, he recorded how many days a month it rained. The table below displays his findings. What is the average amount of days it rained per month during the 9-month period?

Month	Number of Days
March	22
April	23
May	20
June	11
July	12
August	14
September	27
October	24
November	27

(A) 16
(B) 18
(C) 20
(D) 22
(E) 27

4. The table below shows the number of points the Pirates Football Team scored in each game of their season. What is the average number of points they scored per game?

Opponent	Points
The Wolves	21
The Bandits	28
The Trojans	3
The Spartans	42
The Giants	21
The Pumas	17
The Cosmos	36

(A) 21
(B) 24
(C) 25
(D) 28
(E) 39

5. James is raising money for charity and asked his friends to donate. The table below shows how much each of his friends contributed. What is the average donation?

Friend	Donation ($)
Cindy	18
Jack	16
Carlos	12
Bette	22
Amy	18
Sam	10

(A) $6
(B) $8
(C) $12
(D) $16
(E) $24

6. What was the average temperature in the cities below on February 29th?

City	Temperature
Honolulu	78°
Doha	108°
Minsk	0°
Port-au-Prince	94°
Cairo	80°

(A) 54°
(B) 72°
(C) 80°
(D) 90°
(E) 108°

7. The weather service measured annual rainfall in several cities. What is the average annual rainfall in the cities below?

City	Average Annual Rainfall
Calgary	34 in.
Lagos	58 in.
Athens	39 in.
Milan	18 in.
Da Nang	72 in.
Bogota	52 in.
Cape Town	28 in.

(A) 39 in.
(B) 42 in.
(C) 43 in.
(D) 44 in.
(E) 54 in.

Interpreting Tables and Graphs

3rd Grade

Questions 1 and 2 are based on the following chart:

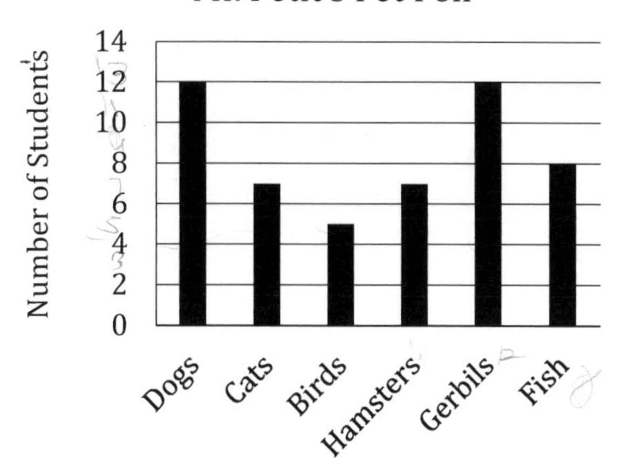

1. How many more students in Mr. Petit's class have gerbils than fish?
   (A) 3
   (B) 4
   (C) 7
   (D) 8
   (E) 12

2. Students in Mr. Petit's class reported the same number of which of the following types of pets?
   (A) birds and hamsters
   (B) birds and cats
   (C) dogs and fish
   (D) hamsters and fish
   (E) hamsters and cats

Questions 3 and 4 are based on the following chart:

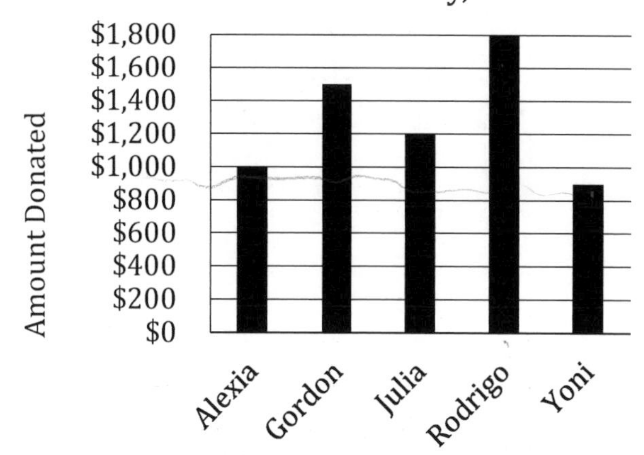

3. Five friends donated money to their favorite charities in 2017. What is the average amount Yoni and Gordon donated?
   (A) $900
   (B) $1,200
   (C) $1,500
   (D) $1,650
   (E) $2,400

4. Which pair of friends together donated the most to charity in 2017?
   (A) Gordon and Julia
   (B) Gordon and Alexia
   (C) Gordon and Yoni
   (D) Alexia and Yoni
   (E) Alexia and Julia

Questions 5 and 6 are based on the following table:

Age	Number of Visitors
0-19	350
20-39	250
40-59	300
60-79	200
Over 79	100

5. On Sunday, visitors of all ages came to the local zoo. How many visitors were 60 or older?
   (A) 100
   (B) 200
   (C) 300
   (D) 400
   (E) 500

6. How many visitors were older than 19 but younger than 60?
   (A) 750
   (B) 550
   (C) 350
   (D) 300
   (E) 250

Questions 7 and 8 are based on the following table:

City	Population
Frannyville	10,000
Mason City	15,000
La Plata	20,000
Dennison	5,000
Plantsburg	25,000

7. What is the combined population of Frannyville, La Plata, and Dennison?
(A) 35,000
(B) 45,000
(C) 50,000
(D) 55,000
(E) 75,000

8. More people live in La Plata than which two cities combined?
(A) Frannyville and Mason City
(B) Mason City and Dennison
(C) Dennison and Plantsburg
(D) Plantsburg and Frannyville
(E) Frannyville and Dennison

4th Grade

Questions 1-2 are based on the following table:

Company	Profits
Bric a Brac Co.	$80 million
Geminex	$65 million
Caplan Corp.	$110 million
Rio and Sons	$135 million

1. A fifth company, Ideologie, earns a profit halfway between the profits of Geminex and Rio and Sons. How much profit does Ideologie earn?
(A) $65 million
(B) $80 million
(C) $100 million
(D) $135 million
(E) $200 million

2. Bric a Brac and Caplan combine their profits. How much more do they now have compared to Rio and Sons?
(A) $25 million
(B) $35 million
(C) $45 million
(D) $55 million
(E) $65 million

Questions 3-4 are based on the following table.

The Merry Hawks basketball team recently won a game. Their four top scoring players were M. Berg, H. Chen B. Lavello, and K. Patrick, whose scores are listed below.

Player	Points
M. Berg	24
H. Chen	15
B. Lavello	31
K. Patrick	14

3. What is the average number of points scored by Chen, Lavello, and Patrick?
(A) 15
(B) 20
(C) 21
(D) 28
(E) 60

4. The Merry Hawks' opponents, the Mooncats, scored 10 more points than the Merry Hawks' top four scorers combined. How many points did the Mooncats score?
(A) 41
(B) 70
(C) 74
(D) 80
(E) 94

Questions 5-6 are based on the following graph:

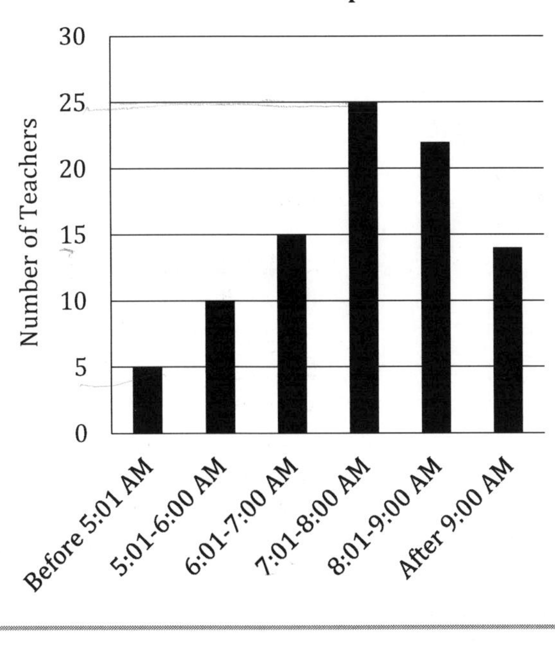

5. Teachers at Natchez High School were polled about the times they wake up on weekends. How many teachers wake up after 5:00 AM but before 8:01 AM on weekends?
   (A) 10
   (B) 25
   (C) 45
   (D) 50
   (E) 66

6. What is the difference between the number of teachers with the most common wake-up time and the least common wake-up time?
   (A) 10
   (B) 15
   (C) 20
   (D) 25
   (E) 30

Questions 7-8 are based on the following graph:

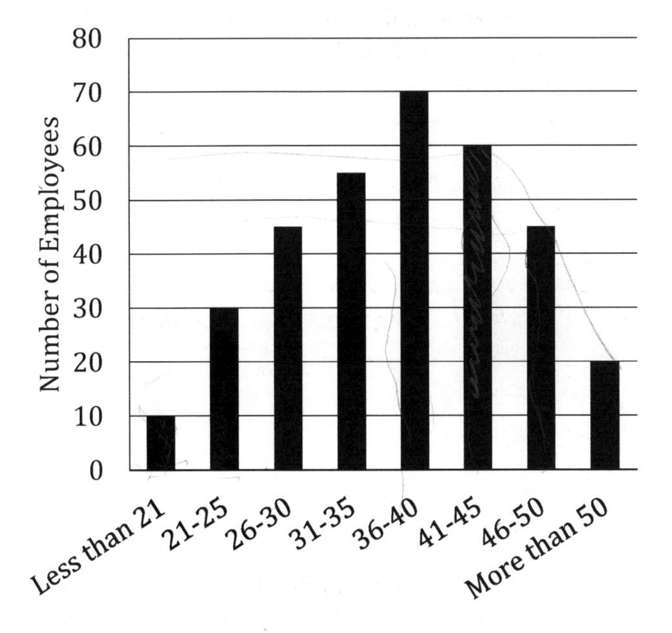

7. How many employees at Kite Co. work more than 40 hours per week?
   (A) 60
   (B) 65
   (C) 105
   (D) 125
   (E) 195

8. How many more employees work 36-40 hours than 0-25 hours?
   (A) 5
   (B) 10
   (C) 30
   (D) 40
   (E) 60

Verbal

Overview

The Verbal section is comprised of synonyms and analogies. Synonym questions assess a student's ability to recognize words and reason through different relationships and subtle differences among words. The analogies measure how well students can relate words and ideas to each other using logic. Together, these questions are designed to test students' vocabulary and reasoning skills.

Students will have 20 minutes to answer 15 synonyms and 15 analogy questions.

On the Actual Test

Synonym questions consist of a single word in capital letters, followed by five answer choices labeled A through E. Students must select the answer choice that has the same or most nearly the same meaning as the word in capital letters.

Analogy questions ask students to look at a pair of words and select another pair of words with a matching relationship. Analogy questions are presented on the Elementary SSAT in two different ways:

- Two-part stem: "A" is to "B" as...
  In these types of questions, students are given two words in the stem of the question, and are asked to select the pair of words with the same relationship as demonstrated between words "A" and "B."

- Three-part stem: "A" is to "B" as "C" is to...
  In these types of questions, students are given three words in the stem of the question; words "A" and "B" form one relationship, and are asked to complete the same relationship between word "C" and your answer choice.

There are many different types of relationships featured in the analogies. The most common ones are described below:

- Antonym relationships: Words that have the opposite, or nearly the opposite, meaning.
- Characteristic relationships: The first word in a pair describes an object, while the second word in the pair indicates a characteristic of that object.
- Part/Whole relationships: The first word in a pair is a part of the second word of the pair.
- Uses relationships: The first word identifies an object, while the second word in the pair describes a use for the object.
- Users relationships: The first word indicates an object, while the second word in the pair indicates a person or type of person who uses that object.
- Category relationships: The first word is a specific example from the category described by the second word in the pair.
- Product/Producer relationships: The first word describes the product, while the second word in the pair describes the person who produces it.
- Degree relationships: One word in a pair is related to the other word by a higher or lower degree.
- Homonyms relationships: Words that sound identical despite being spelled differently.
- Synonym relationships: Words that have very similar meaning (NOTE: not the same as the questions featured in the synonyms portion of the Verbal section).

Unlike in this workbook, the questions on the actual test will **not** indicate which type of relationship each analogy represents.

In This Practice Book

Synonym questions are given their own section and are generally presented in order of difficulty (the harder questions appear toward the end of the section).

Analogy questions are also given their own section and are also generally presented in order from least to most challenging. However, analogy questions are further subdivided as follows:

- Guided Practice – 10 units, one each for the individual types of analogies listed above. Each unit will only include a specific type of analogy. This allows students to focus on a particular type of analogy, if needed.
- Mixed Practice – 2 units of mixed practice, separated by grade level. Each unit will include a mix of analogy types, which mirrors the format of the actual test. This allows students to see how well they know the different types of analogies.

There are additional instructions and recommendations at the beginning of each of the Synonyms and Analogies sections, which students should review before starting.

There are many ways to tackle this section of the test. Use the results from the diagnostic practice test to develop a plan. For instance, students may want to try the analogies Mixed Practice section to get a sense for which areas to focus on. Then, dive into the relevant Guided Practice sections. If students already know what needs further work, they may jump right in to a Guided Practice section.

Remember: if you don't know the answer, skip it and come back to it. If you still don't know, and you're running out of time, just guess!

Synonyms

Overview

Synonym questions consist of a single word in capital letters, followed by five answer choices labeled A through E. Students must select the answer choice that most nearly has the same meaning as the word in capital letters.

How to Use This Section

How much time students should spend on this section should be based on the diagnostic practice test results as well as the student's study plan. For most students, even those who score very well on the diagnostic practice test, we recommend practicing at least 10 questions per week in preparing for the exam. Those who score well on the diagnostic practice test and have an expansive vocabulary may wish to focus more on intermediate and advanced questions, while other students may wish to focus on introductory and intermediate questions.

The purpose of this section is to introduce students to new words. Some may find many of the words in this section to be challenging. Students should not be surprised to have to look up many of the words encountered in this section! We encourage students to make a list of difficult or challenging words, whether they appear in questions or answer choices. Write down the definition of each word as well as a sentence using the word. Students might also want to consider writing down positive or negative associations, any root words that can help them remember the word, or any words that are commonly encountered with that word.

Tutorverse Tips!

Sometimes, words can have more than one meaning. Don't be confused! Look at the answer choices to make an educated guess as to which meaning is being used in the question. Then, use reasoning skills to select the word that most nearly means the same as the word in capital letters.

Use it in a Sentence

As you read the question words in capital letters, think of a word that you might use instead of the question word.

If you don't know what a word means, try using it in a sentence. This will often help you see which word can be used to replace the question word. If this doesn't help, see if you can figure out whether or not the word has any positive or negative associations that match those of the answer choices.

Study Roots, Prefixes, & Suffixes

Many English words are derived from a single Greek or Latin root word. Sometimes, these root words relate to many different English words. In addition, knowing common prefixes and suffixes can help with very long or unfamiliar words, which can inform on the word's connotation or meaning.

Read, Read, Read!

Finally, there is no better preparation for the Synonym section than spending time reading. The practice of reading, whether for school or for pleasure, will help you build up your vocabulary. It will give you practice in utilizing context clues and figuring out what unknown words might mean. Reading at or above your current grade level will help you make better sense of more complicated words and sentences.

3rd Grade

Directions – Select the one word or phrase whose meaning is closest to the word in capital letters.

Introductory

1. FIELD:
   (A) flat
   (B) feel
   (C) fled
   (D) plain
   (E) valley

2. CENTER:
   (A) factory
   (B) separate
   (C) middle
   (D) external
   (E) conclusion

3. UNUSUAL:
   (A) rare
   (B) everyday
   (C) ugly
   (D) unuseful
   (E) wonderful

4. ARGUE:
   (A) wait
   (B) dislike
   (C) disagree
   (D) approve
   (E) shout

5. HELPFUL:
   (A) servant
   (B) friend
   (C) harmful
   (D) grateful
   (E) useful

6. PRANK:
   (A) mock
   (B) play
   (C) foolish
   (D) trick
   (E) plank

7. LEAK:
   (A) drip
   (B) fill
   (C) loose
   (D) break
   (E) liquid

8. INSECT:
   (A) stick
   (B) ant
   (C) bug
   (D) spider
   (E) animal

9. WEALTHY:
   (A) money
   (B) comfort
   (C) dollar
   (D) rich
   (E) boss

10. NECESSARY:
   (A) serious
   (B) extra
   (C) survival
   (D) needed
   (E) neutral

11. GATHER:
   (A) collect
   (B) flowers
   (C) choose
   (D) party
   (E) clutch

12. DANGEROUS:
   (A) predator
   (B) risky
   (C) alarm
   (D) mean
   (E) protected

13. LABEL:
   (A) sticker
   (B) design
   (C) package
   (D) information
   (E) price

14. DISCOVER:
   (A) treasure
   (B) look
   (C) hunt
   (D) find
   (E) track

15. DRIFT:
   (A) river
   (B) drive
   (C) float
   (D) paddle
   (E) slowly

16. FURIOUS:
   (A) fast
   (B) sore
   (C) calm
   (D) angry
   (E) feeling

17. CRUMPLE:
   (A) rip
   (B) paper
   (C) sprinkle
   (D) fail
   (E) wrinkle

18. SWIFT:
   (A) wind
   (B) speed
   (C) fast
   (D) pace
   (E) slow

Intermediate

1. BELIEF:
   (A) religious
   (B) proverb
   (C) accept
   (D) thought
   (E) surprise

2. POKE:
   (A) hole
   (B) jab
   (C) finger
   (D) punch
   (E) tickle

3. COAST:
   (A) ocean
   (B) cliff
   (C) swimming
   (D) shore
   (E) vacation

4. RIDDLE:
   (A) trap
   (B) rhyme
   (C) lullaby
   (D) trickster
   (E) puzzle

5. DEFEND:
   (A) guard
   (B) castle
   (C) defeat
   (D) champion
   (E) challenger

6. REVISE:
   (A) highlight
   (B) rewrite
   (C) editor
   (D) writer
   (E) require

7. INTELLIGENT:
   (A) grades
   (B) school
   (C) slow
   (D) brainy
   (E) sweet

8. OPINION:
   (A) fact
   (B) view
   (C) persuade
   (D) said
   (E) statement

9. POSTER:
   (A) picture
   (B) board
   (C) printer
   (D) booklet
   (E) public

10. CONTAIN:
    (A) within
    (B) release
    (C) cart
    (D) container
    (E) hold

11. GLOBE:
    (A) earth
    (B) model
    (C) moon
    (D) sphere
    (E) history

12. CERTAIN:
    (A) positive
    (B) unsure
    (C) sum
    (D) know
    (E) be

13. PARTLY:
    (A) completely
    (B) totally
    (C) piece
    (D) brokenly
    (E) incompletely

14. DISEASE:
    (A) unwell
    (B) unhealthy
    (C) sickness
    (D) hospital
    (E) nurse

15. REPAIR:
    (A) reduce
    (B) car
    (C) destroy
    (D) fix
    (E) combine

16. NERVOUS:
    (A) brain
    (B) exam
    (C) system
    (D) jumpy
    (E) eager

17. COMMUNITY:
    (A) group
    (B) unequal
    (C) friendship
    (D) member
    (E) city

18. BOTHER:
    (A) distressed
    (B) annoy
    (C) brother
    (D) thrill
    (E) ignore

Advanced

1. GUST:
   (A) stormy
   (B) snow
   (C) puff
   (D) windy
   (E) loud

2. ANCIENT:
   (A) past
   (B) times
   (C) ruins
   (D) old
   (E) religion

3. HARDLY:
   (A) strongly
   (B) sturdily
   (C) barely
   (D) extremely
   (E) only

4. COWARD:
   (A) wimp
   (B) innocent
   (C) brave
   (D) scary
   (E) gloomy

5. EXAMINE:
   (A) questions
   (B) concentrate
   (C) doctor
   (D) quiz
   (E) review

6. TYPICAL:
   (A) type
   (B) uncommon
   (C) unlikely
   (D) ordinary
   (E) bored

7. EXPLORE:
   (A) explorer
   (B) airplane
   (C) explain
   (D) pass
   (E) seek

8. AGREEABLE:
   (A) person
   (B) clumsy
   (C) pleasant
   (D) decide
   (E) arguing

9. CAPTURE:
   (A) seize
   (B) keep
   (C) flag
   (D) prisoner
   (E) hunter

10. VANISH:
    (A) illusion
    (B) faded
    (C) disappear
    (D) bright
    (E) see-through

11. SHELTER:
    (A) flood
    (B) shelf
    (C) homeless
    (D) safe
    (E) shack

12. RESTLESS:
    (A) runner
    (B) active
    (C) sleepy
    (D) peaceful
    (E) motion

13. OBSERVE:
    (A) notice
    (B) science
    (C) telescope
    (D) absorbed
    (E) experimental

14. EXACT:
    (A) estimated
    (B) rounded
    (C) incorrect
    (D) about
    (E) precise

15. UNDERSTAND:
    (A) insight
    (B) gifted
    (C) grasp
    (D) confuse
    (E) knowledge

16. PERSUADE:
    (A) essay
    (B) convince
    (C) believe
    (D) produce
    (E) action

17. MAGNIFICENT:
    (A) beautiful
    (B) magnetic
    (C) enlarge
    (D) dull
    (E) evil

18. ADDITIONAL:
    (A) mathematics
    (B) together
    (C) equal
    (D) extra
    (E) equation

4th Grade

Directions – Select the one word or phrase whose meaning is closest to the word in capital letters.

Introductory

1. ORDINARY:
   (A) custom
   (B) usual
   (C) person
   (D) amazing
   (E) weekly

2. PROVIDE:
   (A) hide
   (B) command
   (C) get
   (D) food
   (E) give

3. RECENTLY:
   (A) lately
   (B) memory
   (C) future
   (D) previous
   (E) yearly

4. BLOSSOM:
   (A) petals
   (B) grain
   (C) cycle
   (D) flower
   (E) plant

5. CONTENT:
   (A) outside
   (B) book
   (C) lonely
   (D) table
   (E) happy

6. ENTIRE:
   (A) partial
   (B) whole
   (C) tired
   (D) divided
   (E) world

7. COUNTRY:
   (A) nation
   (B) continent
   (C) citizen
   (D) flag
   (E) place

8. SURVIVE:
   (A) enjoy
   (B) live
   (C) water
   (D) breathe
   (E) wild

9. DROWSY:
   (A) dream
   (B) medicine
   (C) faint
   (D) wake
   (E) sleepy

10. QUANTITY:
    (A) quality
    (B) items
    (C) plenty
    (D) total
    (E) amount

11. BLIZZARD:
    (A) white
    (B) windy
    (C) snowstorm
    (D) freezing
    (E) gathering

12. CONCEPT:
    (A) idea
    (B) question
    (C) project
    (D) image
    (E) brilliant

13. SELECT:
    (A) weed
    (B) special
    (C) best
    (D) choose
    (E) worst

14. REVEAL:
    (A) tell
    (B) deny
    (C) secret
    (D) password
    (E) cover

15. CONFIDENT:
    (A) afraid
    (B) sure
    (C) noble
    (D) envious
    (E) gentle

16. THREAT:
    (A) danger
    (B) bully
    (C) mild
    (D) insensitive
    (E) frightening

17. DEBATE:
    (A) team
    (B) whisper
    (C) song
    (D) brawl
    (E) argument

18. ENVY:
    (A) admiration
    (B) jealousy
    (C) clingy
    (D) emotion
    (E) wealthy

Intermediate

1. HEROIC:
   (A) powerful
   (B) dramatic
   (C) weak
   (D) superman
   (E) courageous

2. EXHIBIT:
   (A) art
   (B) museum
   (C) display
   (D) hide
   (E) ticket

3. ALTERNATE:
   (A) reality
   (B) twin
   (C) repeat
   (D) another
   (E) translate

4. COMPANION:
   (A) dog
   (B) sibling
   (C) partner
   (D) condition
   (E) foe

5. TRAGIC:
   (A) boring
   (B) sad
   (C) poem
   (D) disappointing
   (E) joking

6. CRAVE:
   (A) buy
   (B) want
   (C) hungry
   (D) cave
   (E) hate

7. PERMIT:
   (A) allow
   (B) driver
   (C) ban
   (D) papers
   (E) improve

8. EXPERIMENT:
   (A) test
   (B) idea
   (C) extreme
   (D) scientist
   (E) lab

9. REQUEST:
   (A) borrow
   (B) question
   (C) library
   (D) refusal
   (E) plea

10. IMPACT:
    (A) tap
    (B) crash
    (C) crater
    (D) boom
    (E) powerful

11. ANXIOUS:
    (A) overjoyed
    (B) nerve
    (C) worried
    (D) crying
    (E) fidget

12. CLAIM:
    (A) reply
    (B) response
    (C) say
    (D) target
    (E) reject

13. MANSION:
    (A) expensive
    (B) room
    (C) hut
    (D) house
    (E) celebrity

14. MODEST:
    (A) shy
    (B) crazy
    (C) modern
    (D) mouse
    (E) clothing

15. DISASTER:
    (A) unlucky
    (B) blessing
    (C) earthquake
    (D) tragedy
    (E) spill

16. COMPETITION:
    (A) racer
    (B) meeting
    (C) trophy
    (D) winner
    (E) contest

17. TRANSFORM:
    (A) maintain
    (B) differ
    (C) alter
    (D) robot
    (E) analyze

18. ROUTINE:
    (A) morning
    (B) pattern
    (C) extraordinary
    (D) instruction
    (E) repeat

Advanced

1. CIRCULAR:
   (A) grouped
   (B) straight
   (C) coin
   (D) round
   (E) ball

2. ACHIEVEMENT:
   (A) celebration
   (B) score
   (C) great
   (D) perform
   (E) accomplishment

3. NUMEROUS:
   (A) many
   (B) handful
   (C) few
   (D) numbers
   (E) mathematical

4. PRACTICALLY:
   (A) slightly
   (B) experienced
   (C) basically
   (D) hands-on
   (E) already

5. ELDERLY:
   (A) aged
   (B) grandparent
   (C) youthful
   (D) wise
   (E) relative

6. NONSENSE:
   (A) foreign
   (B) garbage
   (C) confusion
   (D) gibberish
   (E) language

7. PECULIAR:
   (A) regular
   (B) annoying
   (C) strange
   (D) interesting
   (E) odor

8. UNFAMILIAR:
   (A) conventional
   (B) close
   (C) alien
   (D) stranger
   (E) unsurprised

9. EFFORTLESS:
   (A) easy
   (B) ready
   (C) strain
   (D) demanding
   (E) challenge

10. ABROAD:
   (A) gigantic
   (B) wide
   (C) return
   (D) aboard
   (E) overseas

11. IMPRESSIVE:
   (A) awe
   (B) remarkable
   (C) good
   (D) giant
   (E) sorry

12. SILENTLY:
   (A) loudly
   (B) definitely
   (C) soundlessly
   (D) pure
   (E) evening

13. RARELY:
   (A) infrequently
   (B) fairly
   (C) oddly
   (D) precious
   (E) often

14. CAUTIOUS:
   (A) caring
   (B) cowardly
   (C) careful
   (D) snail
   (E) daring

15. PROTEST:
   (A) stroll
   (B) violent
   (C) annoyed
   (D) disagree
   (E) agreement

16. EXTERIOR:
   (A) behavior
   (B) wilderness
   (C) shell
   (D) wall
   (E) outside

17. MEADOW:
   (A) barn
   (B) deer
   (C) grass
   (D) prairie
   (E) forest

18. VALIANT:
   (A) modest
   (B) heroic
   (C) deviant
   (D) honor
   (E) crafty

Analogies

Overview

Analogy questions ask students to look at a pair of words and select another pair of words with a matching relationship. Analogy questions are presented on the Elementary SSAT in two different ways:

- Two-part stem: "A" is to "B" as…
  In these types of questions, students are given two words in the stem of the question, and are asked to select the pair of words with the same relationship as demonstrated between words "A" and "B."

- Three-part stem: "A" is to "B" as "C" is to…
  In these types of questions, students are given three words in the stem of the question; words "A" and "B" form one relationship, and are asked to complete the same relationship between word "C" and your answer choice.

For the different types of analogy relationships, see the Verbal Overview section.

How to Use This Section

How much time students spend on this section should be based on their diagnostic practice test results as well as their study plan. For most students, even those who score very well on the diagnostic practice test, we recommend practicing at least 10 questions per week in preparing for the exam.

One study plan might be to try a Mixed Practice section to get a sense for which areas to focus on. Based on those results, work on the relevant Guided Practice sections. If students already know what they need to work on, they can jump right in to a Guided Practice section.

The purpose of this section is to introduce students to new words. Some may find many of the words in this section to be challenging. Students should not be surprised to have to look up many of the words encountered in this section! We encourage students to make a list of difficult or challenging words, whether they appear in questions or answer choices. Write down the definition of each word as well as a sentence using the word. Students might also want to consider writing down positive or negative associations, any root words that can help them remember the word, or any words that are commonly encountered with that word.

Tutorverse Tips!

The key to success on the analogies section is practice. Students should know the common types of analogies by heart and be able to quickly categorize the question stem provided into one of these types.

Write down the relationship in the margin and see which of the choices creates an analogy that matches that of the question stem.

Remember: if you don't know the answer, skip it and come back to it. If you still don't know, and you're running out of time, just guess!

Guided Practice

Directions: For each question, select the answer choice that best completes the meaning of the sentence.

Antonyms

3rd Grade

1. Amusing is to boring as
   (A) swimming is to bathing
   (B) strange is to bizarre
   (C) hilarious is to exciting
   (D) delicate is to strong
   (E) circus is to peanuts

2. Final is to first as
   (A) end is to finish
   (B) start is to middle
   (C) arrive is to enter
   (D) baseball is to runner
   (E) long is to brief

3. Scowl is to grin as
   (A) sandwich is to hamburger
   (B) angry is to furious
   (C) dishonest is to sly
   (D) disgusting is to tasty
   (E) agreeable is to pleasant

4. Flood is to drought as
   (A) might is to maybe
   (B) water is to ocean
   (C) argue is to fight
   (D) smooth is to bumpy
   (E) up is to above

5. Arctic is to baking as
   (A) north is to direction
   (B) penguin is to flipper
   (C) light is to dim
   (D) skinny is to thin
   (E) snow is to flake

6. Entrance is to exit as bare is to
   (A) plain
   (B) skin
   (C) pure
   (D) covered
   (E) bald

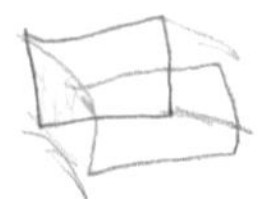

4th Grade

1. Aloft is to grounded as
   (A) scenery is to view
   (B) congratulate is to motivate
   (C) capable is to unable
   (D) get is to receive
   (E) merge is to combine

2. Destructive is to creative as
   (A) alter is to adapt
   (B) artistic is to talented
   (C) sparkle is to shine
   (D) dawn is to morning
   (E) lovely is to dowdy

3. Dormant is to active as
   (A) eager is to uninterested
   (B) coax is to convince
   (C) hibernate is to winter
   (D) monarch is to royalty
   (E) cozy is to comfortable

4. Humble is to conceited as
   (A) debt is to borrow
   (B) captive is to trapped
   (C) polite is to courteous
   (D) difference is to similarity
   (E) tote is to bag

5. Confuse is to simplify as vertical is to
   (A) unclear
   (B) wiggly
   (C) short
   (D) horizontal
   (E) axis

6. Weary is to energetic as reveal is to
   (A) mask
   (B) instruct
   (C) surprise
   (D) alert
   (E) secret

Characteristic

3rd Grade

1. Glass is to clear as
   (A) display is to museum
   (B) junior is to senior
   (C) eye is to face
   (D) road is to flat
   (E) sphere is to globe

2. Elephant is to enormous as
   (A) mall is to shopping
   (B) creature is to animal
   (C) hamster is to furry
   (D) searing is to fire
   (E) grand is to tiny

3. Canyon is to deep as
   (A) random is to ordered
   (B) charming is to animation
   (C) chalkboard is to classroom
   (D) squeaky is to mouse
   (E) cloud is to fluffy

4. Watermelon is to juicy as
   (A) regular is to unusual
   (B) solid is to boulder
   (C) jewel is to gem
   (D) rainbow is to colorful
   (E) protein is to vegetable

5. Maze is to confusing as beach is to
   (A) wet
   (B) island
   (C) secure
   (D) sunlight
   (E) sand

6. Window is to transparent as tentacle is to
   (A) octopus
   (B) slimy
   (C) withered
   (D) hard
   (E) suction

4th Grade

1. Holiday is to festive as
   (A) liquid is to wet
   (B) wide is to land
   (C) remarkable is to performance
   (D) straight is to beam
   (E) celebration is to gathering

2. Sun is to radiant as
   (A) large is to arena
   (B) innocent is to lamb
   (C) story is to mystery
   (D) daylight is to darkness
   (E) foliage is to green

3. Pie is to crusty as
   (A) delicious is to food
   (B) vacation is to relaxation
   (C) dancer is to studio
   (D) vast is to estate
   (E) host is to gracious

4. City is to bustling as
   (A) orchestra is to harmonic
   (B) cup is to bowl
   (C) luxury is to afford
   (D) hurricane is to gust
   (E) massive is to mountain

5. Enemy is to hostile as quilt is to
   (A) carpet
   (B) pattern
   (C) warm
   (D) hard
   (E) patchwork

6. Pole is to thin as thief is to
   (A) wise
   (B) quiet
   (C) amusing
   (D) burglar
   (E) outlaw

Part to Whole

3rd Grade

1. Petal is to rose as
   (A) employee is to company
   (B) bottle is to cap
   (C) traffic is to car
   (D) pack is to wolf
   (E) sandwich is to ham

2. Bird is to flock as
   (A) storm is to raindrop
   (B) word is to sentence
   (C) donkey is to hoof
   (D) wall is to brick
   (E) team is to player

3. Individual is to group as
   (A) room is to windows
   (B) universe is to star
   (C) army is to soldier
   (D) book is to stack
   (E) wing is to feather

4. Zipper is to jacket as
   (A) child is to guardian
   (B) remark is to saying
   (C) arm is to elbow
   (D) outfit is to hat
   (E) stamp is to collection

5. Tip is to highlighter as heel is to
   (A) pointy
   (B) palm
   (C) boot
   (D) words
   (E) obey

6. Member is to tribe as feather is to
   (A) wing
   (B) spine
   (C) down
   (D) bat
   (E) soft

4th Grade

1. Paragraph is to essay as
   (A) continent is to Earth
   (B) distaste is to disgust
   (C) fleet is to ship
   (D) luck is to fortune
   (E) bargain is to trade

2. Bee is to swarm as
   (A) factory is to machine
   (B) show is to puppet
   (C) indicate is to point
   (D) superb is to great
   (E) bristle is to brush

3. Person is to crowd as
   (A) letter is to alphabet
   (B) door is to knob
   (C) calf is to bull
   (D) pizza is to slice
   (E) dollar is to penny

4. Limb is to body as
   (A) shirt is to wardrobe
   (B) include is to invite
   (C) cycle is to stage
   (D) kite is to string
   (E) confirm is to deny

5. Musician is to band as leg is to
   (A) ankle
   (B) jazz
   (C) rhythm
   (D) foot
   (E) table

6. Planet is to galaxy as ant is to
   (A) antennae
   (B) insect
   (C) colony
   (D) strength
   (E) small

Uses

3rd Grade

1. Fan is to cool as
   (A) distribute is to fliers
   (B) shield is to protect
   (C) transfer is to cargo
   (D) astronomy is to stars
   (E) lift is to weights

2. Mirror is to reflect as
   (A) complex is to complicated
   (B) cast is to shadow
   (C) cable is to connect
   (D) bathroom is to basement
   (E) clever is to thoughtless

3. Rollercoaster is to thrill as
   (A) prank is to fool
   (B) block is to dam
   (C) orbit is to planet
   (D) terrify is to nightmare
   (E) fry is to melt

4. Sandbox is to play as
   (A) playground is to children
   (B) lung is to breathe
   (C) diamond is to gold
   (D) painting is to colors
   (E) chew is to gum

5. Soap is to clean as notes is to
   (A) homework
   (B) press
   (C) study
   (D) handwriting
   (E) remove

6. Ink is to write as market is to
   (A) blue
   (B) match
   (C) bustling
   (D) fruit
   (E) sell

4th Grade

1. Teaspoon is to stir as
   (A) solemn is to grave
   (B) teacup is to kettle
   (C) inspire is to speaker
   (D) support is to column
   (E) party is to celebrate

2. Game is to entertain as
   (A) video is to photo
   (B) board is to bored
   (C) mural is to decorate
   (D) enjoyment is to displease
   (E) apple is to orchard

3. Telephone is to communicate as
   (A) flashlight is to illuminate
   (B) weigh is to scale
   (C) converse is to respond
   (D) tell is to bulletin
   (E) forget is to remember

4. Bulldozer is to crush as
   (A) lullaby is to soothe
   (B) moon is to lantern
   (C) record is to microphone
   (D) crane is to huge
   (E) eat is to chopsticks

5. Chair is to sit as satchel is to
   (A) backpack
   (B) carry
   (C) drop
   (D) dining
   (E) empty

6. Magnet is to attract as letter is to
   (A) science
   (B) expect
   (C) gather
   (D) communicate
   (E) signature

Users

3rd Grade

1. Hose is to firefighter as
   (A) hook is to bent
   (B) forbid is to allow
   (C) blaze is to flames
   (D) wrench is to mechanic
   (E) garden is to planting

2. Catcher is to mitt as
   (A) needle is to seamstress
   (B) pencil is to draw
   (C) promise is to pact
   (D) manager is to clerk
   (E) banker is to cash

3. Plow is to farmer as
   (A) tape is to patch
   (B) tractor is to drive
   (C) drill is to dentist
   (D) engineer is to toolbox
   (E) crops is to harvest

4. Uniform is to mailman as
   (A) programmer is to code
   (B) package is to delivery
   (C) astronomer is to telescope
   (D) calculator is to mathematician
   (E) postcard is to envelope

5. Helmet is to astronaut as tray is to
   (A) waiter
   (B) restaurant
   (C) space
   (D) biker
   (E) breakfast

6. Crown is to royalty as suitcase is to
   (A) jewels
   (B) custodian
   (C) tourist
   (D) queen
   (E) poet

my best guess

4th Grade

1. Tightrope is to acrobat as
   (A) whistle is to lifeguard
   (B) camp is to tent
   (C) shove is to push
   (D) crayon is to drawing
   (E) plumber is to plunger

2. Camera is to photographer as
   (A) thinking is to writing
   (B) lens is to film
   (C) disagreeable is to grumpy
   (D) sidewalk is to pedestrian
   (E) captain is to anchor

Go Trinity Tigers!

3. Scissors is to barber as
   (A) razor is to shave
   (B) error is to mistake
   (C) arrow is to archer
   (D) hack is to saw
   (E) haircut is to style

4. Flippers is to diver as
   (A) starfish is to shark
   (B) snorkel is to scuba
   (C) coral is to sea
   (D) trader is to bargains
   (E) textbook is to professor

5. Stroller is to nanny as plane is to
   (A) runway
   (B) pilot
   (C) delay
   (D) officer
   (E) airport

6. Atlas is to explorer as sword is to
   (A) compass
   (B) police
   (C) map
   (D) knight
   (E) nurse

Category

3rd Grade

1. Lizard is to reptile as
   (A) amphibian is to toad
   (B) gecko is to spotted
   (C) French is to language
   (D) snake is to slither
   (E) sound is to thud

2. Earrings is to jewelry as
   (A) stationary is to card
   (B) beetle is to insect
   (C) seasoning is to pepper
   (D) bracelet is to wrist
   (E) necklace is to diamonds

3. Tree is to plant as
   (A) toy is to blocks
   (B) vehicle is to truck
   (C) habitat is to jungle
   (D) vine is to twist
   (E) flute is to instrument

4. Crossword is to puzzle as
   (A) anger is to emotion
   (B) invent is to construct
   (C) clue is to solve
   (D) across is to down
   (E) seafood is to shrimp

5. Salty is to flavor as plastic is to
   (A) wood
   (B) transparent
   (C) tongue
   (D) material
   (E) bitter

6. Smile is to expression as May is to
   (A) movement
   (B) frown
   (C) month
   (D) year
   (E) space

4th Grade

1. Poodle is to dog as
   (A) dairy is to yogurt
   (B) valley is to landform
   (C) helper is to pet
   (D) leash is to walk
   (E) bulldog is to loyal

2. Steel is to metal as
   (A) rust is to ruin
   (B) ingredient is to sugar
   (C) prize is to third
   (D) pigtail is to hairstyle
   (E) copper is to brown

3. Yellow is to color as
   (A) mineral is to iron
   (B) subject is to history
   (C) golden is to shiny
   (D) milkshake is to beverage
   (E) daisy is to white

4. Fork is to utensil as
   (A) transportation is to bike
   (B) placemat is to silverware
   (C) dinner is to lunch
   (D) organ is to heart
   (E) comma is to punctuation

5. Autumn is to season as screwdriver is to
   (A) nails
   (B) handyman
   (C) fix
   (D) tool
   (E) spring

6. Owl is to bird as salmon is to
   (A) ostrich
   (B) fly
   (C) swim
   (D) worm
   (E) fish

Product/Producer

3rd Grade

1. Poem is to poet as
   (A) statue is to sculptor
   (B) rhyme is to beat
   (C) lyrics is to guitar
   (D) writer is to literature
   (E) drill is to coach

2. Nectar is to flower as
   (A) milk is to cow
   (B) blossom is to pollen
   (C) cat is to kitten
   (D) bloom is to wither
   (E) explorer is to pioneer

3. Art is to painter as
   (A) maid is to cleanliness
   (B) pianist is to melody
   (C) bread is to baker
   (D) general is to medal
   (E) gallery is to exhibit

4. Video is to cameraman as
   (A) jailer is to keys
   (B) hairdo is to hairstylist
   (C) carriage is to saddle
   (D) album is to volume
   (E) filming is to camera

5. Key is to locksmith as suit is to
   (A) tailor
   (B) tuxedo
   (C) larva
   (D) father
   (E) slimy

6. Doll is to toymaker as spell is to
   (A) dollhouse
   (B) dresses
   (C) salesman
   (D) witch
   (E) officer

4th Grade

1. Furniture is to carpenter as
   (A) monk is to prayer
   (B) violinist is to harmony
   (C) cabinet is to pantry
   (D) bouquet is to florist
   (E) sofa is to relax

2. Ring is to jeweler as
   (A) foreman is to clipboard
   (B) marriage is to church
   (C) ruby is to red
   (D) diagnosis is to doctor
   (E) cellist is to cello

3. Trick is to magician as
   (A) research is to researcher
   (B) boat is to harbor
   (C) mom is to infant
   (D) barn is to coop
   (E) hat is to rabbit

4. Movie is to director as
   (A) cashier is to groceries
   (B) article is to reporter
   (C) clerk is to helpful
   (D) rider is to jockey
   (E) scary is to humorous

5. Magazine is to editor as dance is to
   (A) jazz
   (B) ballet
   (C) translator
   (D) fashion
   (E) choreographer

6. Sermon is to priest as classwork is to
   (A) secretary
   (B) superintendent
   (C) pupil
   (D) church
   (E) monastery

Degree

3rd Grade

1. Stream is to river as
   (A) identify is to choose
   (B) shrink is to swell
   (C) fatal is to risky
   (D) zigzag is to sway
   (E) hop is to leap

2. Hungry is to starving as
   (A) meal is to share
   (B) moist is to soaked
   (C) bursting is to full
   (D) local is to foreign
   (E) farewell is to goodbye

3. Serious is to severe as
   (A) wander is to stroll
   (B) excess is to extra
   (C) pumpkin is to squash
   (D) core is to center
   (E) bright is to blinding

4. Like is to adore as
   (A) sunny is to cloudless
   (B) catastrophe is to accident
   (C) rainstorm is to drizzle
   (D) nibble is to chomp
   (E) riches is to poverty

5. Dirty is to filthy as
   (A) sink is to float
   (B) tired is to exhausted
   (C) greed is to ambition
   (D) harsh is to mean
   (E) nosy is to curious

6. Chilly is to freezing as fear is to
   (A) afraid
   (B) heights
   (C) terror
   (D) ice
   (E) monsters

4th Grade

1. Village is to city as
   (A) law is to recommendation
   (B) frank is to honest
   (C) mistrust is to believe
   (D) town is to hut
   (E) interested is to obsessed

2. Annoy is to infuriate as
   (A) glimmer is to flicker
   (B) big is to gigantic
   (C) frenzied is to excited
   (D) lurch is to bump
   (E) irritate is to please

3. Speak is to shout as
   (A) satisfactory is to excellent
   (B) temporary is to short
   (C) energetic is to youthful
   (D) booming is to loud
   (E) usual is to likely

4. Uncomfortable is to unbearable as
   (A) priority is to important
   (B) chance is to opportunity
   (C) exert is to effort
   (D) pretty is to gorgeous
   (E) solemn is to serious

5. Alright is to outstanding as content is to
   (A) misery
   (B) contentment
   (C) blissful
   (D) winning
   (E) feeling

6. Fond is to adoring as unsafe is to
   (A) affectionate
   (B) bored
   (C) harm
   (D) doubtful
   (E) deadly

Homonyms

3rd Grade

1. Weak is to week as
   (A) their is to there
   (B) flap is to gap
   (C) powerful is to annual
   (D) feeble is to calendar
   (E) tower is to bower

2. Paws is to pause as
   (A) claws is to nonstop
   (B) about is to doubt
   (C) sight is to bite
   (D) our is to hour
   (E) puppy is to halt

3. Vain is to vein as
   (A) prideful is to vaccine
   (B) too is to two
   (C) bore is to gore
   (D) mile is to file
   (E) handsome is to vessel

4. Maid is to made as
   (A) miss is to build
   (B) servant is to master
   (C) maiden is to produced
   (D) four is to for
   (E) slick is to stick

5. Eight is to ate as
   (A) three is to waffle
   (B) age is to tissue
   (C) threw is to through
   (D) talk is to stalk
   (E) numbers is to drank

6. Wait is to weight as days is to
   (A) daze
   (B) dyes
   (C) time
   (D) pays
   (E) weeks

4th Grade

1. Pare is to pear as
   (A) cut is to ripe
   (B) sew is to so
   (C) ease is to lease
   (D) reduce is to apple
   (E) sow is to seed

2. Loan is to lone as
   (A) return is to together
   (B) single is to one
   (C) listen is to glisten
   (D) library is to alone
   (E) berry is to bury

3. Piece is to peace as
   (A) seen is to invisible
   (B) daunt is to taunt
   (C) cent is to scent
   (D) entire is to war
   (E) section is to serene

4. Throne is to thrown as
   (A) flea is to flee
   (B) lack is to lock
   (C) crown is to hurled
   (D) blue is to blow
   (E) king is to launched

5. Great is to grate as
   (A) where is to wearing
   (B) good is to vent
   (C) wonderful is to sewer
   (D) rain is to reign
   (E) mate is to gate

6. Male is to mail as steel is to
   (A) man
   (B) boy
   (C) deal
   (D) letter
   (E) steal

Synonyms

3rd Grade

1. Doubtful is to unsure as
   (A) base is to bottom
   (B) computer is to technology
   (C) ill is to healthy
   (D) fierce is to mild
   (E) theory is to truth

2. Evening is to night as
   (A) soil is to dirt
   (B) erase is to create
   (C) notice is to ignore
   (D) frail is to tough
   (E) depressed is to cheery

3. Careless is to sloppy as
   (A) sick is to well
   (B) toasty is to frosty
   (C) plate is to bowl
   (D) nation is to country
   (E) gradual is to quickly

4. Fortunate is to lucky as
   (A) unite is to divide
   (B) feast is to lavish
   (C) orange is to grapefruit
   (D) shiver is to tremble
   (E) odd is to typical

5. Belief is to opinion as
   (A) flexible is to rigid
   (B) pain is to numb
   (C) cage is to prisoner
   (D) little is to miniature
   (E) damp is to dry

6. Edit is to change as harm is to
   (A) comfort
   (B) cruel
   (C) hurt
   (D) affect
   (E) hit

4th Grade

1. Ancestor is to elder as
   (A) initial is to last
   (B) broad is to narrow
   (C) blend is to separate
   (D) rough is to gentle
   (E) entirety is to all

2. Dignity is to pride as
   (A) spacy is to careful
   (B) rise is to fall
   (C) grimace is to frown
   (D) fold is to straighten
   (E) rare is to common

3. Clap is to applause as
   (A) agree is to disagree
   (B) crafty is to tricky
   (C) taken is to available
   (D) extraordinary is to average
   (E) pricey is to cheap

4. Panicky is to frantic as
   (A) seller is to customer
   (B) frequent is to rarely
   (C) anticipate is to dread
   (D) peaceful is to calm
   (E) generous is to stingy

5. Concern is to worry as
   (A) giant is to miniscule
   (B) evidence is to proof
   (C) mother is to parent
   (D) anxious is to peaceful
   (E) descend is to ascend

6. Delay is to postpone as contact is to
   (A) touch
   (B) ignore
   (C) agreement
   (D) speed
   (E) reach

Mixed Practice

Directions: For each question, select the answer choice that best completes the meaning of the sentence.

3rd Grade

1. Town is to metropolis as
   (A) human is to elephant
   (B) starving is to thirsty
   (C) deep is to bottomless
   (D) bear is to cub
   (E) anthill is to beehive

2. Armor is to defend as
   (A) mow is to meadow
   (B) basis is to formula
   (C) step is to stomp
   (D) chorus is to together
   (E) party is to celebrate

3. Tornado is to destruction as
   (A) politician is to history
   (B) pleased is to wealthy
   (C) medicine is to health
   (D) opera is to composer
   (E) alternate is to various

4. Rubric is to grades as
   (A) memo is to note
   (B) item is to catalog
   (C) ruler is to length
   (D) curtain is to rod
   (E) lunar is to solar

5. Researcher is to encyclopedia as
   (A) adversary is to enemy
   (B) cartographer is to map
   (C) bewitch is to confuse
   (D) substitute is to replacement
   (E) television is to broadcast

6. Illogical is to nonsensical as
   (A) secede is to join
   (B) impertinent is to important
   (C) conspire is to sweat
   (D) foretell is to anecdote
   (E) divert is to redirect

7. Concoct is to mixture as
   (A) educate is to pupil
   (B) criticize is to empathy
   (C) break is to ruin
   (D) compartment is to sealed
   (E) deserve is to patience

8. Vital is to unnecessary as
   (A) smarts is to intelligence
   (B) universe is to space
   (C) key is to essential
   (D) aged is to elderly
   (E) junior is to senior

9. T-shirt is to outfit as
   (A) cotton is to silk
   (B) rotation is to turn
   (C) wardrobe is to ensemble
   (D) layer is to cake
   (E) style is to flair

10. Graduate is to graduated as
    (A) ceremony is to gown
    (B) finish is to complete
    (C) celebrated is to celebrate
    (D) water is to watered
    (E) instructed is to instruct

11. Fish is to tuna as
    (A) tedious is to devout
    (B) habitat is to unnatural
    (C) sack is to carry
    (D) lure is to catch
    (E) reptile is to chameleon

12. Ballerina is to ballet as singer is to
    (A) orchestra
    (B) opera
    (C) pitch
    (D) voice
    (E) songwriter

4th Grade

1. Discontent is to anguish as quick is to
   (A) rapid
   (B) glacial
   (C) sorrow
   (D) walk
   (E) unhappy

2. Disorderly is to chaotic as
   (A) lost is to found
   (B) messy is to clean
   (C) fabricate is to lie
   (D) leaf is to tree
   (E) disorganized is to section

3. Broccoli is to vegetable as twirl is to
   (A) green
   (B) motion
   (C) spin
   (D) carrots
   (E) dizzying

4. Vacant is to empty as
   (A) hollow is to full
   (B) quiet is to muted
   (C) lot is to parking
   (D) additional is to less
   (E) new is to experienced

5. Aisle is to isle as
   (A) grocery is to store
   (B) will is to while
   (C) hall is to haul
   (D) theatre is to island
   (E) sew is to slow

6. Handle is to mug as
   (A) hold is to drop
   (B) thumb is to hand
   (C) coffee is to steaming
   (D) window is to pane
   (E) harbor is to dock

7. Jagged is to spiky as
   (A) frenzy is to madness
   (B) sorrow is to joy
   (C) leap is to land
   (D) edge is to center
   (E) uneven is to polished

8. Elevator is to lift as
   (A) ride is to escalator
   (B) tablecloth is to cover
   (C) building is to tall
   (D) lobby is to basement
   (E) transport is to ship

9. Victory is to loss as locked is to
   (A) sealed
   (B) middle
   (C) open
   (D) slit
   (E) place

10. Chalk is to powdery as ice is to
   (A) dusty
   (B) frigid
   (C) cube
   (D) melt
   (E) preserve

11. Cushion is to couch as
   (A) glove is to mitten
   (B) exhaust is to tire
   (C) caterpillar is to butterfly
   (D) dictionary is to definition
   (E) year is to century

12. Cancer is to disease as kneeling is to
   (A) chemotherapy
   (B) squatting
   (C) position
   (D) lying
   (E) body

Reading

Overview

In the Reading section, students will read passages and answer questions that pertain to those passages. The passages will vary; some passages will be short poems, while others will be longer essays. All of the questions are designed to measure how well a student understands what he or she reads.

Students will have 30 minutes to read the passages and answer 28 questions.

On the Actual Test

There are two main types of passages on the Elementary SSAT: fiction and non-fiction.

Fiction passages can include short stories, poems, novels, or even personal essays. Non-fiction passages can include informative or persuasive essays and can cover topics ranging from the humanities to the sciences.

The Reading section features questions that highlight the four major topics below. The questions on the test will **not** indicate which topic is being tested. Five answer choices are presented with letters A through E. The questions are **NOT** ordered according to level of difficulty.

- *Main Idea* – What is the general message, lesson, or idea of the passage? What is the author trying to tell the reader?
- *Detail* – What happens in the passage, and why?
- *Inference* – What are some conclusions that can be drawn from the passage? What can a reader infer based on the passage?
- *Vocabulary* – What do certain words mean, in the context of the passage?
- *Story Elements* – What is the problem and solution in the story? Where and when does the story take place?

In This Practice Book

There are 18 passages in this section from a variety of sources, which reflect what students will see on the actual Elementary SSAT. These passages have been divided by grade, as well as Fiction and Non-Fiction sections. The corresponding questions will test students' ability to pinpoint some or all of the major topics that were outlined above.

We recommend that students practice several passages per week in preparing for the exam.

See an unfamiliar word? Look it up! Many words and concepts in this section might be challenging. It's a good habit to keep a list of vocabulary learned in passages, questions, or answer choices. Write down the definition of the word and use it in a sentence. Other notes that might help are positive or negative associations of the word, root words, or any phrases that are commonly encountered with the new word.

Tutorverse Tips!

Practice Active Reading

We recommend that you read the passage first before attempting to answer the questions. As you read, underline or circle key information like main ideas. Draw arrows between related ideas, or examples that support main ideas. Consider outlining the passage to get a sense for the structure of the passage as well as how the different parts of the passage are related to each other.

Because the questions on each passage will be similar to those that you have practiced, you can keep an eye out for important themes and ideas as you read. This will help save time when you answer the questions.

Identifying Main Ideas & Themes

Think about what the main idea might be as you read the passage. Ask yourself these questions as you read:

- What is the point of this passage? What is the author trying to tell me?
- What is the author's point of view on the topic?
- Is there a lesson or moral that I am supposed to learn from the passage?

Referring Back to the Text

- When the question refers back to the text with a quotation, make sure to read a little bit before and after the quoted text. Many times, the quote itself can have an ambiguous meaning if read by itself. Therefore, use context clues to help answer the questions.
- The same advice applies to questions that ask about a word or phrase's meaning. Use context clues, as the word or phrase will almost certainly have more than one possible definition.

Prove It!

Think you have the right answer? Prove it! You should be able to cite evidence from the text to support your answer for <u>every single question</u> – even inference questions! If you can't prove it to yourself, you probably haven't picked the right choice. Ask yourself, "How do I know this is true? What evidence is there from the passage that I can point to?"

Remember: if you don't know the answer, skip it and come back to it. If you still don't know, and you're running out of time, just guess!

Fiction

This section contains fiction passages. These passages have been adapted from short stories, novels, and poems, to help students become comfortable with the types of passages they will encounter on the actual test. Carefully read each passage and then answer the questions about it. For each question, select the choice that best answers the question based on the passage.

3rd Grade

Passage #1

Growing up, we had a pool at our house. I wanted to be in the pool all day long. I didn't know how to swim by myself yet. But I wore floaties on my arms to keep me from drowning. With the floaties on, I wasn't afraid, even though I couldn't swim.

Right after breakfast each morning, I would beg my mom to let me go swimming. She would (5) help me inflate my floaties and I would jump right in.

One really hot day, my father's cousin came to visit. I was already in the pool. Cousin Billy jumped in. Soon I was showing off my swimming skills. "But you aren't swimming! The floaties are helping you!" exclaimed Billy. He was right! My cheeks flamed bright red. Billy told me that he could teach me how to swim by myself. I was unsure, but all he said was, "You'll see."

(10) Billy let a little air out of each floatie. He told me to swim across the pool and back. After each lap, he would let more air out. Soon, the floaties were out of air. I began to worry, but he said the floaties wouldn't sink. Even without air, they stayed above the water. So, I took another lap across the pool. So far, so good!

Next, Billy removed the floaties from my arms. I panicked. But he told me to swim across the (15) pool just the way I had every other time. And I did! I was swimming! Billy had tricked me, but I wasn't mad because I had finally learned how to swim by myself.

1. The main problem the narrator faces is
   - (A) being afraid to go in the pool
   - (B) not knowing how to swim on her own
   - (C) being tricked by her cousin
   - (D) losing her floaties in the house
   - (E) having to teach her cousin to swim

2. In line 5, "inflate" could best be replaced with
   - (A) take off
   - (B) deflate
   - (C) inside
   - (D) blow up
   - (E) arrange

3. In line 8, the narrator's "cheeks flamed bright red" because
   - (A) it was a really hot day
   - (B) she was angry and frustrated by her cousin
   - (C) she was embarrassed because she couldn't really swim
   - (D) she was sunburnt
   - (E) she was wearing red floaties

4. In line 14, the narrator most likely "panicked" because
   - (A) she thought she would sink without the floaties
   - (B) Billy left her alone in the pool
   - (C) the floaties were broken
   - (D) her mom stopped watching her swim
   - (E) she was afraid she would never learn to swim

5. According to the passage, the narrator didn't feel mad about cousin Billy tricking her because
   - (A) she had tricked him first
   - (B) he couldn't swim either
   - (C) they were best friends
   - (D) she had a good sense of humor
   - (E) it had helped her learn to swim

Passage #2

Danny Meadow Mouse walked along one of his little paths very early one morning. He was on his way to get some special grass seed. It was his favorite kind, and he had been looking forward to it for a long time.

"This is going to be an exciting day," said Danny. "If I was really wise, I would stay closer to 5 home and do without that nice seed. Or perhaps that seed will taste better if I have to work hard to get it."

He jogged along his little path. His ears were wide open. His eyes were wide open. His little nose carefully tested the air for any scent of danger. Most of all, he depended on his ears. The grass was so tall, he couldn't see over it.

10 He had gone only a little way when he thought he heard something behind him. He stopped to listen. There it was again. There was only one who could make such a sound as that—Mr. Blacksnake.

Danny could run very fast, but he knew that Mr. Blacksnake could run faster. "I must use my brain to save me!" thought Danny.

15 "If Mr. Blacksnake follows me, he will be sure to think that I have taken the littler path," thought Danny, "so I won't do it."

He ran harder than ever, until he came to a place where two paths branched off: a big one to the right and a little one to the left. He took the left and scampered on. He was sure that Mr. Blacksnake would be so fooled that he would give up the chase, and Danny was right.

20 Whistling cheerfully, he skipped on his way to look for the grass seed he liked so well.

1. Danny Meadow Mouse went so far from home because he wanted to
   (A) work hard
   (B) enjoy the beautiful weather
   (C) find a special grass seed
   (D) trick Mr. Blacksnake
   (E) explore the tall grass

2. The word that best describes how Danny felt about his day is
   (A) scared
   (B) excited
   (C) uninterested
   (D) lonely
   (E) tired

3. Which of the five senses is the most important to Danny Meadow Mouse?
   (A) sight
   (B) smell
   (C) hearing
   (D) touch
   (E) taste

4. How did Danny Meadow Mouse trick Mr. Blacksnake?
   (A) He hid in the tall grass and stayed very quiet.
   (B) He ran faster than Mr. Blacksnake.
   (C) He kept his ears open to hear when Mr. Blacksnake left.
   (D) He took a different path than what Mr. Blacksnake expected.
   (E) He gave up and went home.

5. The word "scampered" in line 18 means
   (A) hurried
   (B) walked
   (C) rested
   (D) stayed
   (E) hid

6. What lesson can we learn from this story?
   (A) Never trust a snake.
   (B) Hard work makes for delicious results.
   (C) The road less taken is the best one.
   (D) Size determines the winner.
   (E) Smarts are more important than speed.

Passage #3

There was once a woman who was very cheerful. But she was old, poor, and lonely. She lived in a tiny cottage. She earned a scant living by running errands for her neighbors.

One summer evening, she was walking when she found a big black pot lying in a ditch. She looked inside. "It's full of gold pieces. This is so lucky!" she shouted.

5 The pot was full of gold coins. She kept saying, "I feel rich!" But the treasure was too heavy for her to carry. She decided to drag it home. "Maybe I'll buy a grand house and just sit by the fire with a cup of tea. I will live like a queen!" she thought.

Soon, she became tired of dragging such a heavy weight. She stopped and looked at her treasure. Alas, it was nothing but a little lump of silver! She rubbed her eyes. She said, "I must have

10 been dreaming. But still, I am so lucky! Silver is less trouble than gold."

She went off again planning what she would do. She still felt rich as rich could be. But when she looked again at her silver, she saw nothing but a big stone.

"I must have been dreaming. But here's luck indeed. This stone can keep my gate open. It's a change for the better!"

15 All of a sudden, the stone was as big as a haystack. It let down four lanky legs and threw out two long ears, had a great long tail. It ran off, laughing like a naughty boy.

The old woman stared after it till it was fairly out of sight, then she burst out laughing too. "Well!" she chuckled, "If it isn't the Bogey Beast himself! What an honor to meet him in person!" She returned to her cottage and spent the evening laughing over her good luck.

1. How did the woman earn her living?
   (A) She begged for money.
   (B) She trades gold and silver.
   (C) She ran errands for neighbors.
   (D) The Bogey Beast paid her.
   (E) She was very lucky.

2. The word "grand" in line 6 means
   (A) fancy
   (B) comfortable
   (C) small
   (D) empty
   (E) haunted

3. Why did the woman think that the lump of silver was better than the gold coins?
   (A) people would not be as envious
   (B) it was lighter and easier to carry
   (C) she didn't want to live like a queen
   (D) she thought the silver was prettier
   (E) it was worth a lot more money

4. According to the passage, what happened when the woman looked at her silver the second time?
   (A) She noticed she was dreaming.
   (B) She wished her silver was gold.
   (C) She thought about what she would do with her silver.
   (D) She saw it had become a bigger piece of silver.
   (E) She realized it was actually a stone.

5. The Bogey-Beast took on all forms EXCEPT
   (A) gold
   (B) silver
   (C) stone
   (D) haystack
   (E) lanky legs, long ears, and a long tail

6. The lesson that the story teaches is
   (A) there is a bright side to everything.
   (B) anything that glitters is not gold.
   (C) change is for the better.
   (D) it is better to live within your means.
   (E) beware of the Bogey Beast.

Passage #4

	I told you before 'twas a stormy night
	When these two little kittens began to fight;
	The old woman seized her sweeping broom,
	And swept the two kittens right out of the room.
5	The ground was covered with frost and snow,
	And the two little kittens had nowhere to go;
	So they laid down on the mat at the door,
	While the old woman finished sweeping the floor.
	Then they crept in, as quiet as mice,
10	All wet with the snow, and cold as ice,
	For they found it was better, that stormy night,
	To lie down and sleep than to quarrel and fight.

1. Why did the old woman sweep the kittens out into the snow?
   (A) They were outdoor cats.
   (B) They were chasing mice.
   (C) She thought they wanted to play outside.
   (D) She wanted to teach them a lesson.
   (E) She did it by accident.

2. In lines 5-8, the kittens are feeling
   (A) proud
   (B) regretful
   (C) angry
   (D) joyful
   (E) playful

3. The phrase "as quiet as mice" (line 9) is used to describe how
   (A) the woman is sweeping
   (B) the snow is falling
   (C) the mice are hiding
   (D) the ice is melting
   (E) the kittens are moving

4. The word "quarrel" (line 12) means
   (A) argue
   (B) agree
   (C) play
   (D) cry
   (E) punch

5. The kittens decide to stop fighting because
   (A) they were exhausted
   (B) the old woman told them to never fight again
   (C) they did not want to be put outside again
   (D) one kitten won the fight
   (E) one kitten gave up

Passage #5 5/7/22

	Slipping softly through the sky Little horned, happy moon, Can you hear me up so high? Will you come down soon?
5	On my nursery window-sill Will you stay your steady flight? And then float away with me Through the summer night?
10	Brushing over tops of trees, Playing hide and seek with stars, Peeping up through shiny clouds At Jupiter or Mars.
15	Little rocking, sailing moon, Do you hear me shout — Ahoy! Just a little nearer, moon, To please a little boy.

1. In this poem, the little boy mostly wants to
   (A) bring the moon closer
   (B) fly up to the moon
   (C) play hide and seek
   (D) catch a balloon
   (E) shout to a friend

2. We can assume from the line, "little horned, happy moon" (line 2) that the moon is
   (A) a full moon
   (B) a half moon
   (C) not visible
   (D) in a good mood
   (E) related to goats

3. In this poem, the boy is
   (A) in the sky
   (B) in a forest
   (C) in his bedroom
   (D) on the moon
   (E) on a boat

4. In line 11, the word "peeping" could be replaced with
   (A) walking
   (B) crying
   (C) feeling
   (D) jumping
   (E) looking

5. In line 13, "little rocking, sailing moon" describes
   (A) what the moon is good for
   (B) what the moon sounds like
   (C) how the moon looks
   (D) how the moon moves
   (E) where the moon is found

4th Grade

Passage #1 5/7/22

The first place that I can well remember was a large, pleasant meadow with a pond of clear water in it. Some shady trees leaned over it. Over the hedge on one side we looked into a plowed field. On the other we looked over a gate at our master's house, which stood by the roadside.

While I was young, I lived upon my mother's milk, as I could not eat grass. In the daytime I ran by her side, and at night I lay down close by her. *5*

There were six young colts in the meadow besides me. They were older than I was. I used to run with them, and had great fun. We used to gallop all together round the field as hard as we could go. Sometimes we had rather rough play, for they would frequently bite and kick as well as gallop.

One day, when there was a good deal of kicking, my mother whinnied to me to come to her, and then she said: *10*

"I wish you to pay attention to what I am going to say to you. The colts who live here are very good colts, but they have not learned manners. Your father has a great name in these parts, and your grandfather won the cup two years at the Newmarket races. I think you have never seen me kick or bite. I hope you will grow up gentle and good, and never learn bad ways. Do your work with a good will, lift your feet up well when you trot, and never bite or kick even in play." *15*

I have never forgotten my mother's advice. I knew our master thought a great deal of her.

1. The narrator of this story is a
   (A) child
   (B) grandmother
   (C) rider
   (D) horse
   (E) master

2. This story takes place mainly
   (A) in a pond
   (B) in a farmhouse
   (C) in a meadow
   (D) at night
   (E) at the Newmarket races

3. In lines 11-15, the narrator gets advice about
   (A) behaving well
   (B) running fast
   (C) respecting his family
   (D) growing up quickly
   (E) listening carefully

4. The narrator's mother called him to come to her because
   (A) it was time to eat
   (B) it was time to sleep
   (C) he was playing on the wrong side of the gate
   (D) he was playing roughly with his friends
   (E) his father wanted to see him

5. Based on the passage, we can assume that the narrator's family
   (A) hates working for the master
   (B) has many accomplishments
   (C) has not learned manners
   (D) lives a lonely life
   (E) does not have to work

6. The word that best describes the narrator's mother is
   (A) playful
   (B) wise
   (C) careless
   (D) boastful
   (E) funny

Passage #2

Once on a dark winter's day, an odd-looking little girl sat in a cab with her father.
She sat with her feet tucked under her, and leaned against her father, as she stared out of the window with a thoughtful and troubled look. She was such a little girl that one did not expect to see such a look on her small face. The fact was, however, that she could not remember any time when
5 she had not been thinking things about grown-up people and the world they belonged to.
At this moment she was remembering the voyage she had just made from India with her father.
She was thinking how strange it was to be in India in the blazing sun, and then in the middle of the ocean, and then driving in a strange car through strange streets where the day was as dark as
10 the night.
"Is this the place?" Sara whispered, cuddling still closer to him. "Is it, Papa?"
"Yes, little Sara, it is. We have reached it at last." And though she was only seven years old, she knew that he felt sad when he said it.
During her short life only one thing had troubled her, and that thing was "the place" she was
15 to be taken to someday. The weather in India was very bad for children, and as soon as possible they were sent away from it. She had seen other children depart. She had known that she would have to go also. She was troubled by the thought that he could not stay with her.
"Couldn't you go to that place with me, papa?" she had asked when she was five years old. "I would help you with your lessons."

1. This story is mainly about
   (A) a father and daughter who dislike each other
   (B) escaping bad weather
   (C) a school for both children and parents
   (D) two travelers making a long journey to India
   (E) a girl on a trip to a mysterious place

2. At the beginning of the story, Sara is remembering
   (A) the long trip she has just made
   (B) lessons she learned in school
   (C) the bad weather in India
   (D) how cold and dark it is outside
   (E) a place where she used to live

3. Which word best describes Sara?
   (A) confused
   (B) carefree
   (C) mature
   (D) helpful
   (E) cold

4. According to the passage, "the place" is most likely a
   (A) house
   (B) ship
   (C) window
   (D) school
   (E) Indian neighborhood

5. The main problem Sara faces in the story is
   (A) not wanting to leave her father
   (B) worry about the grown-up world
   (C) bad weather in India
   (D) fear of her father
   (E) missing her friends

6. In line 16, what does "depart" most likely mean?
   (A) break
   (B) leave
   (C) refuse
   (D) suffer
   (E) worry

Passage #3

Every afternoon, as they were coming from school, the children used to go and play in the Giant's garden.

It was a large lovely garden, with soft green grass. Here and there over the grass stood beautiful flowers like stars. There were twelve peach-trees that in the spring-time broke out into (5) delicate blossoms of pink and pearl, and in the autumn bore rich fruit. The birds sat on the trees and sang so sweetly that the children used to stop their games in order to listen to them. "How happy we are here!" they cried to each other.

One day the Giant came back. He had been to visit his friend the Cornish ogre, and had stayed for seven years. After the seven years were over, he had said all that he had to say, for his (10) conversation was limited. He determined to return to his own castle. When he arrived, he saw the children playing in the garden.

"What are you doing here?" he cried in a very gruff voice, and the children ran away.

"My garden is my own garden," said the Giant; "anyone can understand that, and I will allow nobody to play in it but myself." So, he built a high wall all round it, and put up a notice-board.

(15) TRESPASSERS
WILL BE
PROSECUTED

The poor children had now nowhere to play. They tried to play on the road, but the road was very dusty and full of hard stones, and they did not like it. They used to wander round the high wall (20) when their lessons were over, and talk about the beautiful garden inside. "How happy we were there," they said to each other.

1. The main problem the children face is
   (A) the road has too many rocks in it
   (B) they no longer have a place to play
   (C) they are scared of the Cornish ogre
   (D) the Giant did not tend to his garden
   (E) the birds in the garden stopped singing

2. We can assume the children were once able to play in the Giant's garden because
   (A) they got out of school early
   (B) the peach trees bore fruit
   (C) they had tricked the Giant
   (D) the Giant was not there
   (E) they got along with the Giant

3. "Flowers like stars" in line 4 probably means the flowers were
   (A) very old
   (B) small and brightly colored
   (C) only visible at night
   (D) from outer space
   (E) growing in the shape of constellations

4. In line 12, what does "gruff" mean?
   (A) sad
   (B) loud
   (C) harsh
   (D) polite
   (E) funny

5. According to the passage, the Giant leaves the ogre's house because the two
   (A) had nothing to talk about
   (B) had to find fruit to eat
   (C) argued with one another
   (D) missed the Giant's garden
   (E) wanted to find the children

6. What word best describes the Giant?
   (A) friendly
   (B) kind
   (C) selfish
   (D) talkative
   (E) lonely

Passage #4

Under this loop of honeysuckle,
A creeping, colored caterpillar,
I gnaw the fresh green hawthorn spray,
I nibble it leaf by leaf away.

5 Down beneath grow dandelions,
Daisies, old-man's-looking-glasses;
Rooks flap croaking across the lane.
I eat and swallow and eat again.

Here come raindrops helter-skelter;
10 I munch and nibble unregarding:
Hawthorn leaves are juicy and firm.
I'll mind my business: I'm a good worm.

1. The speaker in the poem would most likely agree with which statement?
   (A) Rain is annoying.
   (B) Flowers are pretty.
   (C) Plants make good meals.
   (D) Worms are nosy animals.
   (E) Leaves are good hiding spots.

2. We can assume the speaker in the poem is
   (A) a frog
   (B) a child
   (C) an old man
   (D) a dandelion
   (E) a caterpillar

3. In line 2, "creeping" could best be replaced with
   (A) crawling
   (B) sleeping
   (C) jumping
   (D) talking
   (E) resting

4. The word that best describes the speaker in the poem is
   (A) lazy
   (B) angry
   (C) loving
   (D) determined
   (E) weary

5. What did the speaker in the poem do when it rained?
   (A) He drank it.
   (B) He ignored it.
   (C) He went inside.
   (D) He went to sleep.
   (E) He stopped eating.

Passage #5

It snows! It snows! From out of the sky,
The feathered flakes fly, how fast they fly!
Like little birds, that don't know why
They're on the chase, from place to place,
5 Fluttering in the sky without a trace.
It snows! It snows! A merry place
Is over us, on this heavy day!

But now the wind comes whistling loud,
To snatch and waft it, as a cloud,
10 Or giant phantom in a shroud;
It spreads, it twirls, it mounts and whirls,
At length a mighty wing unfurls,
And then, away! but where, none knows,
Or ever will.—It snows! it snows!

15 Tomorrow will the storm be done?
Then out will come the golden sun,
And thus, with life, it ever goes
In shade or shine! – It snows! It snows!

1. The main idea of the passage is
    (A) life is always changing
    (B) bad things are always followed by good things
    (C) snow exists all over the world
    (D) sun will melt away snow
    (E) snowfall makes people merry

2. What does the poet mean by saying, "Like little birds, that don't know why / They're on the chase" (lines 3-4)?
    (A) The snow is the same color as some birds' feathers.
    (B) The snow has wings.
    (C) The snow is chasing birds.
    (D) The snow is moving randomly.
    (E) Birds enjoy snow.

3. How is the storm different in stanza 2 than in stanza 1?
    (A) The birds turn into clouds.
    (B) The snowfall becomes lighter.
    (C) The wind becomes much stronger.
    (D) The storm stops and the sun is out.
    (E) There is no change.

4. The word "mounts" (line 11) means
    (A) falls
    (B) rises
    (C) freezes
    (D) rides
    (E) whistles

5. All of the following words are used to describe the storm EXCEPT
    (A) fast
    (B) fluttering
    (C) feathered
    (D) whistling
    (E) sparkling

Passage #6

I have a little shadow that goes in and out with me,
And what can be the use of him is more than I can see.
He is very, very like me from the heels up to the head;
And I see him jump before me, when I jump into my bed.

5 The funniest thing about him is the way he likes to grow—
Not at all like proper children, which is always very slow;
For he sometimes shoots up taller like a bouncy rubber ball,
And he sometimes gets so little that there's none of him at all.

He hasn't got a notion of how children ought to play,
10 And can only make a fool of me in every sort of way.
He stays so close beside me, he's a coward, you can see;
I'd think shame to stick to nursie as that shadow sticks to me!

One morning, very early, before the sun was up,
I rose and found the shining dew on every buttercup;
15 But my lazy little shadow, like a silly sleepy-head,
Had stayed at home behind me and was fast asleep in bed.

1. The word that best describes the poet is
   (A) wise
   (B) simpleminded
   (C) kind
   (D) imaginative
   (E) disobedient

2. In line 9, "notion" could be replaced with
   (A) understanding
   (B) motion
   (C) game
   (D) wish
   (E) morning

3. In lines 7-8, the speaker compares his shadow to a "bouncy rubber ball" to show how it
   (A) moves
   (B) changes size
   (C) disappears
   (D) becomes round
   (E) is dangerous

4. Because the shadow stays close to the speaker, the speaker thinks that it is
   (A) small
   (B) ashamed
   (C) cowardly
   (D) loving
   (E) friendly

5. How does the poet feel about his shadow?
   (A) Loving.
   (B) Frightened.
   (C) Silent.
   (D) Confused.
   (E) Amused.

6. Why does the shadow "stay at home" (line 16) before the sun is up?
   (A) It is sleepy and lazy.
   (B) It didn't know the speaker had gone out.
   (C) It didn't want to get wet.
   (D) It doesn't appear when there is no light.
   (E) It can't go out without permission.

Non-Fiction

This section contains non-fiction passages that can explain an idea or attempt to persuade the reader. Carefully read each passage and then answer the questions about it. For each question, select the choice that best answers the question based on the passage.

3rd Grade

Passage #1

Before there were books, movies, or TV shows, people told stories to each other. These stories made life more interesting. One famous storyteller was named Aesop. He lived a very long time ago in ancient Greece. He is known for his fables. Aesop's fables are stories that each teach a life lesson. The characters are animals who seem like humans. The stories show that people can learn
5 from their mistakes.

There are many famous fables. Have you heard the story of the tortoise and the hare? The hare was making fun of the tortoise. He said the tortoise was too slow. Upset, the tortoise challenged him to a race. The hare was so sure he would win that he lay down and took a nap in the middle of the race. The tortoise never stopped. When the hare woke up, the tortoise had won. This story
10 teaches us the lesson that slow and steady wins the race. Another well-known story is the town mouse and the country mouse. The country mouse has little to eat. Yet he is happy and carefree. When he visits the city mouse, he is amazed by how much food the city mouse can get. Then, they meet the house cat. After this scare, the country mouse decides to go back home. This fable shows us that it is better to live happily even if you are poor than be rich and full of worries. Aesop's fables
15 teach us many different life lessons. Some of Aesop's fables are funny. Others are more solemn. All of the fables make you think. They help us learn how to think and how to treat others.

Aesop's fables have been told to many generations. The fables are still told around the world today. Children and adults continue to enjoy the fables.

1. The author wrote this passage to
   (A) give information about Aesop's fables
   (B) convince people to read stories rather than watch TV
   (C) tell different stories including animals
   (D) teach children to treat others nicely
   (E) show that slow and steady wins the race

2. What happened to make the country mouse decide to go home?
   (A) he does not like the city mouse's food
   (B) he is frightened by meeting the house cat
   (C) he is happy and carefree
   (D) he would rather be poor than rich
   (E) he learns an important life lesson

3. We can assume that Aesop's fables are
   (A) interesting to adults but not kids
   (B) written for Greek people only
   (C) made into books and movies
   (D) still helpful many years later
   (E) only about hares, tortoises and mice

4. In line 15, what does the word "solemn" mean?
   (A) hilarious
   (B) good
   (C) serious
   (D) strange
   (E) exciting

5. From this passage, you can assume that Aesop was
   (A) determined
   (B) sly
   (C) quiet
   (D) imaginative
   (E) carefree

Passage #2

The sky gets gray. Snow begins to fall. At first, there are just a few snowflakes, but soon there are more and more. The wind begins to howl. People and animals search for warm and safe places. It's a blizzard!

Not every winter storm is a blizzard. To be called a blizzard, the storm has to have strong
5 winds that blow the snow around. Blowing snow often makes it very hard to see. This is called a 'whiteout.' Imagine trying to see through a white bed sheet that is right in front of your face. That is what a whiteout can be like. When there is a whiteout, it isn't safe to drive in a car or even to go for a walk.

Three things have to happen to make a storm a blizzard. First, the wind must blow at 35
10 miles an hour or more. That's a very strong wind! It is hard to walk against, and it makes whole trees move. Second, it must be hard to see farther than one-fourth of a mile. Third, the wind and blowing snow must last three hours or more. Snow will often fall during a blizzard, but it doesn't have to. A blizzard can go on even after the snow stops falling. That happens when the wind keeps whipping up the fallen snow.

15 A big snowstorm looks like fun. But blizzards are the most dangerous form of winter weather. People and animals outside can freeze or get lost. They can get into accidents. When there is a blizzard warning, the best thing is to stay inside and keep warm until the foul weather ends. You can have fun in the snow when the danger is over.

1. The main idea of this passage is
   (A) blizzards are a special kind of storm
   (B) it's safe to walk your dog in a blizzard
   (C) snow is dangerous to play in
   (D) blizzards last for only a few minutes
   (E) blizzards are over when snow stops falling

2. In this passage, the author compares a whiteout to a
   (A) howling animal
   (B) bedsheet
   (C) bucket of white paint
   (D) strong wind
   (E) falling snowflake

3. A whiteout happens when
   (A) the sky gets gray and snow falls
   (B) people look for warm places
   (C) blowing snow makes it hard to see
   (D) a person looks at a white bed sheet
   (E) snow falls for three hours or more

4. In line 13, "whipping up" the snow probably means
   (A) smoothing it out
   (B) hitting it again and again
   (C) blowing it into the air
   (D) setting it straight
   (E) changing its direction

5. In line 17, the word "foul" could best be replaced with
   (A) dirty
   (B) broken
   (C) fresh
   (D) strange
   (E) unpleasant

6. The author of this passage would probably agree that
   (A) playing outside in a blizzard is fun
   (B) cold is not the greatest danger of a blizzard
   (C) blizzards can also occur on non-windy days
   (D) the best place to enjoy a blizzard is from inside your house
   (E) you should tie your dog up outside during blizzards

Passage #3

Some people do not like when their food touches other food. Bento boxes, from Japan, can help keep foods separate. They are a type of lunch box. Different foods can go in each section of a bento box.

Bento boxes have been around for ages. Most people think they started in Japan over one (5) thousand years ago. People left home to hunt, fish, or farm. They often packed bento boxes with rice to eat for lunch.

The word 'bento' has meant different things over time. Around 1185, people started to eat hoshi-ii for lunch. Hoshi-ii is a meal made of dried rice in a bag. At the time, the bag was called a 'bento.' In the 1500s, people added a shiny varnish to bento boxes. These kinds of boxes (10) were used to store food.

After that, bento boxes were once again used for lunches. People put many kinds of foods in bento boxes. Bento boxes could have rice balls, seafood, and vegetables.

Japan built many railroads in the 1800s. Crowds gathered to ride the trains. People started selling bento boxes at the train stations. People could eat the bento boxes on the train. (15) Soon, stores and restaurants sold bento boxes. This made bento boxes even more popular.

Today, bento boxes are made out of wood, metal, or plastic. They are sold all over the world. Many have different shapes and colors. However, they are used the same way. These bento boxes still have separate sections for different foods, and people still pack lunches in them.

1. This passage was probably written to
   (A) tell the history of bento boxes
   (B) describe how bento boxes look
   (C) show how to make a bento box
   (D) explain who invented bento boxes
   (E) reveal why people stopped using bento boxes

2. We can assume that bento boxes were first used because people
   (A) needed bait when they went fishing
   (B) ate most meals with their close friends
   (C) started to grow rice on their farms
   (D) did not like using bags to carry rice
   (E) were unable to come home for lunch

3. The phrase "around for ages" (line 4) could be best replaced with
   (A) grown in size
   (B) discovered in the past
   (C) in use for a long time
   (D) made for young people
   (E) discovered recently

4. How was the bento for hoshi-ii different from bento boxes today?
   (A) It had different compartments.
   (B) It was a sack instead of a box.
   (C) It was used to store food for lunch.
   (D) It was filled with things made from rice.
   (E) It had a layer of shiny varnish.

5. According to the passage, bento boxes at train stations were
   (A) made for farmers, hunters and fishermen
   (B) used to transport food on trains
   (C) sold to people who rode on the train
   (D) bought at restaurant cars on the train
   (E) more popular than restaurant bento boxes

Passage #4

National parks are an important part of America. They were first created by President Roosevelt. Roosevelt passed the Antiquities Act. He passed it in 1906. This act used public lands to save the environment. It helped protect plants and animals.

There are now 59 national parks across the nation. All parks are protected by the U.S. government. The government watches over forests, mountains, and caves. It even preserves old Civil War battlefields. (5)

These parks have become popular with tourists. Thousands of people visit the parks each year. They go hiking and sight-seeing. They fall in love with the parks' beauty. They visit places like Yellowstone and the Grand Canyon.

(10) The national parks are also a good way for the government to earn money. Visitors spend billions of dollars each year at national parks. This creates nearly 300,000 jobs.

Some groups want to close down parts of these parks. They want to use the lands for oil and mining. These people have created an 'anti-park caucus.' They want to convince the government to change the law. They plan to build a mine in the Grand Canyon.

(15) However, pollution would ruin the parks' beauty. To make mines, we would lose many clean water sources. Even worse, we would lose an important part of our history. We must save our national parks from these groups.

1. The author would most likely agree with which statement?
   (A) Tourism pollutes national parks.
   (B) The Grand Canyon should be converted into a mine.
   (C) There are too many national parks in the U.S.
   (D) National parks are an important part of American history.
   (E) Theodore Roosevelt was the greatest president.

2. According to the passage, Theodore Roosevelt protected plants and animals by
   (A) passing the Antiquities Act
   (B) creating 59 national parks
   (C) preserving Civil War battlefields
   (D) going hiking and sight-seeing
   (E) creating a caucus

3. Which detail does NOT support the idea that national parks should be preserved?
   (A) They relate to historical events.
   (B) People enjoy sightseeing and visiting nature.
   (C) Many special plants and animals live there.
   (D) Private companies make a great deal of money from them each year.
   (E) They create jobs for local people.

4. In line 13, what does the word "caucus" most likely mean?
   (A) group
   (B) park
   (C) law
   (D) paper
   (E) mine

5. According to the passage, people want to shut down parts of national parks because they want to
   (A) protect the wildlife living in the parks from tourism
   (B) honor the presidency of Theodore Roosevelt
   (C) go hiking and sight-seeing without other visitors
   (D) use the billions of dollars for charity
   (E) build mines and drill for oil

4th Grade

Passage #1

A resolution is a promise to fix a problem or find a solution. Many people make New Year's resolutions by deciding to change themselves. They hope to make their lives better.

This tradition is thousands of years old. However, January 1st has not always been the start of the New Year. Long ago, the new year was celebrated in the spring. Back then, people lived by
5 eating what they planted. In the winter, few plants grew and animals went into hiding. There was very little to eat. The warmth of spring gave people hope again. They saw the land and its animals come back to life. People knew how important this time of year was. It meant their families would have food.

Soon, they saw spring as a fresh start for themselves, too. People from Babylon celebrated by
10 choosing new kings. Early Christians read from the Bible and sang songs. The tradition of making resolutions began. People would think about mistakes they had made in the past. They would use the start of a new year to make changes for the better.

Later, people changed the day of New Year's to January 1st. Even though the date is not the same, people still believe in making resolutions to have a better year. Nowadays, some people eat a
15 bunch of grapes. Others bake a gold coin into a cake. Many of us watch a huge ball drop to the ground. Though people celebrate New Year's in different ways, it is still an important way for millions of people to get a fresh start.

1. What is the main idea of the passage?
   (A) New Year's is celebrated the same way all around the world.
   (B) People should always make New Year's resolutions.
   (C) Some people's New Year's resolutions are better than others.
   (D) New Year's resolutions have become an important part of New Year's.
   (E) Resolutions can be made any time.

2. Why are the "grapes," the "gold coin" and the "huge ball" mentioned in lines 14-15?
   (A) They are gifts given on New Year's.
   (B) They are things people buy for themselves on New Year's.
   (C) They are examples of different ways people celebrate the New Year now.
   (D) They are examples of crops that people plant in the spring.
   (E) They are ways to definitely have a good year.

3. In line 10, the word "tradition" means
   (A) habit
   (B) swap
   (C) sign
   (D) party
   (E) old

4. In the past, what happened during the spring to make people hopeful?
   (A) The moon became full.
   (B) The tradition of making resolutions began.
   (C) The crops became mature and ready for harvest.
   (D) They could plant new crops and see them grow.
   (E) They could choose a new king and sing songs.

5. What does the author mean by "the land and its animals come back to life" in lines 6-7?
   (A) The earth's creatures came back from the dead.
   (B) Many animals returned from a trip.
   (C) Plants started to grow again and animals came out of hiding.
   (D) The sun came out after months of darkness.
   (E) The animals were sad but then became happy again.

Passage #2

Parents always tell their children, "Eat your vegetables!" But children still don't want to eat them. We think vegetables are celery, carrots, or lettuce. Fruits are apples, oranges, or bananas. But what is a vegetable? Many things we think are vegetables aren't what they seem. Some of things we think are vegetables are actually fruit. What are tomatoes, peppers, peas, and
5 beans? They are fruits!

Usually we use taste to decide if something is a fruit or vegetable. But sometimes we are wrong. Fruits aren't all sweet. Vegetables aren't always bland. Fruits and vegetables are actually different parts of plants. A fruit is the part with seeds. The seeds are so the plant can reproduce. It can make more plants like itself. Vegetables are the other parts of the plant. A vegetable might
10 be the leaves, stalk, or root.

People say you can't judge a book by its cover. You also can't judge a vegetable by its taste. You should not decide if something is a fruit or vegetable because of taste. You should decide when you know what part of the plant they are. Parents should start saying "eat your fruits and vegetables!"

1. The main idea of this passage is
   (A) parents nag kids about eating vegetables too much.
   (B) fruits and vegetables are delicious.
   (C) tomatoes and peppers are fruits.
   (D) fruits help plants reproduce.
   (E) people often mix up fruits and vegetables.

2. According to the passage, a fruit is
   (A) celery, carrots or lettuce
   (B) part of a healthy diet
   (C) the seed part of a plant
   (D) tastier than vegetables
   (E) very colorful

3. In line 4, why does the author mention tomatoes?
   (A) Kids don't like eating tomatoes.
   (B) People think of it as a vegetable, but it's actually a fruit.
   (C) Not many vegetables are red.
   (D) Tomatoes are easy to grow.
   (E) It grows with peppers, peas and beans.

4. In line 11, the author says "People say you can't judge a book by its cover" because
   (A) you can't judge a fruit or vegetable by taste.
   (B) books are like fruits and vegetables.
   (C) you never know what you're going to eat for dinner.
   (D) it's not safe to say that a tomato is a vegetable.
   (E) parents don't know when their children will eat their vegetables.

5. In line 10, what does the word "stalk" mean?
   (A) top
   (B) stem
   (C) thin
   (D) color
   (E) follow

Passage #3

Raise money for others. Buy groceries for the elderly. Donate canned goods to the homeless. Clean up your local park. There are many ways, big and small, to help your community. In fact, every child should *want* to be a volunteer. Volunteering can help you change the world. It can also help you build your character.

5 Volunteers are important for communities because they work 'pro bono.' That means they offer services without any costs. It can reward the community with cleaner spaces and new developments. It also makes people feel cared for. Working for free can have its rewards for you, too. It can also reward the volunteer with new skills. By planning an event, volunteers learn leadership skills. Volunteers also have the chance to meet many different people.

10 There are many ways to volunteer in your hometown. You can join a school club, or you can help clean your neighborhood park. You can also make a lemonade stand or start a bake sale. After you sell the goodies, you can donate the money to charity. Another idea is a food drive. This means collecting food from neighbors, then giving it to people who need it. You can even start your own volunteer program or organization. Volunteering is as simple as deciding to help another person.

15 Do not wait for the world to bring you kindness. Give compassion to the world first! Become a volunteer today. You can create a better life for yourself and others.

1. The author would most likely agree with which statement?
   (A) Volunteering is a way to develop yourself.
   (B) Volunteering should not be pro bono.
   (C) Volunteering is the same as donating money.
   (D) Volunteering helps communities and not individual people.
   (E) Volunteering is difficult.

2. In line 5, the Latin phrase pro bono means that the work is
   (A) costly
   (B) discounted
   (C) positive
   (D) unpaid
   (E) difficult

3. The author claims that volunteering rewards the community with all of the following EXCEPT
   (A) feeling cared for
   (B) cleaner spaces
   (C) new developments
   (D) less hunger
   (E) new skills

4. According to the passage, we can assume that what kind of person chooses to volunteer?
   (A) homeless
   (B) kindhearted
   (C) selfish
   (D) bored
   (E) competitive

5. Running a lemonade stand can be a type of volunteering because
   (A) you donate the profits to charity
   (B) you give the lemonade away for free
   (C) you can run it in your hometown
   (D) you get rewards for doing it
   (E) you make a personal profit

The Writing Sample

Overview

Before students begin the multiple-choice section of the Elementary SSAT, they will be asked to complete a writing sample. This must be completed in 15 minutes. While this writing sample is **not** scored, it will be sent to the admissions officers at the schools to which students apply. The writing sample will be used by schools to assess a student's writing skills and learn more about him or her. A copy of the writing sample will **not** be included in the scores provided unless separately purchased from the SSAT.

On the Actual Test

Students will see a picture prompt, and directions to write a story based on the image. The picture is intended to spark a student's imagination.

Students will have 15 minutes to write the sample. Consider mapping out time as follows:

2 minutes – *Plan*. Brainstorm ideas and jot down notes or sketches on the scrap paper that will be provided. Students should organize their stories, and have a clear beginning, middle, and end.

12 minutes – *Write*. If students have planned well, the actual writing of the sample should be a breeze. Remember to infuse your story with personality – schools are looking to get to know you through your story!

1 minute – *Proofread*. This is crucial! Reread the sample to look for and correct any punctuation, spelling, and grammar errors.

How to Use This Section

Below are 5 essay prompts. Treat each one as a prompt you might see on the real test.

1. Set a timer for 15 minutes.
2. Make your notes on a separate piece of paper.
3. Write your essay on a sheet of lined paper.
4. Remember to proofread!

Directions: Look one of the pictures on the next two pages. Tell a story about what happened in that picture. Make sure your story includes a beginning, a middle, and an end.

3rd Grade Final Practice Test (Form C)

Section 1: Quantitative

1	ⒶⒷⒸⒹⒺ	7	ⒶⒷⒸⒹⒺ	13	ⒶⒷⒸⒹⒺ	19	ⒶⒷⒸⒹⒺ	25	ⒶⒷⒸⒹⒺ
2	ⒶⒷⒸⒹⒺ	8	ⒶⒷⒸⒹⒺ	14	ⒶⒷⒸⒹⒺ	20	ⒶⒷⒸⒹⒺ	26	ⒶⒷⒸⒹⒺ
3	ⒶⒷⒸⒹⒺ	9	ⒶⒷⒸⒹⒺ	15	ⒶⒷⒸⒹⒺ	21	ⒶⒷⒸⒹⒺ	27	ⒶⒷⒸⒹⒺ
4	ⒶⒷⒸⒹⒺ	10	ⒶⒷⒸⒹⒺ	16	ⒶⒷⒸⒹⒺ	22	ⒶⒷⒸⒹⒺ	28	ⒶⒷⒸⒹⒺ
5	ⒶⒷⒸⒹⒺ	11	ⒶⒷⒸⒹⒺ	17	ⒶⒷⒸⒹⒺ	23	ⒶⒷⒸⒹⒺ	29	ⒶⒷⒸⒹⒺ
6	ⒶⒷⒸⒹⒺ	12	ⒶⒷⒸⒹⒺ	18	ⒶⒷⒸⒹⒺ	24	ⒶⒷⒸⒹⒺ	30	ⒶⒷⒸⒹⒺ

Section 2: Verbal

1	ⒶⒷⒸⒹⒺ	7	ⒶⒷⒸⒹⒺ	13	ⒶⒷⒸⒹⒺ	19	ⒶⒷⒸⒹⒺ	25	ⒶⒷⒸⒹⒺ
2	ⒶⒷⒸⒹⒺ	8	ⒶⒷⒸⒹⒺ	14	ⒶⒷⒸⒹⒺ	20	ⒶⒷⒸⒹⒺ	26	ⒶⒷⒸⒹⒺ
3	ⒶⒷⒸⒹⒺ	9	ⒶⒷⒸⒹⒺ	15	ⒶⒷⒸⒹⒺ	21	ⒶⒷⒸⒹⒺ	27	ⒶⒷⒸⒹⒺ
4	ⒶⒷⒸⒹⒺ	10	ⒶⒷⒸⒹⒺ	16	ⒶⒷⒸⒹⒺ	22	ⒶⒷⒸⒹⒺ	28	ⒶⒷⒸⒹⒺ
5	ⒶⒷⒸⒹⒺ	11	ⒶⒷⒸⒹⒺ	17	ⒶⒷⒸⒹⒺ	23	ⒶⒷⒸⒹⒺ	29	ⒶⒷⒸⒹⒺ
6	ⒶⒷⒸⒹⒺ	12	ⒶⒷⒸⒹⒺ	18	ⒶⒷⒸⒹⒺ	24	ⒶⒷⒸⒹⒺ	30	ⒶⒷⒸⒹⒺ

Section 3: Reading

1	ⒶⒷⒸⒹⒺ	7	ⒶⒷⒸⒹⒺ	13	ⒶⒷⒸⒹⒺ	19	ⒶⒷⒸⒹⒺ	25	ⒶⒷⒸⒹⒺ
2	ⒶⒷⒸⒹⒺ	8	ⒶⒷⒸⒹⒺ	14	ⒶⒷⒸⒹⒺ	20	ⒶⒷⒸⒹⒺ	26	ⒶⒷⒸⒹⒺ
3	ⒶⒷⒸⒹⒺ	9	ⒶⒷⒸⒹⒺ	15	ⒶⒷⒸⒹⒺ	21	ⒶⒷⒸⒹⒺ	27	ⒶⒷⒸⒹⒺ
4	ⒶⒷⒸⒹⒺ	10	ⒶⒷⒸⒹⒺ	16	ⒶⒷⒸⒹⒺ	22	ⒶⒷⒸⒹⒺ	28	ⒶⒷⒸⒹⒺ
5	ⒶⒷⒸⒹⒺ	11	ⒶⒷⒸⒹⒺ	17	ⒶⒷⒸⒹⒺ	23	ⒶⒷⒸⒹⒺ		
6	ⒶⒷⒸⒹⒺ	12	ⒶⒷⒸⒹⒺ	18	ⒶⒷⒸⒹⒺ	24	ⒶⒷⒸⒹⒺ		

Section 4: Writing Sample

[Use space provided in the test. Do not write your sample here]

Section 5: Experimental

1	ⒶⒷⒸⒹⒺ	5	ⒶⒷⒸⒹⒺ	9	ⒶⒷⒸⒹⒺ	13	ⒶⒷⒸⒹⒺ
2	ⒶⒷⒸⒹⒺ	6	ⒶⒷⒸⒹⒺ	10	ⒶⒷⒸⒹⒺ	14	ⒶⒷⒸⒹⒺ
3	ⒶⒷⒸⒹⒺ	7	ⒶⒷⒸⒹⒺ	11	ⒶⒷⒸⒹⒺ	15	ⒶⒷⒸⒹⒺ
4	ⒶⒷⒸⒹⒺ	8	ⒶⒷⒸⒹⒺ	12	ⒶⒷⒸⒹⒺ		

Overview

An important part of an effective study plan is to determine how a student has progressed. This practice test assesses a student's existing knowledge and grasp of concepts that may be seen on the actual exam.

Keep in mind that this practice test will be scored differently from the actual exam. On the actual Elementary SSAT, **certain questions will not count towards a student's actual score (i.e. the experimental section).** Also, the student's score will be determined by comparing his or her performance with those of other students in the same grade. On this practice test, however, every question is scored in order to accurately gauge the student's current ability level. Therefore, **this practice test should NOT be used as a gauge of how a student will score on the actual test**. This test should only be used to help students reevaluate his/her study plan.

Format

The format of this practice test is similar to that of the actual exam and includes 15 questions in a mock-experimental section. **For practice purposes only, students should treat the mock experimental section of the practice test as any other.**

The format of the practice test is below.

Scoring	Section	Number of Questions	Time Limit
Scored Section	Section 1: Quantitative	30	30 minutes
	Section 2: Verbal	30	20 minutes
	15-Minute Break		
	Section 3: Reading	28	30 minutes
	Total Scored Exam (Sections 1-3)	88	**1 hour, 20 minutes**
Unscored Section (sent to schools)	Writing Sample	1	15 minutes
Unscored Section	Section 5: Experimental	15	15 minutes

Answering

Use the answer sheet provided on the previous page to record answers. Students may wish to tear it out of the workbook.

SECTION 1
30 Questions

There are five suggested answers after each problem in this section. Solve each problem in your head or in the space provided to the right of the problem. Then, look at the suggested answers and pick the best one.

Note: Any figures or shapes that accompany problems in Section 1 are drawn as accurately as possible EXCEPT when it is stated that the figure is NOT drawn to scale.

Sample Question:

11 × 14 = ●ⒷⒸⒹⒺ
(A) 154 (B) 196 (C) 1,114 (D) 1,554 (E) 1,969

DO WORK IN THIS SPACE

1. Lorenzo purchased gifts for his friends. The gifts he bought cost \$38, \$23, \$16, and \$47. What was the average amount he spent?
   (A) \$31
   (B) \$37
   (C) \$38
   (D) \$39
   (E) \$40

2. Jack and Stacy both have stamp collections. If they have 35 stamps together and Stacy has 23 stamps herself, how many stamps does Jack have?
   (A) 11
   (B) 12
   (C) 21
   (D) 22
   (E) 58

3. Of the shapes shown on the right, which shape has the GREATEST chance of being selected at random?
   (A) a square
   (B) a triangle
   (C) a circle
   (D) a moon
   (E) a star

4. Which of the following is closest in value to 17?
   (A) 16.89
   (B) 16.95
   (C) 17.04
   (D) 17.09
   (E) 17.1

GO ON TO THE NEXT PAGE.

DO WORK IN THIS SPACE

5. Which of the following statements MUST be true about a parallelogram?
   (A) It has four or more sides.
   (B) It has four right angles.
   (C) It has two pairs of parallel sides.
   (D) It has four equal sides.
   (E) It has only one pair of sides that is parallel.

---

6. Which of these shapes is a quadrilateral but not a rhombus?

   (A)  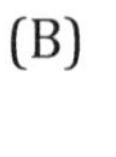

   (B) 

   (C) 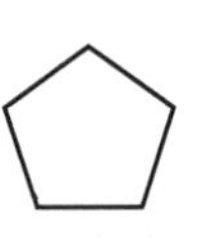

   (D) 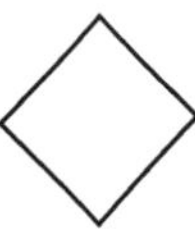

   (E) 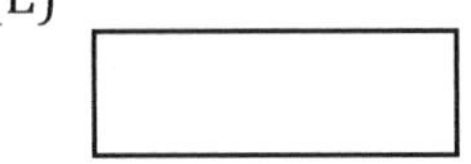

---

7. 126 + 245 =
   (A) 351
   (B) 361
   (C) 362
   (D) 371
   (E) 372

---

8. Aja bought a milkshake that cost $3.20. She handed the cashier $4.00. If the cashier gave her the correct amount of change, which combination of coins could she have received?
   (A) 1 quarter and 3 dimes
   (B) 2 quarters and 3 nickels
   (C) 2 quarters and 3 dimes
   (D) 3 quarters and 1 dime
   (E) 3 quarters and 2 nickels

---

9. A child is holding 5 helium balloons: 2 red balloons, 2 yellow balloons, and 1 green balloon. If one balloon accidentally flies away, which color is that balloon LEAST likely to be?
   (A) red
   (B) yellow
   (C) green
   (D) no color is less likely to fly away than the others
   (E) all colors would have an equal chance of flying away

GO ON TO THE NEXT PAGE.

DO WORK IN THIS SPACE

10. $86 \times 15 =$
    (A) 101
    (B) 860
    (C) 1,260
    (D) 1,290
    (E) 9,030

11. Which fractions below are ordered from greatest to least?
    (A) $\frac{1}{100}, \frac{1}{50}, \frac{1}{40}, \frac{1}{20}, \frac{1}{10}$
    (B) $\frac{1}{100}, \frac{1}{50}, \frac{1}{20}, \frac{1}{40}, \frac{1}{10}$
    (C) $\frac{1}{10}, \frac{1}{40}, \frac{1}{50}, \frac{1}{20}, \frac{1}{100}$
    (D) $\frac{1}{10}, \frac{1}{20}, \frac{1}{40}, \frac{1}{50}, \frac{1}{100}$
    (E) $\frac{1}{10}, \frac{1}{40}, \frac{1}{20}, \frac{1}{50}, \frac{1}{100}$

12. In a chess set, there is one black piece to every one white piece. If there are 16 black pieces, then how many white pieces are there in this set?
    (A) 8
    (B) 16
    (C) 18
    (D) 24
    (E) 32

13. Remi saw 84 purple bicycles last week. This week, he saw 26 more than half the number of purple bicycles he saw last week. How many purple bicycles did he see this week?
    (A) 55
    (B) 68
    (C) 110
    (D) 194
    (E) 220

14. If the area of this rectangle is 30 square units, what is the length of w?

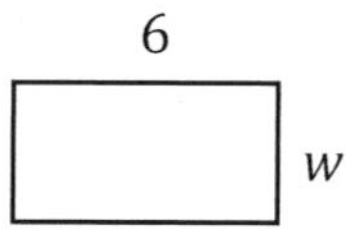

    (A) 4
    (B) 5
    (C) 6
    (D) 10
    (E) 22

GO ON TO THE NEXT PAGE.

DO WORK IN THIS SPACE

Questions 15 and 16 are based on the bar graph shown on the right:

15. A youth group offers four sports: Baseball, Basketball, Football, and Soccer. According to the graph, the number of people who play baseball is closest to:
   (A) 8
   (B) 10
   (C) 12
   (D) 15
   (E) 17

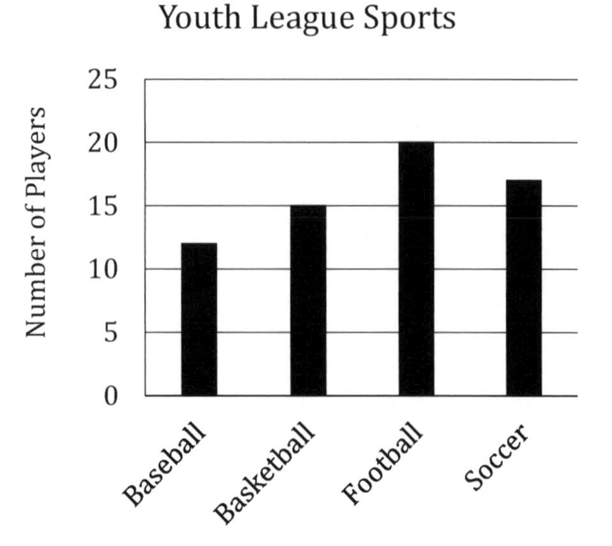

16. How many more people play football than basketball?
   (A) 35
   (B) 20
   (C) 15
   (D) 8
   (E) 5

---

17. Linus owns 37 DVDs. If he gives some DVDs to his sister and has 28 left, how many DVDs did he give to his sister?
   (A) 9
   (B) 11
   (C) 19
   (D) 55
   (E) 65

---

18. In the polygon shown on the right, all sides are equal. What is the perimeter of the polygon?
   (A) 35 in.
   (B) 36 in.
   (C) 42 in.
   (D) 49 in.
   (E) 56 in.

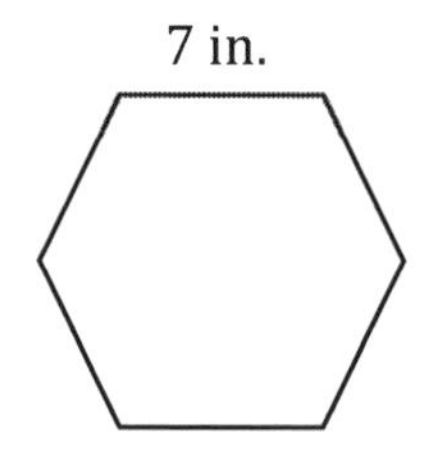

---

19. Maisey exercised for $\frac{3}{4}$ of an hour. She then stretched for $\frac{1}{8}$ of an hour. How much time in total did she spend exercising and stretching?
   (A) $\frac{1}{8}$
   (B) $\frac{1}{3}$
   (C) $\frac{1}{2}$
   (D) $\frac{7}{8}$
   (E) 1

GO ON TO THE NEXT PAGE.

DO WORK IN THIS SPACE

20. A sketch pad has 10 sheets of paper. A box holds 20 sketch pads. How many sheets of paper are in 5 boxes?
    (A) 50
    (B) 100
    (C) 200
    (D) 1,000
    (E) 10,000

21. 23 + 9 = ___ + 10
    (A) 13
    (B) 21
    (C) 22
    (D) 23
    (E) 32

22. Which number falls between $\frac{1}{2}$ and 1?
    (A) $\frac{1}{4}$
    (B) $\frac{3}{4}$
    (C) $\frac{3}{2}$
    (D) $\frac{4}{2}$
    (E) $\frac{5}{4}$

23. Shana has 100 pencils. The pencils have a total mass of 4 kilograms. What is the mass of each pencil in grams?
    (A) 4,000
    (B) 400
    (C) 40
    (D) 4
    (E) 0.4

24. Which of the following is a prime number?
    (A) 6
    (B) 9
    (C) 10
    (D) 17
    (E) 21

25. What is $\frac{9}{4}$ written as a mixed number?
    (A) $6\frac{3}{4}$
    (B) $5\frac{1}{4}$
    (C) $2\frac{1}{4}$
    (D) $1\frac{3}{4}$
    (E) $1\frac{1}{8}$

GO ON TO THE NEXT PAGE.

DO WORK IN THIS SPACE

26. Each school day Ann starts lunch at 11:40 a.m. Ann's lunch period is 45 minutes long. What time does Ann's lunch period end?
    (A) 11:25 a.m.
    (B) 12:05 p.m.
    (C) 12:15 p.m.
    (D) 12:25 p.m.
    (E) 12:45 p.m.

---

27. In an airplane, the first 6 rows have 4 seats each and the last 10 rows have 6 seats each. How may total seats are there?
    (A) 24
    (B) 40
    (C) 60
    (D) 84
    (E) 160

---

28. $\frac{9}{10} - \frac{3}{5} =$
    (A) $\frac{3}{10}$
    (B) $\frac{1}{5}$
    (C) $\frac{3}{5}$
    (D) $1\frac{1}{5}$
    (E) $1\frac{1}{2}$

---

29. Ellen's birthday is 3 weeks and 1 day before Jacob's birthday. If Jacob's birthday is July 29th, when is Ellen's birthday?
    (A) June 28
    (B) June 29
    (C) July 7
    (D) July 8
    (E) July 14

---

30. Mike finished a race in $\frac{4}{5}$ of an hour. Jennifer finished the race in $\frac{3}{5}$ of an hour. How much longer, in hours, did it take Mike to finish the race?
    (A) $\frac{1}{25}$
    (B) $\frac{1}{5}$
    (C) $\frac{7}{25}$
    (D) $\frac{12}{25}$
    (E) $1\frac{2}{5}$

STOP

IF YOU FINISH BEFORE TIME IS UP,
CHECK YOUR WORK IN THIS SECTION ONLY.
YOU MAY NOT TURN TO ANY OTHER SECTION.

SECTION 2
30 Questions

There are two different types of questions in this section: synonyms and analogies. Read the directions and sample question for each type.

Synonyms
Each of the questions that follow consist of one capitalized word. Each word is followed by five words or phrases. Select the one word or phrase whose meaning is closest to the word in capital letters.

Sample Question:

HOT: ●ⒷⒸⒹⒺ

(A) warm
(B) sunny
(C) open
(D) enjoyable
(E) unfriendly

---

1. POSSIBILITY:
   (A) hopeful
   (B) chance
   (C) difficult
   (D) beyond
   (E) likely

2. VISION:
   (A) sight
   (B) glasses
   (C) visor
   (D) eyes
   (E) blind

3. CLEVER:
   (A) slow
   (B) clear
   (C) competitive
   (D) smart
   (E) polite

4. SKILL:
   (A) expert
   (B) unable
   (C) ability
   (D) leader
   (E) job

5. EXCHANGE:
   (A) repeat
   (B) mimic
   (C) pay
   (D) extreme
   (E) trade

6. IRRITATE:
   (A) support
   (B) disturb
   (C) grumpy
   (D) nerves
   (E) brother

7. MISERY:
   (A) monstrous
   (B) unhappiness
   (C) joy
   (D) numb
   (E) cheap

8. AUTOMATICALLY:
   (A) reflex
   (B) manually
   (C) naturally
   (D) speed
   (E) automobile

9. ASSIST:
   (A) assistant
   (B) favor
   (C) relief
   (D) help
   (E) hand

10. OPPONENT:
    (A) ally
    (B) aggressive
    (C) boxing
    (D) compete
    (E) enemy

11. ESCAPE:
    (A) jog
    (B) free
    (C) cage
    (D) prison
    (E) flee

12. LIMIT:
    (A) border
    (B) infinite
    (C) outer
    (D) roof
    (E) push

13. SPOIL:
    (A) sport
    (B) love
    (C) ruin
    (D) fruit
    (E) child

14. FRIENDLY:
    (A) neighbor
    (B) nice
    (C) traitor
    (D) buddy
    (E) socialize

15. PEAK:
    (A) mountain
    (B) top
    (C) cold
    (D) high
    (E) sneak

GO ON TO THE NEXT PAGE.

Analogies

The questions that follow ask you to find relationships between words. For each question, select the answer choice that best completes the meaning of the sentence.

Sample Question:

Dance is to dancer as: 

(A) lesson is to teacher
(B) cat is to yarn
(C) fish is to water
(D) umbrella is to rain
(E) shovel is to snow

Choice (A) is the best answer because a dancer dances a dance, just as a teacher teaches a lesson. This choice states a relationship that is most like the relationship between dance and dancer.

---

16. Oven is to bake as
    (A) steer is to wheel
    (B) frighten is to mask
    (C) chocolate is to brownie
    (D) cookie is to chewy
    (E) rope is to tie

17. Dome is to round as river is to
    (A) stream
    (B) water
    (C) flowing
    (D) circle
    (E) brittle

18. Continue is to interrupt as
    (A) further is to ahead
    (B) balanced is to stable
    (C) bind is to wrap
    (D) noisy is to silent
    (E) joyful is to cheerful

19. Blade is to sharp as
    (A) buzz is to beehive
    (B) layered is to onion
    (C) arcade is to fun
    (D) dull is to blunt
    (E) dye is to paint

20. Ugly is to hideous as
    (A) valuable is to expensive
    (B) sprint is to jog
    (C) some is to numerous
    (D) abandoned is to lonely
    (E) hitch is to hesitation

21. Cake is to dessert as
    (A) steak is to potatoes
    (B) sense is to hearing
    (C) cream is to butter
    (D) inch is to unit
    (E) size is to medium

22. Sponge is to absorb as closet is to
    (A) consume
    (B) store
    (C) bedroom
    (D) monster
    (E) shelves

23. Strand is to braid as
    (A) hand is to pinky
    (B) thread is to fabric
    (C) club is to member
    (D) container is to lid
    (E) crew is to sailor

24. Flashcard is to teacher as
    (A) learner is to thinker
    (B) late is to tardy
    (C) tutor is to professor
    (D) passenger is to bus
    (E) ball is to athlete

GO ON TO THE NEXT PAGE.

25. Wool is to sheep as
    (A) crochet is to scarf
    (B) tiger is to cub
    (C) farm is to hay
    (D) novel is to author
    (E) hen is to chick

26. Say is to exclaim as cold is to
    (A) refrigerator
    (B) frigid
    (C) surprise
    (D) shivering
    (E) chat

27. Hear is to here as
    (A) nose is to eyes
    (B) tune is to ton
    (C) chain is to main
    (D) ear is to where
    (E) break is to brake

28. Song is to composer as honey is to
    (A) darling
    (B) singer
    (C) jam
    (D) bumblebee
    (E) bear

29. Tusk is to horn as
    (A) quarter is to dime
    (B) unfair is to fair
    (C) pebble is to stone
    (D) stranger is to buddy
    (E) energetic is to passive

30. Spicy is to bland as fasten is to
    (A) separate
    (B) attach
    (C) wires
    (D) link
    (E) join

STOP

IF YOU FINISH BEFORE TIME IS UP,
CHECK YOUR WORK IN THIS SECTION ONLY.
YOU MAY NOT TURN TO ANY OTHER SECTION.

SECTION 3
28 Questions

Carefully read each passage and then answer the questions about it. For each question, select the choice that best answers the question based on the passage.

I am the wind,
And I come very fast;
Through the tall wood
I blow a loud blast.

5 Sometimes I am soft
As a sweet, gentle child,
I play with the flowers
I'm quiet and mild.

And then out so loud
10 All at once I can roar
If you wish to be quiet,
Close window and door.

I am the wind
And I come very fast
15 Through the tall wood
I blow a loud blast.

1. From the passage, you can assume that the narrator is
   (A) a child
   (B) a flower
   (C) a person
   (D) the tall tree
   (E) the wind

2. The main idea of the passage is
   (A) the wind is very soft
   (B) the wind is like a child
   (C) the wind can roar and blow a loud blast
   (D) the wind can change a great deal
   (E) the wind is very fast

3. In lines 5-6, the poet compares the wind to a child to show how
   (A) mischievous the wind can be
   (B) children love playing outside on windy days
   (C) gentle and sweet the wind can be
   (D) greatly the wind loves children
   (E) how loud the wind can be

4. The word "mild" (line 8) means
   (A) shy
   (B) boring
   (C) sugary
   (D) fast
   (E) sleepy

GO ON TO THE NEXT PAGE.

Seven out of ten households have some kind of pet. But there are still millions of animals that are strays or live in shelters. Adopting a pet is a way to give an animal a real home. But that isn't the only reason to adopt a pet!

Bringing a pet into your home can be good for you. Pets are fun to play with, 5 but they also teach people things. Caring for a pet, like feeding or cleaning up after it, can help children learn to be responsible. It can also teach kids to be more patient and considerate. For older people, pets make great company if they live alone. Best of all, pets are loyal, and will love their owners no matter what.

Just like humans, animals need a home. They also need a group to feel a part 10 of. Pets will bond even with humans. They will come to consider their owners as a part of their tribe or family. As a part of a family, some pets will try to protect their owners if they sense danger. One dog woke up his owners when he realized the house was on fire, and saved their lives!

Pet adoption makes sense for humans and animals. If you aren't sure if you 15 should adopt a pet, ask yourself these questions: "Would I like to make my life better? Do I want to do something nice for someone else?" If you answered "Yes" both times, then adopting a pet is a good idea for you!

5. The main idea of this passage is
   (A) too many animals don't have homes
   (B) pets can help children learn good habits
   (C) pets are loyal to their owners
   (D) all older people should own pets
   (E) pet adoption is good for many reasons

6. The author would most likely agree with which statement?
   (A) Caring for pets is hard work.
   (B) Only dogs are loyal pets.
   (C) Too many animals don't have homes.
   (D) Every human should have a pet.
   (E) Different pet species can bond with one another.

7. In line 8, "loyal" could best be replaced with
   (A) fond
   (B) needy
   (C) royal
   (D) faithful
   (E) companion

8. According to the passage, pets will protect their owners because they
   (A) feel grateful for being adopted
   (B) are afraid of danger
   (C) don't want to be alone
   (D) were trained to do so
   (E) think of their owners as a part of their tribe

GO ON TO THE NEXT PAGE.

Raggedy Ann heard some of the boys talk of "The Kite," so Raggedy Ann knew this must be a kite.

When a tail had been fastened to the kite and a large ball of heavy twine tied to the front, one of the boys held the kite up in the air and another boy walked off, (5) unwinding the ball of twine.

There was a nice breeze blowing, so the boy with the twine called, "Let 'er go" and started running.

Marcella held Raggedy up so that she could watch the kite sail through the air.

How nicely it climbed! But suddenly the kite acted strangely. As all the (10) children shouted advice to the boy with the ball of twine, the kite began darting this way and that. Finally making four or five loop-the-loops, it crashed to the ground.

"It needs more tail on it!" one boy shouted.

Then the children asked each other where they might get more rags to fasten to the tail of the kite.

(15) "Let's tie Raggedy Ann to the tail!" suggested Marcella. "I know she would enjoy a trip 'way up in the sky!"

The boys all shouted with delight at this new suggestion. So Raggedy Ann was tied to the tail of the kite.

This time the kite rose straight in the air and remained steady. The boy with (20) the ball of twine unwound it until the kite and Raggedy Ann were 'way, 'way up and far away. How Raggedy Ann enjoyed being up there! She could see for miles and miles! And how tiny the children looked!

9. We can assume that Raggedy Ann is Marcella's
   (A) pet
   (B) doll
   (C) sister
   (D) neighbor
   (E) classmate

10. In line 5, "twine" could best be replaced with
   (A) wax
   (B) rags
   (C) string
   (D) paper
   (E) plastic

11. According to the passage, why does the kite crash?
   (A) It is covered in rags.
   (B) It does not have enough tail.
   (C) It is too heavy to fly.
   (D) The boys ran this way and that.
   (E) There was too much wind.

12. The word that best describes Raggedy Ann while she is attached to the kite is
   (A) relaxed
   (B) amazed
   (C) annoyed
   (D) generous
   (E) frightened

GO ON TO THE NEXT PAGE.

Doctors know that having a healthy diet isn't easy. To help, they created a picture of a dinner plate. It is separated into four colored sections. Each section is a different size. These sizes tell us how much we should eat of each food type. They call this 'MyPlate.' Doctors think that MyPlate can help people make better food choices.

5 Vegetables and grains are the biggest sections on MyPlate. These should make up most of the food we eat. Doctors tell us that our vegetables should be a rainbow. Tomatoes, carrots, and lettuce are some colorful choices. Grains are things like bread and pasta. Doctors tell us to make sure these are whole grain.

Fruits and proteins are smaller sections on MyPlate. Eat a little less of these. 10 Fruits are things like bananas and apples. Proteins are things like meat or nuts. MyPlate also comes with a drink glass. This small section is for dairy. Yogurt and low-fat milk are examples of healthy dairy.

Ice cream, chips and soda taste good. But doctors tell us that too much of these is not good for us. They know it can be very easy to eat unhealthy food. Doctors use 15 MyPlate because it is a reminder. People look at MyPlate and remember that what they eat affects their bodies.

13. The main idea of this passage is that
    - (A) it is not easy to eat healthy
    - (B) our food should be colorful
    - (C) MyPlate helps people eat healthier
    - (D) we should divide our food into sections on our plate
    - (E) ice cream is not good for you

14. In line 6, "our vegetables should be a rainbow" most likely means
    - (A) we should color our vegetables before we eat them
    - (B) we should arrange our vegetables in rainbow color order
    - (C) we should only eat tomatoes, carrots and lettuce
    - (D) fruits can be all the same color
    - (E) different colored vegetables have different health benefits

15. According to the passage, we should eat mostly
    - (A) different colored fruits
    - (B) low-fat milk and yogurt
    - (C) meats and nuts
    - (D) vegetables and grains
    - (E) potato chips and ice cream

16. In line 2, "sections" most likely means
    - (A) parts
    - (B) halves
    - (C) wholes
    - (D) squares
    - (E) triangles

GO ON TO THE NEXT PAGE.

In the evening Peter as usual paid his visit to Heidi.

The minute he opened the door she ran up to him, saying: "Peter, I have to tell you something."

"Say it," he replied.

5 "You must learn to read now," said the child.

"I have done it already."

"Yes, yes, Peter, but I don't mean it that way," Heidi eagerly continued; "you must learn so that you really know how afterwards."

"I can't," Peter remarked.

10 "Nobody believes you about that any more, and I won't either," Heidi said resolutely. "When I was in Frankfurt, grandmama told me that it wasn't true and that I shouldn't believe you."

Peter's astonishment was great.

"I'll teach you, for I know how; when you have learnt it, you must read one or 15 two songs to grandmother every day."

"I shan't!" grumbled the boy.

This obstinate refusal made Heidi very angry. With flaming eyes, she planted herself before the boy and said: "I'll tell you what will happen, if you don't want to learn. Your mother has often said that she'll send you to Frankfurt. Clara showed me 20 the terrible, large boys' school there, where you'll have to go. You must stay there till you are a man, Peter! You mustn't think that there is only one teacher there, and such a kind one as we have here. No, indeed! There are whole rows of them, and when they are out walking, they have high black hats on their heads. I saw them myself, when I was out driving!"

17. The main problem Peter faces is
    (A) Heidi will not help him with his studies
    (B) he has trouble learning how to read
    (C) Heidi does not visit him enough
    (D) he doesn't get along with Heidi
    (E) he must sing songs for his grandma

18. "With flaming eyes" in line 17 probably means Heidi is feeling
    (A) blind
    (B) afraid
    (C) determined
    (D) amazed
    (E) on fire

19. In line 13, the word "astonishment" means
    (A) joy
    (B) fear
    (C) relief
    (D) anger
    (E) shock

20. According to the passage, what will happen to Peter if he does not learn to read?
    (A) He will be sent to a boy's school.
    (B) He will have to live with his grandma.
    (C) He will be taught by only one teacher.
    (D) He will move to Frankfurt with Heidi.
    (E) He will have to wear a black hat.

GO ON TO THE NEXT PAGE.

A hike is a long walk that people take outdoors for fun. Anyone, young or old, can go on a hike. Hiking is fun. People hike for many different reasons.

Some people like watching nature. Seeing plants, birds and other animals up close is one reason people hike. Other people hike for exercise. Climbing hills or
5 following trails can be a good way to work your whole body. Some people hike for a break from jobs or chores. The fresh air and warm sun can give you the energy you need to go back to work if you are feeling tired.

To have a good hike, first make sure you are dressed right. Good shoes, like boots with treads, will keep you from slipping. On cold days, wear a hat, gloves, and
10 layers of warm clothing. On hot, sunny days, you still need good shoes, but you can wear shorts and short sleeves. You should also wear sunscreen and bug spray when hiking in warm weather.

The right clothes are important, but there are also other things you will need before hiking. A map will keep you from getting lost. A bottle of water and some nuts
15 or dried fruit will give you energy for the long walk. Don't forget to bring a friend or adult to hike with you, in case you get lost or need help.

Hiking is a popular hobby. It is very easy for people of all ages to go on a hike.

21. The author wrote this passage to
    - (A) warn people about the dangers of hiking
    - (B) discuss why people hike and how people prepare for it
    - (C) list the many different kinds of clothes people should wear for hiking
    - (D) convince people that hiking is the best activity
    - (E) describe the different types of people who hike and how old they are

22. According to the passage, people go hiking because
    - (A) they don't like to work
    - (B) they are bored
    - (C) it gives them energy
    - (D) they don't like being indoors
    - (E) they can be alone

23. We can assume that hiking can be done at any time of year because the author
    - (A) mentions the importance of wearing good shoes
    - (B) says that hiking can make you tired
    - (C) tells the reader to bring water and snacks on a hike
    - (D) talks about what clothing to wear on a hike in warm and cold weather
    - (E) says that hiking lets people enjoy nature

24. In lines 14-15, the phrases "map," "nuts or dried fruit" and "bring a friend" let us know that
    - (A) it is normal to get tired during a long hike
    - (B) it takes a long time to prepare for a hike, but the hike itself is short
    - (C) hikes are extremely exciting
    - (D) it's boring to go hiking alone
    - (E) going unprepared on a hike can be dangerous.

GO ON TO THE NEXT PAGE.

My Very Educated Mother Just Served Us Nine Pizzas. What is this silly sentence? It is a way to remember there were once nine planets: Mercury, Venus, Earth, Mars, Jupiter, Saturn, Uranus, Neptune and Pluto. We live on planet Earth. Earth is part of the solar system. The solar system is full of planets, moons, and other
5 objects. All of the planets orbit the Sun.

Pluto is the smallest of them all. It is smaller than Earth's moon. Its width is half the size of the United States. Since Pluto is so small, scientists now call Pluto a dwarf planet. A dwarf planet is not a moon. A moon travels around a bigger object, like a planet. Pluto moves around the sun.

10 It takes one year for Earth to orbit the sun. It takes almost 250 years for Pluto to go all around the sun. Pluto is the planet farthest away from the sun. Pluto is very cold. There is no life on Pluto. It is not like Earth. It is mostly rock and ice on Pluto. Charon is the name of one of Pluto's moons. It takes about one week for Charon to circle Pluto. You can only see Charon from one side of Pluto.

15 Next time someone asks you about the solar system, you can tell them all about Pluto, the dwarf planet of our solar system.

25. The main idea of this passage is that
- (A) the solar system is full of planets, moons, and other objects
- (B) all planets orbit the Sun
- (C) life only exists on planet Earth
- (D) Pluto is a unique planet
- (E) Pluto's moon is Charon

26. In line 5, the word "orbit" can be replaced by
- (A) pass
- (B) fly
- (C) circle
- (D) stay
- (E) view

27. Pluto is different from Earth for all of the following reasons EXCEPT
- (A) Pluto takes 250 years to make an orbit.
- (B) Pluto has no living creatures on it.
- (C) Pluto is mostly icy and rocky.
- (D) Pluto is the furthest away from the sun.
- (E) Pluto orbits around the sun.

28. Based only on the passage, we can infer that nothing lives on Pluto because
- (A) its moon is only visible from one side
- (B) it is a dwarf planet
- (C) it is too far away from the sun
- (D) it is a moon, not a planet
- (E) it is too small

STOP

IF YOU FINISH BEFORE TIME IS UP,
CHECK YOUR WORK IN THIS SECTION ONLY.
YOU MAY NOT TURN TO ANY OTHER SECTION.

SECTION 4
Writing Sample

Look at the picture and tell a story about what happened. Make sure your story includes a beginning, middle and end.

GO ON TO THE NEXT PAGE.

STOP

IF YOU FINISH BEFORE TIME IS UP,
CHECK YOUR WORK IN THIS SECTION ONLY.
YOU MAY NOT TURN TO ANY OTHER SECTION.

SECTION 5
15 Questions

Where the acorn tumbles down,
Where the ash tree sheds its berry,
With your fur so soft and brown,
With your eye so round and merry,
5 Scarcely moving the long grass,
Field Mouse, I can see you pass.

Little thing, in what dark den,
Lie you all the winter sleeping?
Till warm weather comes again,
10 Then once more I see you peeping
Round about the tall tree roots
Nibbling at their fallen fruits.

1. The poet is
   (A) watching a field mouse
   (B) thinking about sleeping in a den
   (C) petting the field mouse's fur
   (D) dreaming of warm weather
   (E) hiding near the roots of tall trees

2. What season is the first stanza most likely happening in?
   (A) spring
   (B) summer
   (C) autumn
   (D) winter
   (E) any season of the year

3. Each the following words are used by the author to describe traits of the Field Mouse EXCEPT
   (A) soft
   (B) brown
   (C) round
   (D) dark
   (E) merry

4. The phrase "Scarcely moving the long grass" (line 5) shows that the Field Mouse is
   (A) fast
   (B) hungry
   (C) sleepy
   (D) merry
   (E) careful

5. The word "sheds" (line 2) most nearly means
   (A) gets
   (B) keeps
   (C) drops
   (D) stores
   (E) remembers

---

6. STURDY:
   (A) building
   (B) strong
   (C) skinny
   (D) stumpy
   (E) hard

7. ATTEMPT:
   (A) fail
   (B) try
   (C) climb
   (D) tempt
   (E) hesitate

GO ON TO THE NEXT PAGE.

8. PREDICT:
   (A) prevent
   (B) next
   (C) psychic
   (D) ending
   (E) guess

9. Map is to locate as
   (A) fish is to tackle
   (B) parrot is to pirate
   (C) contain is to jar
   (D) banner is to announce
   (E) baby is to adult

10. Instructor is to job as
   (A) teach is to grasp
   (B) music is to opera
   (C) directions is to commands
   (D) January is to month
   (E) learned is to confused

11. What is the area of the triangle below?
   (Note: Area = $\frac{1}{2}$ *(base × height))*

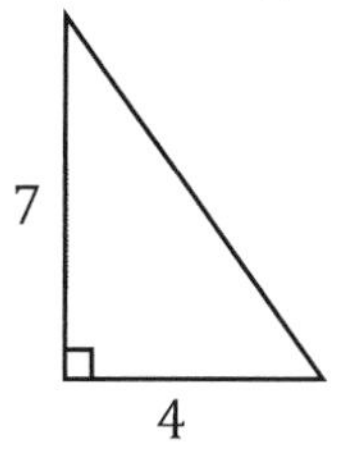

   (A) 4 square units
   (B) 7 square units
   (C) 11 square units
   (D) 14 square units
   (E) 28 square units

12. The local theatre is showing a play from 9:15p.m. to 11:45 p.m. How long is the play?
   (A) 1 hour and 30 minutes
   (B) 2 hours and 15 minutes
   (C) 2 hours and 30 minutes
   (D) 2 hours and 45 minutes
   (E) 3 hours and 15 minutes

13. Jorja is running a race. If the racetrack is 2 kilometers long, how many meters will Jorja run if she finishes the race?
   (A) 2 meters
   (B) 20 meters
   (C) 200 meters
   (D) 2,000 meters
   (E) 20,000 meters

14. Daniella has a jar full of 100 marbles. 43 are blue, 39 are red, and the rest are yellow. If she drops in 11 more yellow marbles, how many yellow marbles will be in the jar altogether?
   (A) 11
   (B) 18
   (C) 29
   (D) 82
   (E) 111

15. Kiley built a pizza with five different toppings. There are 2 pepperoni slices, 1 with spicy chicken, 3 plain cheese, 1 with vegetables, and 1 with white cheese. If she grabs a slice randomly, which topping will she most likely get?
   (A) pepperoni
   (B) spicy
   (C) vegetables
   (D) plain cheese
   (E) white cheese

STOP

IF YOU FINISH BEFORE TIME IS UP,
CHECK YOUR WORK IN THIS SECTION ONLY.
YOU MAY NOT TURN TO ANY OTHER SECTION.

Scoring the 3rd Grade Final Practice Test (Form C)

Sections 1-3 – Scored

Score the test using the answer sheet and *referring to the answer key in the back of the book (see table of contents).*

For each section, record the number of questions answered correctly. This will give you the raw score for each section. Note that the actual test will convert the raw score to a scaled score by comparing the student's performance with all other students in the same grade who took the test.

Section	Questions Correct (Raw Score)
Quantitative *Section 1*	___________
Verbal *Section 2*	___________
Reading *Section 3*	___________

Carefully consider the results from the practice test when forming a study plan. Remember, the Elementary SSAT is given to students in grades 3-4. Unless the student has finished 4th grade, chances are that there is material on this test that he or she has not yet been taught. If this is the case, and the student would like to improve beyond what is expected of his or her grade, consider working with a tutor or teacher, who can help the student learn more about new topics.

Section 4 – Writing Sample – Unscored

Have a parent or trusted educator review the essay or story written for the writing sample. Important areas to focus on include organization, clarity of ideas, originality, and technical precision (spelling, grammar, etc.).

Section 5 – Unscored

On the real test, the Experimental section will NOT be scored. Consider the student's performance on this section for practice purposes only. Did he or she do better on one section than another? Use this information along with the information from Sections 1-3 to form the study plan.

4th Grade Final Practice Test (Form D)

Overview

An important part of an effective study plan is to determine how a student has progressed. This practice test assesses a student's existing knowledge and grasp of concepts that may be seen on the actual exam.

Keep in mind that this practice test will be scored differently from the actual exam. On the actual Elementary SSAT, **certain questions will not count towards a student's actual score (i.e. the experimental section).** Also, the student's score will be determined by comparing his or her performance with those of other students in the same grade. On this practice test, however, every question is scored in order to accurately gauge the student's current ability level. Therefore, **this practice test should NOT be used as a gauge of how a student will score on the actual test**. This test should only be used to help students reevaluate his/her study plan.

Format

The format of this practice test is similar to that of the actual exam and includes 15 questions in a mock-experimental section. **For practice purposes only, students should treat the mock experimental section of the practice test as any other.**

The format of the practice test is below.

<table>
<tr><th>Scoring</th><th>Section</th><th>Number of Questions</th><th>Time Limit</th></tr>
<tr><td rowspan="5">Scored Section</td><td>Section 1: Quantitative</td><td>30</td><td>30 minutes</td></tr>
<tr><td>Section 2: Verbal</td><td>30</td><td>20 minutes</td></tr>
<tr><td colspan="3">15-Minute Break</td></tr>
<tr><td>Section 3: Reading</td><td>28</td><td>30 minutes</td></tr>
<tr><td>Total Scored Exam (Sections 1-3)</td><td>88</td><td>1 hour, 20 minutes</td></tr>
<tr><td>Unscored Section (sent to schools)</td><td>Writing Sample</td><td>1</td><td>15 minutes</td></tr>
<tr><td>Unscored Section</td><td>Section 5: Experimental</td><td>15</td><td>15 minutes</td></tr>
</table>

Answering

Use the answer sheet provided on the next page to record answers. Students may wish to tear it out of the workbook.

Section 1: Quantitative

1 ⒶⒷⒸⒹⒺ	7 ⒶⒷⒸⒹⒺ	13 ⒶⒷⒸⒹⒺ	19 ⒶⒷⒸⒹⒺ	25 ⒶⒷⒸⒹⒺ
2 ⒶⒷⒸⒹⒺ	8 ⒶⒷⒸⒹⒺ	14 ⒶⒷⒸⒹⒺ	20 ⒶⒷⒸⒹⒺ	26 ⒶⒷⒸⒹⒺ
3 ⒶⒷⒸⒹⒺ	9 ⒶⒷⒸⒹⒺ	15 ⒶⒷⒸⒹⒺ	21 ⒶⒷⒸⒹⒺ	27 ⒶⒷⒸⒹⒺ
4 ⒶⒷⒸⒹⒺ	10 ⒶⒷⒸⒹⒺ	16 ⒶⒷⒸⒹⒺ	22 ⒶⒷⒸⒹⒺ	28 ⒶⒷⒸⒹⒺ
5 ⒶⒷⒸⒹⒺ	11 ⒶⒷⒸⒹⒺ	17 ⒶⒷⒸⒹⒺ	23 ⒶⒷⒸⒹⒺ	29 ⒶⒷⒸⒹⒺ
6 ⒶⒷⒸⒹⒺ	12 ⒶⒷⒸⒹⒺ	18 ⒶⒷⒸⒹⒺ	24 ⒶⒷⒸⒹⒺ	30 ⒶⒷⒸⒹⒺ

Section 2: Verbal

1 ⒶⒷⒸⒹⒺ	7 ⒶⒷⒸⒹⒺ	13 ⒶⒷⒸⒹⒺ	19 ⒶⒷⒸⒹⒺ	25 ⒶⒷⒸⒹⒺ
2 ⒶⒷⒸⒹⒺ	8 ⒶⒷⒸⒹⒺ	14 ⒶⒷⒸⒹⒺ	20 ⒶⒷⒸⒹⒺ	26 ⒶⒷⒸⒹⒺ
3 ⒶⒷⒸⒹⒺ	9 ⒶⒷⒸⒹⒺ	15 ⒶⒷⒸⒹⒺ	21 ⒶⒷⒸⒹⒺ	27 ⒶⒷⒸⒹⒺ
4 ⒶⒷⒸⒹⒺ	10 ⒶⒷⒸⒹⒺ	16 ⒶⒷⒸⒹⒺ	22 ⒶⒷⒸⒹⒺ	28 ⒶⒷⒸⒹⒺ
5 ⒶⒷⒸⒹⒺ	11 ⒶⒷⒸⒹⒺ	17 ⒶⒷⒸⒹⒺ	23 ⒶⒷⒸⒹⒺ	29 ⒶⒷⒸⒹⒺ
6 ⒶⒷⒸⒹⒺ	12 ⒶⒷⒸⒹⒺ	18 ⒶⒷⒸⒹⒺ	24 ⒶⒷⒸⒹⒺ	30 ⒶⒷⒸⒹⒺ

Section 3: Reading

1 ⒶⒷⒸⒹⒺ	7 ⒶⒷⒸⒹⒺ	13 ⒶⒷⒸⒹⒺ	19 ⒶⒷⒸⒹⒺ	25 ⒶⒷⒸⒹⒺ
2 ⒶⒷⒸⒹⒺ	8 ⒶⒷⒸⒹⒺ	14 ⒶⒷⒸⒹⒺ	20 ⒶⒷⒸⒹⒺ	26 ⒶⒷⒸⒹⒺ
3 ⒶⒷⒸⒹⒺ	9 ⒶⒷⒸⒹⒺ	15 ⒶⒷⒸⒹⒺ	21 ⒶⒷⒸⒹⒺ	27 ⒶⒷⒸⒹⒺ
4 ⒶⒷⒸⒹⒺ	10 ⒶⒷⒸⒹⒺ	16 ⒶⒷⒸⒹⒺ	22 ⒶⒷⒸⒹⒺ	28 ⒶⒷⒸⒹⒺ
5 ⒶⒷⒸⒹⒺ	11 ⒶⒷⒸⒹⒺ	17 ⒶⒷⒸⒹⒺ	23 ⒶⒷⒸⒹⒺ	
6 ⒶⒷⒸⒹⒺ	12 ⒶⒷⒸⒹⒺ	18 ⒶⒷⒸⒹⒺ	24 ⒶⒷⒸⒹⒺ	

Section 4: Writing Sample

[Use space provided in the test. Do not write your sample here]

Section 5: Experimental

1 ⒶⒷⒸⒹⒺ	5 ⒶⒷⒸⒹⒺ	9 ⒶⒷⒸⒹⒺ	13 ⒶⒷⒸⒹⒺ
2 ⒶⒷⒸⒹⒺ	6 ⒶⒷⒸⒹⒺ	10 ⒶⒷⒸⒹⒺ	14 ⒶⒷⒸⒹⒺ
3 ⒶⒷⒸⒹⒺ	7 ⒶⒷⒸⒹⒺ	11 ⒶⒷⒸⒹⒺ	15 ⒶⒷⒸⒹⒺ
4 ⒶⒷⒸⒹⒺ	8 ⒶⒷⒸⒹⒺ	12 ⒶⒷⒸⒹⒺ	

SECTION 1
30 Questions

There are five suggested answers after each problem in this section. Solve each problem in your head or in the space provided to the right of the problem. Then, look at the suggested answers and pick the best one.

Note: Any figures or shapes that accompany problems in Section 1 are drawn as accurately as possible EXCEPT when it is stated that the figure is NOT drawn to scale.

Sample Question:

$11 \times 14 =$ ●ⒷⒸⒹⒺ

(A) 154
(B) 196
(C) 1,114
(D) 1,554
(E) 1,969

DO WORK IN THIS SPACE

1. Tamika bought 4.75 liters of apple juice. How many milliliters of juice did Tamika buy?
   (A) 0.0475
   (B) 0.475
   (C) 475
   (D) 4,750
   (E) 47,500

2. The digit 5 in the decimal 0.8201534 is equivalent to which of the following?
   (A) $\frac{5}{10}$
   (B) $\frac{5}{100}$
   (C) $\frac{5}{1,000}$
   (D) $\frac{5}{10,000}$
   (E) $\frac{5}{100,000}$

3. Soren had a yard sale. In the first hour, she received $42, $51, $11, $60, and $51 for items sold. What was the average price of the items she sold during that hour?
   (A) $31
   (B) $42
   (C) $43
   (D) $44
   (E) $51

4. If $k - 29 = 13$, then $k + 16 = ?$
   (A) 13
   (B) 29
   (C) 32
   (D) 48
   (E) 58

GO ON TO THE NEXT PAGE.

DO WORK IN THIS SPACE

5. Two taxi companies operate in Caesar City. Yellow Cab has 48 taxis and Red Cab has 4 more than twice as many taxis as Yellow Cab. How many taxis does Red Cab have?
   (A) 28
   (B) 52
   (C) 96
   (D) 100
   (E) 104

---

6. Which fractions below are ordered from smallest to largest?
   (A) $1, \frac{1}{3}, \frac{2}{3}, \frac{4}{3}, 2$
   (B) $\frac{1}{3}, \frac{2}{3}, 1, \frac{4}{3}, 2$
   (C) $1, 2, \frac{1}{3}, \frac{2}{3}, \frac{4}{3}$
   (D) $\frac{4}{3}, \frac{2}{3}, \frac{1}{3}, 2, 1$
   (E) $2, \frac{4}{3}, 1, \frac{2}{3}, \frac{1}{3}$

---

7. Two equal rectangles are put together to make a square. If the area of the square is 64 square units, what is the perimeter of one of the rectangles?
   (A) 16 units
   (B) 24 units
   (C) 30 units
   (D) 32 units
   (E) 48 units

---

8. A cube with sides labeled 1, 1, 2, 3, 5, 8. When rolled, which number will it MOST likely land on?
   (A) 1
   (B) 2
   (C) 3
   (D) 5
   (E) 8

---

9. Mark has basketball practice today after school at 3:15 p.m. His basketball coach said practice would end at 4:30 p.m. Mark has been at basketball practice for 25 minutes. How much more time will he be at practice if he says until the end?
   (A) 25 minutes
   (B) 40 minutes
   (C) 50 minutes
   (D) 1 hour and 15 minutes
   (E) 1 hour and 30 minutes

GO ON TO THE NEXT PAGE.

DO WORK IN THIS SPACE

10. Which best describes the triangle?
    (A) acute
    (B) isosceles
    (C) equilateral
    (D) right
    (E) obtuse

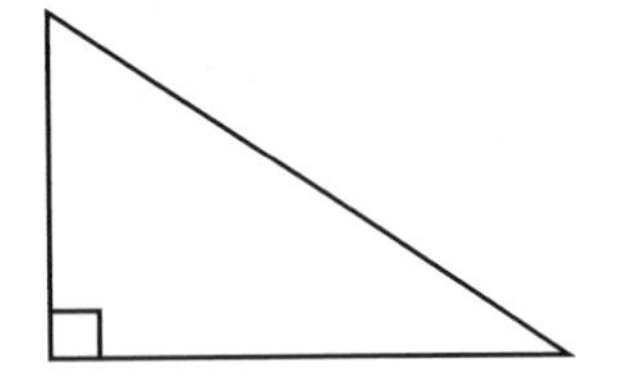

11. Amy and Allen's grandmother gave them each $2.00. They decide to put their money together and buy candy to share. If the candy costs a total of $2.80, how much money will they have leftover?
    (A) $0.60
    (B) $0.80
    (C) $1.20
    (D) $1.40
    (E) $1.60

12. 6,254 + 197 =
    (A) 6,321
    (B) 6,341
    (C) 6,351
    (D) 6,451
    (E) 6,461

13. Which is a line of symmetry?
    (A) line A
    (B) line B
    (C) line C
    (D) line D
    (E) none of these

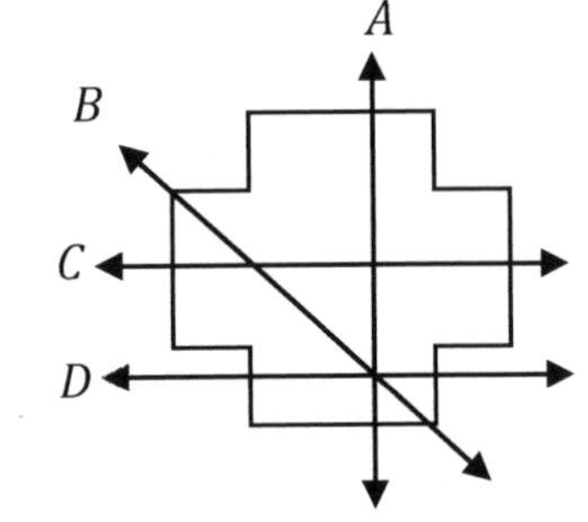

14. 5 is to 25 as 6 is to ___
    (A) 12
    (B) 15
    (C) 18
    (D) 36
    (E) 64

15. If a grocery store has 412 oranges and it sells 268 oranges, how many oranges are left?
    (A) 680
    (B) 356
    (C) 256
    (D) 154
    (E) 144

GO ON TO THE NEXT PAGE.

DO WORK IN THIS SPACE

16. Nika is baking a cake and needs more than $1\frac{1}{2}$ cups of flour but less than 2 cups of flour. A possible number of cups that she could need is:
   (A) 1
   (B) $1\frac{1}{4}$
   (C) $1\frac{1}{2}$
   (D) $1\frac{3}{4}$
   (E) 2

17. Chris plays running back for her football team and recorded how many yards she ran in each game she played this season. What is the average number of yards that Chris ran per game?
   (A) 22 yds.
   (B) 48 yds.
   (C) 54 yds.
   (D) 55 yds.
   (E) 56 yds.

Game	Points
The Chargers	21
The Steelers	28
The Jaguars	3
The Rams	42
The Buccaneers	21
The Bills	17

18. What is the area of the triangle shown on the right?
   (Note: Area = $\frac{1}{2}$ (base × vertical height))
   (A) 6 square units
   (B) 10 square units
   (C) 12 square units
   (D) 15 square units
   (E) 24 square units

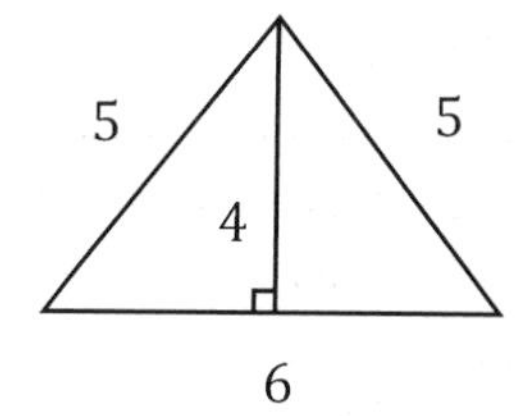

19. Megan's dog weighs 480 ounces. What is this weight, in pounds?
   (Note: 1 pound = 16 ounces)
   (A) 16
   (B) 30
   (C) 48
   (D) 4,800
   (E) 7,680

20. The students in Mrs. Smith's class will each give a $2\frac{1}{2}$-minute presentation. If there are 8 students who will present in one day, how much time, in minutes, will all the presentations take?
   (A) $5\frac{1}{2}$
   (B) 8
   (C) $10\frac{1}{2}$
   (D) 20
   (E) 40

GO ON TO THE NEXT PAGE.

DO WORK IN THIS SPACE

21. What is $\frac{3}{4}$ multiplied by $\frac{5}{8}$?
    (A) $1\frac{7}{8}$
    (B) $1\frac{3}{8}$
    (C) $\frac{15}{32}$
    (D) $\frac{3}{8}$
    (E) $\frac{1}{8}$

Questions 22-23 are based on the table shown on the right:

Borough	Percent of Applicants
Bronx	22
Brooklyn	25
Manhattan	18
Queens	26
Staten Island	9

22. Residents from New York's five boroughs apply to a city job. What percent of applicants are from the Bronx or Queens?
    (A) 4
    (B) 22
    (C) 26
    (D) 48
    (E) 51

23. Which pairs of boroughs had the most applicants combined?
    (A) Bronx and Staten Island
    (B) Brooklyn and Staten Island
    (C) Bronx and Manhattan
    (D) Brooklyn and Manhattan
    (E) Manhattan and Queens

---

24. Which of the following can NOT be represented by the equation $12 \div y = 4$?
    (A) Find the number of students in each row if 12 students are seated in 4 rows.
    (B) Find the number of presents that can be wrapped with 12 inches of ribbon if each present requires 4 inches of ribbon.
    (C) Find how many candies each person receives if there are 4 people and 12 candies.
    (D) Find how many children remain on the school bus if there are 12 children and 4 children get off the bus.
    (E) Find how many fish a tank can hold if there are 12 fish and 4 fish tanks.

---

25. How many cars would it take to transport 115 people if 5 people can fit in a car?
    (A) 15
    (B) 23
    (C) 30
    (D) 33
    (E) 110

GO ON TO THE NEXT PAGE.

DO WORK IN THIS SPACE

26. In a diagram, if one triangle represents 300 people, then how many people would 4 triangles represent?
   (A) 304
   (B) 600
   (C) 900
   (D) 1,200
   (E) 1,300

27. 630 ÷ 9 =
   (A) 60
   (B) 70
   (C) 80
   (D) 90
   (E) 100

28. If a dump truck can transport 6 tons of gravel, how many dump trucks are needed to transport 108 tons of gravel?
   (A) 8
   (B) 10
   (C) 16
   (D) 18
   (E) 20

29. A spinner is to be created from the image at right. Which number is the spinner LEAST likely to land on?
   (A) an even number
   (B) an odd number
   (C) a prime number
   (D) a composite number
   (E) a number greater than 6

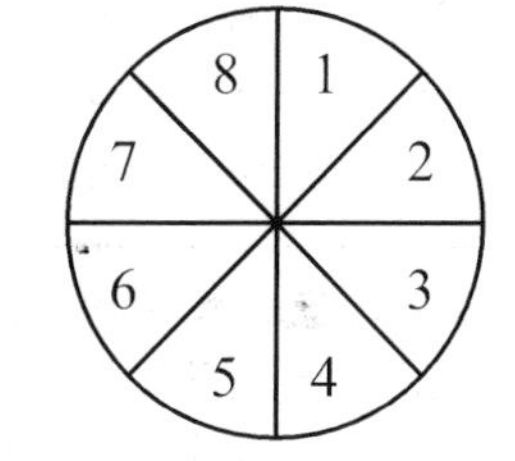

30. $\frac{7}{12} - \frac{1}{6} =$
   (A) 0
   (B) $\frac{5}{12}$
   (C) $\frac{9}{12}$
   (D) 3
   (E) 5

STOP

IF YOU FINISH BEFORE TIME IS UP,
CHECK YOUR WORK IN THIS SECTION ONLY.
YOU MAY NOT TURN TO ANY OTHER SECTION.

SECTION 2
30 Questions

There are two different types of questions in this section: synonyms and analogies. Read the directions and sample question for each type.

Synonyms

Each of the questions that follow consist of one capitalized word. Each word is followed by five words or phrases. Select the one word or phrase whose meaning is closest to the word in capital letters.

Sample Question:

HOT: ●ⒷⒸⒹⒺ

(A) warm
(B) sunny
(C) open
(D) enjoyable
(E) unfriendly

---

1. MAGICALLY:
(A) incredible
(B) fantastically
(C) awfully
(D) quickly
(E) wizard

2. STRATEGY:
(A) coach
(B) game
(C) succeed
(D) plan
(E) victory

3. FABLE:
(A) turtle
(B) hare
(C) moral
(D) lesson
(E) tale

4. CONVERT:
(A) units
(B) beliefs
(C) change
(D) number
(E) cash

5. RELIABLE:
(A) random
(B) family
(C) real
(D) dependable
(E) trust

6. VOYAGE:
(A) ship
(B) space
(C) crew
(D) road
(E) journey

7. DISTRACT:
(A) distinct
(B) sidetrack
(C) sibling
(D) focus
(E) emphasize

8. HILARIOUS:
(A) funny
(B) giggle
(C) joke
(D) bland
(E) comedy

GO ON TO THE NEXT PAGE.

9. CREEP:
   (A) skip
   (B) camouflage
   (C) crawl
   (D) weird
   (E) normal

10. REVOLT:
   (A) rebellion
   (B) unite
   (C) obey
   (D) fight
   (E) pirate

11. GUARDIAN:
   (A) insurance
   (B) protector
   (C) ward
   (D) helper
   (E) angel

12. MYTH:
   (A) magic
   (B) nonfiction
   (C) magazine
   (D) story
   (E) gods

13. PRESERVE:
   (A) jungle
   (B) save
   (C) care
   (D) outlast
   (E) fruity

14. TAUNT:
   (A) praise
   (B) loose
   (C) abominable
   (D) tease
   (E) absent

15. IDENTICAL:
   (A) identity
   (B) unique
   (C) twins
   (D) differ
   (E) alike

GO ON TO THE NEXT PAGE.

Analogies

The questions that follow ask you to find relationships between words. For each question, select the answer choice that best completes the meaning of the sentence.

Sample Question:

Dance is to dancer as: ●Ⓑ©ⒹⒺ

(A) lesson is to teacher
(B) cat is to yarn
(C) fish is to water
(D) umbrella is to rain
(E) shovel is to snow

Choice (A) is the best answer because a dancer dances a dance, just as a teacher teaches a lesson. This choice states a relationship that is most like the relationship between dance and dancer.

16. Baggage is to heavy as porcupine is to
    (A) feathery
    (B) zoo
    (C) prickly
    (D) claim
    (E) purple

17. Desire is to want as
    (A) immense is to small
    (B) hate is to enjoy
    (C) success is to failure
    (D) hopeless is to despairing
    (E) make is to damage

18. Soccer is to sport as
    (A) disaster is to earthquake
    (B) cleats is to run
    (C) villain is to character
    (D) mammal is to panda
    (E) goalie is to defend

19. Picture is to illustrator as experiment is to
    (A) scientist
    (B) explosion
    (C) image
    (D) police
    (E) beaker

20. Seam is to seem as principle is to
    (A) school
    (B) headmaster
    (C) particular
    (D) principal
    (E) appear

21. Cave is to dark as
    (A) garbage is to foul
    (B) shady is to forest
    (C) brink is to edge
    (D) complaint is to praise
    (E) civilized is to wilderness

22. Lukewarm is to steaming as
    (A) nauseous is to queasy
    (B) scorching is to hot
    (C) nice is to exquisite
    (D) restful is to soothing
    (E) timid is to shy

23. Thermometer is to nurse as taxi is to
    (A) cab
    (B) salesman
    (C) flu
    (D) fever
    (E) driver

24. Basic is to advanced as
    (A) easy is to simple
    (B) pleasing is to attractive
    (C) home is to address
    (D) grubby is to spotless
    (E) spoon is to napkin

GO ON TO THE NEXT PAGE.

25. Dungeon is to castle as
    (A) handle is to suitcase
    (B) chatter is to gossip
    (C) window is to sill
    (D) increase is to lessen
    (E) television is to screen

26. Newspaper is to inform as
    (A) climb is to stairs
    (B) cart is to transport
    (C) headline is to article
    (D) heat is to pan
    (E) lava is to volcano

27. Costume is to actor as
    (A) fiction is to fact
    (B) purchase is to buy
    (C) phone is to secretary
    (D) drama is to theatre
    (E) prop is to object

28. Books is to publisher as
    (A) binder is to binding
    (B) reader is to fairytales
    (C) paperback is to blurb
    (D) official is to governor
    (E) contract is to lawyer

29. Which is to witch as
    (A) lean is to sheen
    (B) suite is to sweet
    (C) when is to broomstick
    (D) grow is to improve
    (E) select is to spell

30. Envious is to jealous as explain is to
    (A) complicate
    (B) reply
    (C) learn
    (D) state
    (E) elaborate

STOP

IF YOU FINISH BEFORE TIME IS UP,
CHECK YOUR WORK IN THIS SECTION ONLY.
YOU MAY NOT TURN TO ANY OTHER SECTION.

SECTION 3
28 Questions

Carefully read each passage and then answer the questions about it. For each question, select the choice that best answers the question based on the passage.

Zoos first became popular in the 1800s. Back then, animals were not treated very well in zoos. They were often not fed properly. Many people still believe zoos are bad for animals. But modern zoos are much better. They help many animals survive. Zoos have also become a place for learning about wildlife.

5 Modern zoos offer more space for animals. They are not crammed in tight cages. These zoos are designed to look like an animal's natural home. They use sand, water and trees. Many 'cages' look just like the animal's habitat. That's because these zoos are trying to save certain animals. For example, golden frogs have died out in some places in the world. Many zoos still raise them to keep the species alive.

10 Zoos also teach people. They show how beautiful many animals are. People do many things that hurt wild animals without knowing it. Zoos teach people how to make better choices. Each year, thousands of students visit zoos on field trips. Some zoos even offer summer camps. Zoos have become outdoor classrooms. They get students excited about science and helping animals.

15 The zoos of today are different from the zoos of the past. They are important for the future of both people and animals.

1. The main idea of the passage is that
   - (A) people should pay more for zoos
   - (B) zoos have improved over time
   - (C) zoos have gotten worse over time
   - (D) all zoos should save animals
   - (E) animals are not treated well in zoos

2. The word "crammed" (line 5) most likely means
   - (A) crowded
   - (B) released
   - (C) fed
   - (D) captured
   - (E) freed

3. Zoos changed the design of their cages in order to
   - (A) use up extra sand, water and trees
   - (B) make golden frogs happier
   - (C) attract more paying viewers
   - (D) teach children what natural habitats look like
   - (E) save animals that are dying in the wild

4. From reading the passage, we can assume that golden frogs are
   - (A) poisonous to humans
   - (B) thriving in the wild
   - (C) in danger of dying out completely
   - (D) a popular animal for students
   - (E) an important topic of study

GO ON TO THE NEXT PAGE.

When I was a kid, we took vacations to many different places. My favorite one came every summer. My parents and me and my little brother and sister would pile into the car. We passed the time by playing I Spy and trying to spot out-of-state license plates. Two hours later we would feel the warm sun and smell the salty air. *5* Our family shore vacation was always the best week of the year.

Everyone was relaxed down the shore. Even my parents! They gave us kids a little more freedom. They trusted us to walk the two blocks to the beach alone. And we were there all day. Food trucks came around every hour. Lunch was a sandy hotdog in between riding the waves. And ice pops cooled us off after chasing each *10* other in the hot sun. Mom and Dad would drag us back to the house for dinner. But afterward we ran back to the beach to fly our kites. We would stay out until it got dark.

The best part of the shore trip was reuniting with family. Cousins who lived far away would rent a beach house on the same block as us. And we spent the whole *15* week as a big gang. From five to fifteen years old, everyone was included in our adventures. We buried each other in the sand. We hunted for lost pirate treasure. We had sand-castle-building contests. We told jokes, shared secrets and even played pranks on the adults!

Some years, we only saw these cousins at this shore vacation. But the time we *20* spent together there made us best friends for the whole year.

5. The narrator wrote this passage to
   (A) convince people to vacation at the shore
   (B) explain why shore vacations were so special to her
   (C) warn people about swimming in the ocean
   (D) show how special each of her cousins were
   (E) encourage people to spend time with their cousins

6. In lines 7-12, the author describes walking to the beach alone and staying out until dark to show
   (A) how she had more freedom at the shore
   (B) that the beach was a scary place
   (C) why her parents were relaxed
   (D) why she loved her cousins
   (E) what she had to do to buy an ice pop

7. The narrator and her cousins engaged in all the following activities EXCEPT:
   (A) burying each other in the sand
   (B) hunting for lost treasure
   (C) having sand castle building contests
   (D) playing I Spy
   (E) sharing secrets

8. In line 18, "pranks" most likely means.
   (A) music
   (B) games
   (C) tricks
   (D) cranks
   (E) hooky

GO ON TO THE NEXT PAGE.

She's brought many much-loved characters to life: Henry Huggins, Ramona Quimby, Ralph S. Mouse. Her books are among the most popular in every library. She has received many honors and awards. But who is she?

Her name is Beverly Cleary.

5 When Beverly Cleary started first grade, she already loved books and reading. But she was placed in the lowest reading circle at school. She had to learn long lists of sounds and words. The stories she had to read were too simple. It made Beverly feel bad about herself. But Beverly didn't give up. By third grade, she was carrying big stacks of books from the library and back. In high school, the librarian suggested 10 she try writing her own books. Beverly promised herself that she would, someday. She would write stories that kids like her wanted to read.

After college, Beverly worked in a children's library. Her first published book was *Henry Huggins*. She was 34 years old when she wrote it. She kept writing new books and stories until she was over 80 years old. You may have even read some of 15 them! *Henry and Ribsy, Ramona the Pest,* and *The Mouse and the Motorcycle* are just a few. These books helped Beverly win many writing awards. A school in Oregon is named after her. Portland has put statues of Henry, his dog Ribsy, and Ramona in a park. Of course, the best honor for a writer is being remembered and loved by readers. Beverly Cleary certainly is.

9. The main idea of this passage is
   (A) why Beverly Clearly became a librarian
   (B) why some writers win awards
   (C) why people should spend more time reading
   (D) what happened in the life of a popular author
   (E) how Beverly Cleary wrote many books

10. In line 6, a reading circle is most likely a
   (A) class
   (B) room
   (C) cushion
   (D) library
   (E) book series

11. According to the passage, what is the best honor a writer can receive?
   (A) having a building named after you
   (B) getting your statue in a park
   (C) selling lots of books
   (D) being loved and remembered
   (E) being able to write for 50 years

12. The word that best describes Beverly Clearly is
   (A) gentle
   (B) committed
   (C) peaceful
   (D) unrewarded
   (E) weak

GO ON TO THE NEXT PAGE.

I know the song that the bluebird is singing,
Out in the apple-tree where he is swinging;
Brave little fellow, the skies may look dreary;
But he does not care while his heart is so cheery.

5 Listen awhile and you'll hear what he's saying,
Up in the apple-tree swinging and swaying.
"Dear little blossoms down under the snow,
You must be weary of winter, I know;
Listen, while I sing you a message of cheer;
10 Summer is coming and Springtime is here!"

"Little white snowdrop! I pray that you melt;
Bright yellow flower! Come, open your eyes;
Sweet little violets, hid from the cold,
Put on your tables of purple and gold;
15 Daffodils! Daffodils! Say, do you hear?
Summer is coming and Springtime is here!"

13. The main idea of the poem is
    (A) winter is almost over and there is excitement about springtime
    (B) there are many different colored flowers blooming
    (C) bluebirds like to sing in the snow
    (D) apple trees are growing fruit
    (E) winter skies are beautiful and cheery

14. The word "dreary" (line 3) most likely means
    (A) cheery
    (B) bright
    (C) gloomy
    (D) sunny
    (E) snowy

15. The author uses all of the following aspects of Nature as signs of springtime EXCEPT
    (A) the bluebird
    (B) violets
    (C) daffodils
    (D) blossoms
    (E) the skies

16. What does the author mean by "Come, open your eyes!" (line 12)?
    (A) the bluebird should open its eyes to springtime
    (B) the flowers should finally bloom
    (C) everyone should open their eyes to the coming of summer
    (D) the skies should finally clear so everyone can see the sun
    (E) winter is a time to take the time to notice the beauty of the world

GO ON TO THE NEXT PAGE.

Research shows that some kids watch almost 4 hours of TV every day. That includes advertisements. Many of these ads are for fast food restaurants. Others focus on sugary, salty snacks. Children see the ads play over and over. It makes them want those unhealthy foods. Should ads for unhealthy foods be shown during kids' TV shows? Many people argue no. *5*

Kids' brains take many years to grow. Most young children do not realize that ads are not always true. They don't know that ads try to make them buy things they do not need. Kids like the bright colors and music of ads. They think the food in ads looks delicious. What kids don't realize is that those foods have too much salt, fat and sugar. *10* They can make children overweight or even sick. So, trying to sell these products to children can be dangerous.

Some countries already have laws about this. They do not allow junk food companies to advertise during kids' TV shows. These countries know these foods can be harmful to children's health. The US does not have any laws to protect children from these ads. *15* So, many American kids see these foods and ask their parents for them.

Having a good diet is important for children. It helps them grow up to be healthy adults. If kids are tricked into eating junk food, this is not fair. Keeping junk food ads out of children's TV watching will make kids want less unhealthy food and snacks. *20*

17. The author would most likely agree with which statement?
    - (A) All advertising is harmful.
    - (B) Advertising helps people know what they should buy.
    - (C) Children should not watch so much TV.
    - (D) The US should have laws about advertising on children's TV.
    - (E) Children's TV shows can be educational.

18. According to the passage, kids don't realize that ads are not always true because
    - (A) they are not smart
    - (B) their brains are not fully grown yet
    - (C) ads are fun to watch
    - (D) they like junk food
    - (E) they don't know junk foods are unhealthy

19. In line 8, why are "bright colors and music" most likely mentioned?
    - (A) to tell readers what fast food restaurants are like
    - (B) to describe kids' TV shows
    - (C) as reasons ads are not true
    - (D) as reasons kids are overweight
    - (E) as reasons kids like TV ads

20. From the passage, we can assume the author thinks that advertising is
    - (A) beneficial
    - (B) uncommon
    - (C) problematic
    - (D) necessary
    - (E) healthy

GO ON TO THE NEXT PAGE.

A little grey mouse once asked his mother why people put such good food in the pantry for them. With a twinkle in her eye, his mother replied: "Well, Greywhiskers, I don't think they like us as much as you seem to think. Now remember, I have absolutely forbidden you to put your nose above the ground unless
5 I am with you. As kind as the people are, I wouldn't be surprised if they tried to catch you."

Greywhiskers twitched his tail with scorn. He was quite sure he knew how to take care of himself. He didn't want to follow his mother's tail all his life. So as soon as she had curled herself up for an afternoon nap he snuck away, and scampered
10 across the pantry shelves.

Then he found a little wooden house. Just inside, there hung cheese.

Greywhiskers ran in, but, oh! "click" went the little wooden house. He was caught fast in a trap.

When the morning came, the cook, who had set the trap, lifted it from the
15 shelf. Then he called a little girl to come and see the thief who had eaten her cake.

"What are you going to do with him?" asked Ethel.

"Why, drown him, my dear, for sure."

The tears came into the little girl's blue eyes.

"You didn't know it was stealing, did you, mousie dear?" she said.

20 "No," squeaked Greywhiskers sadly, "I didn't."

The cook's back was turned for a moment. Then, the tender-hearted little Ethel lifted the lid of the trap, and out popped mousie.

Oh! how quickly he ran home to his mother, and how she comforted him until he began to forget his fright.

21. Why did Greywhiskers' mother forbid him from putting his nose above the ground?
    (A) He could not take care of himself.
    (B) He might smell something unpleasant.
    (C) She did not want him to eat delicious food without her.
    (D) She did not want him to grow up.
    (E) The people might try to catch him.

22. The word "scorn" in line 7 means
    (A) admiration
    (B) contentment
    (C) dislike
    (D) excitement
    (E) heaviness

23. Why did Greywhiskers go to the pantry?
    (A) He found a little wooden house.
    (B) He wanted to prove himself.
    (C) He wanted to eat delicious food.
    (D) He wanted to meet the people.
    (E) He was bored.

24. We can assume Ethel freed Greywhiskers from the trap because
    (A) she felt sorry for him
    (B) she wanted him for a pet
    (C) she was angry at the cook
    (D) she liked to watch him eat cheese
    (E) the cook told her to free him

GO ON TO THE NEXT PAGE.

In southern Los Angeles, seventeen strange towers rise up from the ground. They look like upside down ice cream cones. They are made out of wire. The tallest tower is almost one hundred feet tall! These are known as the Watts Towers. One man built them by himself.

5 Simon Rodia moved from Italy to the United States. In 1921, he started building the Watts Towers in his spare time. He used scrap metal and other objects he found. He covered the metal with mortar, or cement. Then he decorated the mortar with glass, seashells, and other colorful materials. Some came from the Malibu Pottery. Rodia worked there for many years. After work, he would take the 10 broken pieces of pottery home for his tower.

The towers kept growing over the years. Rodia had to climb them to keep working. When he climbed, he stuck a window-washer's belt to the tower. This belt made sure he didn't fall.

Rodia called the art project "Nuestro Pueblo." This means "our town" in 15 Spanish. He worked on the towers for 34 years. In 1955, he moved to northern California to be closer to his family. He gave away his land and the towers. Today, the city of Los Angeles owns the towers. People now take art classes at the local art center. It is attached to the towers, and gives people a close-up view of Rodia's amazing creation.

25. The author wrote this passage to
    - (A) give instructions on how to build a tower
    - (B) explain why Rodia built the Watts Towers
    - (C) tell stories about Rodia's life in Italy and Los Angeles
    - (D) describe the Watts Towers and how Rodia built them
    - (E) inform people about the art classes at the Watts Tower

26. We can assume that Rodia made the Watts Towers out of materials that
    - (A) he could use for free
    - (B) were in perfect condition
    - (C) he bought at pottery stores
    - (D) looked like ice cream cones
    - (E) matched the color of the mortar

27. Rodia most likely wanted the Watts Towers to represent
    - (A) the beauty of the beach
    - (B) the importance of family
    - (C) togetherness in his city
    - (D) a love of Italy
    - (E) the importance of teamwork

28. According to the passage, Rodia started to use a window-washer's belt because
    - (A) he needed to wash his tower
    - (B) his towers had become very tall
    - (C) he wanted to add it to his tower
    - (D) he built windows into his tower
    - (E) his towers were made with glass

STOP

IF YOU FINISH BEFORE TIME IS UP,
CHECK YOUR WORK IN THIS SECTION ONLY.
YOU MAY NOT TURN TO ANY OTHER SECTION.

SECTION 4
Writing Sample

Look at the picture and tell a story about what happened. Make sure your story includes a beginning, middle and end.

STOP

IF YOU FINISH BEFORE TIME IS UP,
CHECK YOUR WORK IN THIS SECTION ONLY.
YOU MAY NOT TURN TO ANY OTHER SECTION.

SECTION 5
15 Questions

Sojourner Truth was once a slave. After she was freed from slavery, she began fighting for all slaves to be free. Truth also hated the fact that many people believed women were less important than men. She often gave speeches about the importance of women's rights. In her famous 1851 speech, she said:

5 "I want to say a few words about women's equality. I believe in equality – I believe women are just as important as men. I *am* equality. I have as much muscle as any man. I can do as much work as any man. I have plowed and reaped and husked and chopped and mowed the fields as much as any man. And what more can a man do than I? I can carry as much as any man. And I can eat as much, too. I am as strong
10 as any man out there."

This speech shows that Sojourner Truth fought for women's rights as much as slaves' rights. Few people discuss this part of her beliefs. It is important to understand this side of her. Her speeches show how many people who wanted to end slavery also fought for the equality of women.

1. The main idea of the passage is that
   (A) all people should be freed from slavery
   (B) women should be paid equally as men
   (C) the people who fought for freedom also cared about women's rights
   (D) intelligence is more important than strength
   (E) Sojourner Truth was very brave

2. When Sojourner Truth says "I *am* equality" (line 6), she means that she
   (A) is proof that women can work as hard as men
   (B) believes that all humans are equal
   (C) wanted to free all slaves
   (D) thinks women are better than men
   (E) thinks women's rights are the most important issue

3. From her speech, we can assume that Sojourner Truth once worked as a
   (A) postmaster
   (B) seamstress
   (C) cook
   (D) poet
   (E) farmer

4. In line 12, the word "discuss" may be replaced with
   (A) love
   (B) argue
   (C) know
   (D) disagree
   (E) repeat

5. In the passage, women's equality is supported by all of the following EXCEPT
   (A) "I want to say a few words about women's equality" (line 5)
   (B) "I have as much muscle as any man" (lines 6-7)
   (C) "I have plowed and reaped...the fields as much as any man" (lines 7-8)
   (D) "I can eat as much, too" (line 9)
   (E) "I can carry as much as any man" (line 9)

6. The word that best describes Sojourner Truth is
   (A) honest
   (B) determined
   (C) weak
   (D) passive
   (E) quiet

GO ON TO THE NEXT PAGE.

7. MINIMUM:
   (A) lower
   (B) least
   (C) medium
   (D) zero
   (E) maximum

8. EQUIVALENT:
   (A) equal
   (B) regular
   (C) triple
   (D) parallel
   (E) related

9. Frontier is to unknown as
   (A) attentive is to distracted
   (B) shaggy is to animal
   (C) sandy is to desert
   (D) cozy is to burrow
   (E) vinegar is to sour

10. Broom is to sweep as
   (A) vacuum is to floor
   (B) heal is to medicine
   (C) money is to purchase
   (D) future is to past
   (E) math is to science

11. Podium is to mayor as
   (A) judge is to robes
   (B) give is to grant
   (C) politician is to speech
   (D) knife is to butcher
   (E) win is to lose

12. Building is to architect as
   (A) hotel is to warehouse
   (B) putty is to mold
   (C) clothing is to designer
   (D) doorman is to greeting
   (E) electrician is to wiring

13. Samantha, Alice, and Joe are buying snacks to share after school. Samantha has $2.43, Alice has $1.67 and Joe has 92¢. How much money do they have altogether?
   (A) $3.92
   (B) $4.02
   (C) $4.92
   (D) $5.02
   (E) $5.92

14. Which shape is a parallelogram but not a rectangle?
   (A)
   (B) 
   (C) 
   (D) 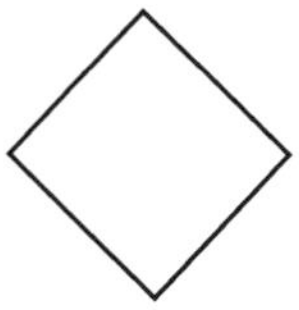
   (E)

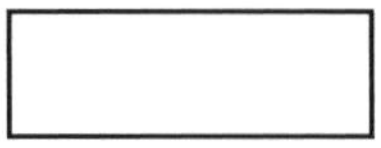

15. Place the following numbers in order from least to greatest: nine million, five hundred thirty-two thousand, eighty-nine, twenty-two thousand.
   (A) 89; 22,000; 532,000; 9,000,000
   (B) 89; 532; 22,000; 9,000,000
   (C) 89; 5,320; 22,000; 9,000,000
   (D) 9,000,000; 22,000; 5,320; 89
   (E) 9,000,000; 532,000; 22,000; 89

STOP

IF YOU FINISH BEFORE TIME IS UP,
CHECK YOUR WORK IN THIS SECTION ONLY.
YOU MAY NOT TURN TO ANY OTHER SECTION.

Scoring the 4th Grade Final Practice Test (Form D)

Sections 1-3 – Scored

Score the test using the answer sheet and *referring to the answer key in the back of the book (see table of contents).*

For each section, record the number of questions answered correctly. This will give you the raw score for each section. Note that the actual test will convert the raw score to a scaled score by comparing the student's performance with all other students in the same grade who took the test.

Section	Questions Correct (Raw Score)
Quantitative *Section 1*	__________
Verbal *Section 2*	__________
Reading *Section 3*	__________

Carefully consider the results from the practice test when forming a study plan. Remember, the Elementary SSAT is given to students in grades 3-4. Unless the student has finished 4th grade, chances are that there is material on this test that he or she has not yet been taught. If this is the case, and the student would like to improve beyond what is expected of his or her grade, consider working with a tutor or teacher, who can help the student learn more about new topics.

Section 4 – Writing Sample – Unscored

Have a parent or trusted educator review the essay or story written for the writing sample. Important areas to focus on include organization, clarity of ideas, originality, and technical precision (spelling, grammar, etc.).

Section 5 – Unscored

On the real test, the Experimental section will NOT be scored. Consider the student's performance on this section for practice purposes only. Did he or she do better on one section than another? Use this information along with the information from Sections 1-3 to form the study plan.

Answer Keys

This section provides the answer solutions to the practice questions in each section of the workbook. There are no answers provided to the writing sample section. Instead, consider having a tutor, teacher, or other educator review your writing and give you constructive feedback.

Remember: detailed answer explanations are available online at **www.thetutorverse.com**. Students should ask a parent or guardian's permission before going online.

3rd Grade Diagnostic Practice Test (Form A) Answer Key

Section 1: Quantitative

1. B	5. D	9. D	13. B	17. B	21. B	25. B	29. E
2. A	6. B	10. C	14. C	18. B	22. E	26. D	30. C
3. C	7. D	11. E	15. E	19. C	23. C	27. B	
4. D	8. B	12. D	16. E	20. A	24. B	28. D	

Section 2 – Verbal

1. D	5. A	9. C	13. E	17. D	21. C	25. D	29. E
2. C	6. B	10. C	14. E	18. B	22. B	26. D	30. D
3. B	7. E	11. A	15. B	19. B	23. A	27. B	
4. D	8. D	12. D	16. A	20. A	24. E	28. E	

Section 3 – Reading

1. B	5. E	9. B	13. B	17. E	21. A	25. C
2. C	6. D	10. C	14. E	18. D	22. D	26. E
3. A	7. B	11. C	15. B	19. B	23. C	27. E
4. C	8. C	12. D	16. E	20. E	24. B	28. A

Section 4 – Writing Sample

Responses may vary. Have an experienced tutor or educator review the writing sample.

Section 5 – "Experimental"

1. A	3. E	5. C	7. D	9. A	11. B	13. E	15. D
2. B	4. B	6. E	8. E	10. C	12. B	14. D	

4th Grade Diagnostic Practice Test (Form B) Answer Key

Section 1: Quantitative

1. A	5. E	9. B	13. E	17. E	21. D	25. C	29. B
2. D	6. C	10. C	14. D	18. C	22. A	26. A	30. C
3. C	7. E	11. D	15. B	19. B	23. E	27. C	
4. C	8. B	12. B	16. A	20. E	24. A	28. B	

Section 2 – Verbal

1. B	5. C	9. E	13. E	17. E	21. D	25. D	29. E
2. D	6. B	10. B	14. A	18. D	22. C	26. E	30. E
3. A	7. E	11. B	15. C	19. A	23. A	27. D	
4. D	8. D	12. A	16. B	20. C	24. B	28. A	

Section 3 – Reading

1. B	5. D	9. D	13. B	17. A	21. A	25. B
2. D	6. A	10. A	14. D	18. C	22. E	26. E
3. E	7. A	11. E	15. E	19. E	23. D	27. D
4. D	8. E	12. B	16. A	20. B	24. C	28. E

Section 4 – Writing Sample

Responses may vary. Have an experienced tutor or educator review the writing sample.

Section 5 – "Experimental"

1. A	3. A	5. B	7. D	9. D	11. A	13. E	15. C
2. B	4. C	6. E	8. E	10. A	12. B	14. C	

Quantitative

Number Concepts & Operations

Place Value – 3rd Grade

1. B	2. D	3. B	4. E	5. E	6. B	7. D	8. E

Place Value – 4th Grade

1. D	2. B	3. A	4. D	5. C	6. E	7. E	8. E

Basic Concepts – 3rd Grade

1. B	3. E	5. B	7. D	9. D
2. C	4. C	6. C	8. E	10. B

Basic Concepts – 4th Grade

1. E	3. C	5. E	7. D	9. D	11. A	13. C
2. D	4. A	6. C	8. E	10. C	12. B	14. C

Ordering Numbers and Fractions – 3rd Grade

1. C	2. B	3. A	4. C	5. C	6. B	7. C

Ordering Numbers and Fractions – 4th Grade

1. D	2. B	3. E	4. E	5. A	6. C	7. D

Fractions – 3rd Grade

1. E	3. D	5. E	7. C	9. C	11. E	13. D
2. C	4. B	6. A	8. A	10. C	12. E	

Fractions – 4th Grade

1. C	3. E	5. C	7. B	9. E	11. D	13. D
2. A	4. E	6. C	8. A	10. C	12. D	14. C

Arithmetic Word Problems – 3rd Grade

1. C 2. C 3. B 4. D 5. E 6. D 7. E 8. C 9. B 10. A 11. E 12. D 13. E 14. C 15. A 16. E 17. D

Arithmetic Word Problems – 4th Grade

1. A 2. B 3. A 4. E 5. E 6. C 7. D 8. D 9. E 10. B 11. A 12. A 13. A 14. C 15. C 16. B

Algebraic Principles

Solving Equations and Inequalities – 3rd Grade

1. D 2. B 3. D 4. C 5. D

Solving Equations and Inequalities – 4th Grade

1. B 2. C 3. B 4. A 5. B

Ratios and Proportions – 3rd Grade

1. E 2. D 3. D 4. B

Ratios and Proportions – 4th Grade

1. B 2. D 3. C 4. B 5. C

Geometry

Shapes and Attributes – 3rd Grade

1. C 2. C 3. A 4. A 5. B 6. D 7. B

Shapes and Attributes – 4th Grade

1. C 2. C 3. D 4. E 5. B 6. A 7. A

Area and Perimeter – 3rd Grade

1. D 2. C 3. B 4. B 5. B 6. C 7. B

Area and Perimeter – 4th Grade

1. C 2. D 3. A 4. A 5. B 6. B 7. C 8. B 9. D 10. C

Measurement

Time and Money – 3rd Grade

1. C 2. B 3. B 4. D 5. C 6. C 7. E 8. B 9. C 10. B 11. E 12. E 13. D 14. B

Time and Money – 4th Grade

1. C 2. B 3. B 4. E 5. A 6. D 7. B 8. B 9. E 10. D

Unit Analysis – 3rd Grade

1. A 2. C 3. A 4. C 5. B 6. E

Unit Analysis – 4th Grade

1. D 2. D 3. C 4. B 5. D 6. D

Statistics & Probability

Probability – 3rd Grade

1. D 2. C 3. B 4. A 5. B

Probability – 4th Grade

1. B 2. D 3. B 4. C 5. A 6. E 7. D 8. D

Mean – 3rd Grade

1. C 2. B 3. C 4. D

Mean – 4th Grade

1. E 2. B 3. C 4. B 5. D 6. B 7. C

Interpreting Tables and Graphs – 3rd Grade

1. B 2. E 3. B 4. A 5. C 6. B 7. A 8. E

Interpreting Tables and Graphs – 4th Grade

1. C 2. D 3. B 4. E 5. D 6. C 7. D 8. C

Verbal – Synonyms

3rd Grade

Introductory

1. D	4. C	7. A	10. D	13. A	16. D
2. C	5. E	8. C	11. A	14. D	17. E
3. A	6. D	9. D	12. B	15. C	18. C

Intermediate

1. D	4. E	7. D	10. E	13. E	16. D
2. B	5. A	8. B	11. D	14. C	17. A
3. D	6. B	9. A	12. A	15. D	18. B

Advanced

1. C	4. A	7. E	10. C	13. A	16. B
2. D	5. E	8. C	11. E	14. E	17. A
3. C	6. D	9. A	12. B	15. C	18. D

4th Grade

Introductory

1. B	4. D	7. A	10. E	13. D	16. A
2. E	5. E	8. B	11. C	14. A	17. E
3. A	6. B	9. E	12. A	15. B	18. B

Intermediate

1. E	4. C	7. A	10. B	13. D	16. E
2. C	5. B	8. A	11. C	14. A	17. C
3. D	6. B	9. E	12. C	15. D	18. B

Advanced

1. D	4. C	7. C	10. E	13. A	16. E
2. E	5. A	8. C	11. B	14. C	17. D
3. A	6. D	9. A	12. C	15. D	18. B

Verbal – Analogies

Guided Practice – Antonyms – 3rd Grade

1. D 2. E 3. D 4. D 5. C 6. D

Guided Practice – Antonyms – 4th Grade

1. C 2. E 3. A 4. D 5. D 6. A

Guided Practice – Characteristic – 3rd Grade

1. D 2. C 3. E 4. D 5. A 6. B

Guided Practice – Characteristic – 4th Grade

1. A 2. E 3. E 4. A 5. C 6. B

Guided Practice – Part to Whole – 3rd Grade

1. A	2. B	3. D	4. E	5. C	6. A

Guided Practice – Part to Whole – 4th Grade

1. A	2. E	3. A	4. A	5. E	6. C

Guided Practice – Uses – 3rd Grade

1. B	2. C	3. A	4. B	5. C	6. E

Guided Practice – Uses – 4th Grade

1. E	2. C	3. A	4. A	5. B	6. D

Guided Practice – Users – 3rd Grade

1. D	2. E	3. C	4. D	5. A	6. C

Guided Practice – Users – 4th Grade

1. A	2. D	3. C	4. E	5. B	6. D

Guided Practice – Category – 3rd Grade

1. C	2. B	3. E	4. A	5. D	6. C

Guided Practice – Category – 4th Grade

1. B	2. D	3. D	4. E	5. D	6. E

Guided Practice – Product/Producer – 3rd Grade

1. A	2. A	3. C	4. B	5. A	6. D

Guided Practice – Product/Producer – 4th Grade

1. D	2. D	3. A	4. B	5. E	6. C

Guided Practice – Degree – 3rd Grade

1. E	2. B	3. E	4. D	5. B	6. C

Guided Practice – Degree – 4th Grade

1. E	2. B	3. A	4. D	5. C	6. E

Guided Practice – Homonyms – 3rd Grade

1. A	2. D	3. B	4. D	5. C	6. A

Guided Practice – Homonyms – 4th Grade

1. B	2. E	3. C	4. A	5. D	6. E

Guided Practice – Synonyms – 3rd Grade

1. A	2. A	3. D	4. D	5. D	6. C

Guided Practice – Synonyms – 4th Grade

1. E	2. C	3. B	4. D	5. B	6. A

Mixed Practice – 3rd Grade

1. C	3. C	5. B	7. A	9. D	11. E
2. E	4. C	6. E	8. E	10. D	12. B

Mixed Practice – 4th Grade

1. A	3. B	5. C	7. A	9. C	11. E
2. C	4. B	6. B	8. B	10. B	12. C

Reading Comprehension

Fiction – 3rd Grade

Passage #1

1. B	2. D	3. C	4. A	5. E

Passage #2

1. C 2. B 3. C 4. D 5. A 6. E

Passage #3

1. C 2. A 3. B 4. E 5. D 6. A

Passage #4

1. D 2. B 3. E 4. A 5. C

Passage #5

1. A 2. B 3. C 4. E 5. D

Fiction – 4th Grade

Passage #1

1. D 2. C 3. A 4. D 5. B 6. B

Passage #2

1. E 2. A 3. C 4. D 5. A 6. B

Passage #3

1. B 2. D 3. B 4. C 5. A 6. C

Passage #4

1. C 2. E 3. A 4. D 5. B

Passage #5

1. A 2. D 3. C 4. B 5. E

Passage #6

1. D 2. A 3. B 4. C 5. E 6. D

Non-Fiction – 3rd Grade

Passage #1

1. A 2. B 3. D 4. C 5. D

Passage #2

1. A 2. B 3. C 4. C 5. E 6. D

Passage #3

1. A 2. E 3. C 4. B 5. C

Passage #4

1. D 2. A 3. D 4. A 5. E

Non-Fiction – 4th Grade

Passage #1

1. D 2. C 3. A 4. D 5. C

Passage #2

1. E 2. C 3. B 4. A 5. B

Passage #3

1. A 2. D 3. E 4. B 5. A

3rd Grade Final Practice Test (Form C) Answer Key

Section 1: Quantitative

1. A	5. C	9. C	13. B	17. A	21. C	25. C	29. C
2. B	6. E	10. D	14. B	18. C	22. B	26. D	30. B
3. A	7. D	11. D	15. C	19. D	23. C	27. D	
4. C	8. C	12. B	16. E	20. D	24. D	28. A	

Section 2 – Verbal

1. B	5. E	9. D	13. C	17. C	21. D	25. D	29. C
2. A	6. B	10. E	14. B	18. D	22. B	26. B	30. A
3. D	7. B	11. E	15. B	19. C	23. B	27. E	
4. C	8. C	12. A	16. E	20. C	24. E	28. D	

Section 3 – Reading

1. E	5. E	9. B	13. C	17. B	21. B	25. D
2. D	6. C	10. C	14. E	18. C	22. C	26. C
3. C	7. D	11. B	15. D	19. E	23. D	27. E
4. A	8. E	12. B	16. A	20. A	24. E	28. C

Section 4 – Writing Sample

Responses may vary. Have an experienced tutor or educator review the writing sample.

Section 5 – "Experimental"

1. A	3. D	5. C	7. B	9. D	11. D	13. D	15. D
2. C	4. E	6. B	8. E	10. D	12. C	14. C	

4th Grade Final Practice Test (Form D) Answer Key

Section 1: Quantitative

1. D	5. D	9. C	13. C	17. A	21. C	25. B	29. E
2. E	6. B	10. D	14. D	18. C	22. D	26. D	30. B
3. C	7. B	11. C	15. E	19. B	23. E	27. B	
4. E	8. A	12. D	16. D	20. D	24. D	28. D	

Section 2 – Verbal

1. B	5. D	9. C	13. B	17. D	21. A	25. A	29. B
2. D	6. E	10. A	14. D	18. C	22. C	26. B	30. E
3. E	7. B	11. B	15. E	19. A	23. E	27. C	
4. C	8. A	12. D	16. C	20. D	24. D	28. E	

Section 3 – Reading

1. B	5. B	9. D	13. A	17. D	21. E	25. D
2. A	6. A	10. A	14. C	18. B	22. C	26. A
3. E	7. D	11. D	15. E	19. E	23. B	27. C
4. C	8. C	12. B	16. B	20. C	24. A	28. B

Section 4 – Writing Sample

Responses may vary. Have an experienced tutor or educator review the writing sample.

Section 5 – "Experimental"

1. C	3. E	5. A	7. B	9. E	11. D	13. D	15. A
2. A	4. C	6. B	8. A	10. C	12. C	14. B	

Made in the USA
Columbia, SC
16 September 2021